AN INSIDER'S VIEW OF

Mormon Origins

AN INSIDER'S VIEW OF
Mormon Origins

Grant H. Palmer

SALT LAKE CITY

In loving memory of my wife,
Kathy Dahlin Palmer,
1944-92

Digital scans by Tyson Stokes.

Illustrations of Joseph Smith dictating the Book of Mormon by Kurt Gray.

Cover design by Ron Stucki.

The cover includes, in the background, a selection of books available in Joseph Smith's youth.

An Insider's View of Mormon Origins was printed on acid-free paper and was composed, printed, and bound in the United States of America.

2022   2021   2020   2019   2018   18   17   16   15   14

Library of Congress Cataloging-in-Publication Data
Palmer, Grant H.
     An insider's view of Mormon origins / by Grant H. Palmer
       p. cm.
     Includes bibliographical references and index.
     ISBN 1-56085-157-0 (pbk.)
     1. Mormon Church--History--19th century. I. Title
  BX8611 .P32 2002
  289.3'034--dc21
                       2002030201

Contents

Preface

For thirty-four years I was primarily an Institute director for the Church Educational System (CES) of the Church of Jesus Christ of Latter-day Saints. There is much to like about the college-level discussions that sometimes occur in the Institute setting. Unfortunately, our adult lessons and discussions at church rarely rise above the seminary level, even though many of our members are well educated. Our discussions are usually an inch deep and a mile wide as they say. We seem to have a lingering desire for simple religion. We like to hear confirmations that everything is as we assumed it was: our pioneer ancestors were heroic and inspired and the Bible and Book of Mormon are in perfect harmony, for instance. We never learn in church that the Book of Abraham papyri were discovered and translated by Egyptologists or that researchers have studied Native American genes and what the implications are for the Book of Mormon. Questions about such topics are discouraged because they create tension; they are considered inappropriate or even heretical. This approach has isolated many of us from the rest of the world or from reality itself in those instances when we insist on things that are simply untrue.

All the while, such remarkable research has been conducted over the past thirty years into Mormon origins. It is exciting to see what has been done collaboratively by church historians—the faculty of the Joseph Fielding Smith Institute for Church History at Brigham Young University, BYU history and religion professors and scholars from other disciplines and other church schools, and seminary and institute faculty—and by unaffiliated scholars. Together, they have painstakingly collated and compared accounts of the most important events in church history from the original minutes and diaries; gathered data from the environment to better understand the circumstances under which activities occurred; studied the language of the revelations and scriptures and compared it to the general idiom and to literary expressions; excavated and restored sites; scoured archives; translated documents; gathered genealogical records and pursued traces of people's lives for additional testaments. They have published, critiqued, and reevaluated a veritable mountain of evidence. Too much of this escapes the view of the rank-and-file in the church.

There was a day when Latter-day Saint history was considered unworthy of this kind of attention by professional historians. In large part, due to the Mormon History Association and the involvement by LDS scholars in other professional groups, this is no longer the case. Today, publishers, both academic and general interest presses, accept and publish Mormon topics on a regular basis. Yet the relatively modest print runs these books usually receive indicate that they sell mostly to other professionals rather than to the LDS public at large. There is a lingering distrust of anything that hasn't come directly from, or with an endorsement by, the church leadership.

Some of this research has been conducted by critics of the church. Some of it contains distortions and is unreliable. But much of what even the critics have written is backed by solid investigation and sound reasoning and should not be dismissed. Your friends don't always tell you what you need to hear. Furthermore, it is untrue that non-Mormons who write about the church are de facto anti-Mormon. Many outside historians are good friends and supporters of the church, and many find the topics interesting for their own sake without any agenda.

About a decade and a half ago, there was some consternation and confusion over Mark Hofmann's forgeries and murders. In fact, it has taken a while to sort through and correct the damage he caused. Ironically, while the LDS church supported the forgeries, two of the church's most visible critics never accepted their validity. Despite the setback to history caused by Hofmann, the ranks of honest and earnest historians have continued their research and writing.

Over the years, scholars of all stripes have made contributions and counterbalanced each other by critiquing each other's works. We now have a body of authentic, reliable documents and a near-consensus on many of the details. From this base, the overall picture of Mormon origins begins to unfold. This picture is much different from what we hear in the modified versions that are taught in Sunday school. But demythologized—placed in its original time and place, amid all the twists and turns that exist in the real world—it rings true. There has not been an attempt to eliminate the spiritual from the secular. Far from that, the foundational stories are in many cases more spiritual, less temporal, and more stirring. Whatever else, they are also fascinating. To know the personalities involved in these events and to hear them tell their experiences in their own original words before everything was recast for hierarchical and proselyting purposes is to see it all in an entirely new and exciting perspective.

That said, I have wondered how I should introduce my work. How should I convey what I feel in my soul? First, this book is not intended for children or investigators. So much of our attention is directed toward children and potential converts that long-standing adult members rarely have an opportunity to speak freely to each other. We worry that tender ears may overhear. I am a fourth-generation Mormon, and I want to address this discussion to other second-, third-, and fourth-generation Mormons who will better understand where I am coming from. Lest there be any question, let me say that my intent is to increase faith, not to diminish it. Still, faith needs to be built on truth—what is, in fact, true and believable. After that comes the great leap. We too often confuse faith with knowledge. Faith has to do with the unknown, not about what can be proven or can be shown to be reasonably based on the evidence. I have always thought that an unwillingness to submit one's beliefs to rigorous scrutiny is a manifestation of weakness of faith. Otherwise, everything becomes a matter of orthodoxy rather than truth.

These are matters that I wrestled with for years. As a young man, I became involved in CES because of my commitment to the gospel and my love of the scriptures and also because of my passion for church history. These remain priorities today. I see a number of things differently now than I did before I embarked on this lifelong study of, and service to, the church. I volunteered toward the end of my career to be the LDS Institute director at the Salt Lake County jail. I looked forward to focusing on basic Bible teachings and doing some counseling. I also hoped that I might resolve some of my own questions in an atmosphere where I could freely contemplate them. Now that I am retired, I find myself compelled to discuss in public what I pondered mostly in private at that time.

I have two purposes in writing. One is to introduce church members who have not followed the developments in church history during the last thirty years to issues that are central to the topic of Mormon origins. I hope my survey will be enlightening and useful to anyone who has wanted to understand what has been termed the New Mormon History.

Second, I would like church members to understand historians and religion teachers like myself. When I or my colleagues talk or write about the LDS past, we tend to avoid superlatives that members expect when hearing a recital of our history. Their ears finely tuned to the nuances of such parlance, they assume that we have secularized the story, that we are intentionally obtuse, or that we split hairs. They have heard that we are revisionists, and by this they understand that we are rewriting history in a way that was never intended. In truth, we are salvaging the earliest, authentic versions of these stories from the ravages of well-meaning censors who have abridged and polished them for institutional purposes.

Wallace B. Smith, president-emeritus of the RLDS church (now the Community of Christ), writing about "the foundation experiences" of Mormonism, observed: "One thing is clear. The genie is out of the bottle and it cannot be put back. Facts uncovered and the questions raised by the new Mormon historians will not go away. They will have to be dealt with if we are to maintain a position of honesty and integrity in our dealings with our own members as well as our friends in the larger religious community."[1] I find this position to be both refreshing and healthy. I also agree with Thomas Jefferson who taught that however discomfiting a free exchange may be, truth will ultimately emerge the victor.[2] President Hugh B. Brown, a counselor in the LDS presidency during the 1960s, echoed on behalf of the church:

> I admire men and women who have developed the questing spirit, who are unafraid of new ideas as stepping stones to progress. We should, of course, respect the opinions of others, but we should also be unafraid to dissent—if we are informed. Thoughts and expressions compete in the marketplace of thought, and in that competition truth emerges triumphant. Only error fears freedom of expression ... This free exchange of ideas is not to be deplored as long as men and women remain humble and teachable. Neither fear of consequence or any kind of coercion should ever be used to secure uniformity of thought in the church. People should express their problems and opinions and be unafraid to think without fear of ill consequences. ... We must preserve freedom of the mind in the church and resist all efforts to suppress it.[3]

---

1. Wallace B. Smith, "Exiles in Time," *Saints' Herald* 139 (Apr. 1992): 8.
2. On the study of religion, Jefferson advised his nephew, "[Y]ou are answerable, not for the rightness, but uprightness, of the decision"; qtd. in Merrill D. Peterson, ed., *Thomas Jefferson: A Profile* (New York: Hill and Wang, 1967), 247.
3. Hugh B. Brown, *An Abundant Life: The Memoirs of Hugh B. Brown,* ed. Edwin B. Firmage (Salt Lake City: Signature Books, 1988), 137-39; Hugh B. Brown, "An Eternal Quest—Freedom of the Mind," a speech delivered at Brigham Young University, 13 May 1969, in *Speeches of the Year* (Provo, UT:

These and similar sentiments motivate me in my current endeavor. I do not believe that what I have written is flawless, but I lay out the evidence and state the implications of what I see as clearly as possible. My years of teaching have taught me that if I am not direct, my point is missed. However, there is also a downside to such straightforwardness. If I seem provocative or insensitive, or if I offend, it is not my intention. These are issues that are deeply important to me. I do not treat them lightly, whatever the shortcomings of my prose. Yet, I feel good that I do not cloak the issues in ambiguities, with an overdose of qualifiers and disclaimers. I find these matters to be so engaging that, for me, they bring church history to life for the first time. If nothing else, the reader may sense my enthusiasm, which can be boundless, I admit.

Perhaps the reader is already puzzled by this lengthy dialogue on historiography and freedom of belief. If so, let me state clearly what can be expected from this book. I, along with colleagues, and drawing from years of research, find the evidence employed to support many traditional claims about the church to be either nonexistent or problematic. In other words, it didn't all happen the way we've been told. For the sake of accuracy and honesty, I think we need to address and ultimately correct this disparity between historical narratives and the inspirational stories that are told in church. Hopefully my book will be received in the spirit in which it is intended. As English philosopher John Stuart Mill said, any attempt to resist another opinion is a "peculiar evil." If the opinion is right, we are robbed of the "opportunity of exchanging error for truth." If it is wrong, we are deprived of a deeper understanding of the truth in "its collision with error."[4]

On 4-5 January 1922, B. H. Roberts, senior president of the church's seven presidents of the seventy, presented to ranking church leaders what he called "Book of Mormon Difficulties," discussed in

Brigham Young University Press, 1969); rpt. in *Dialogue: A Journal of Mormon Thought* 17 (Spring 1984): 77-83.

4. John Stuart Mill, *On Liberty*, ed. Currin V. Shields (Indianapolis: Bobbs-Merrill Co., Inc., 1956), 21.

chapter two of this book. Elder Roberts said: "In a church which claimed continuous revelation, a crisis had arisen where revelation was necessary." He hoped his brethren would bring "the inspiration of the Lord" to solve these problems. However, after his presentations, his colleagues reaffirmed their testimonies of the Book of Mormon and offered no solutions.[5]

I would like to renew Elder Roberts's call for a more candid discussion of the foundations of the church beginning with the Book of Mormon. I discuss these issues in eight chapters, the first of which evaluates Joseph Smith's efforts at translation. Chapters 2-4 examine Joseph's intellectual environment, including the King James Bible, evangelical religion, and American antiquities, all of which influenced the content of the Book of Mormon. Chapter 4 also discusses religious feelings and the Holy Ghost. Chapters 5-6 reveal the impact of folk beliefs on two early claims of Mormonism. Chapters 7-8 investigate priesthood restoration and Joseph's first vision, detailing the developments and what precipitated the changes in the history of these two experiences.

I wish to thank my friends and colleagues who agreed to be readers of my first and subsequent drafts for their many helpful suggestions and encouragement. It is good to have critics, but it is also good to have such reassuring friends.

---

5. B. H. Roberts, *Studies of the Book of Mormon,* ed. Brigham D. Madsen (Urbana: University of Illinois Press, 1985), 21-23, 46.

Fig. 1. Joseph Smith (1805-44), from Frederick Piercy's *Route from Liverpool to Great Salt Lake Valley* (Liverpool and London, 1855).

1.
Joseph Smith as Translator/Revelator

One of Joseph Smith's primary prophetic gifts was the translation of ancient documents by the power of God. He used the word "translate" to explain his work on the Book of Mormon, the Bible, Egyptian papyri, the Kinderhook plates, a Greek psalter, and a lost parchment written by the apostle John. Although the word "translate" may be as useful as any other, it inadequately explains the process by which these scriptures came to be. In this chapter I will examine the historical record—specifically what Joseph Smith, his family, and other early church leaders had to say on this topic—and consider what we can conclude about the way in which the Book of Mormon was dictated.

The Book of Mormon

The church teaches that the golden plates were an ancient record received and translated into English by Joseph Smith.[1] Illustrations in the church magazine, the *Ensign*, depict the prophet studying the

---

1. See Doctrine and Covenants 20:8 (hereafter D&C); "Joseph Smith—History," The Pearl of Great Price, 1:33-35, 53, 59-62 (hereafter JS—History). These verses imply that Joseph needed the plates to translate. Joseph said that the "Title Page of the Book of Mormon is a literal translation" from the gold plates. Some have argued that since he said the plates

plates much like an archaeologist or classicist might.[2] This view is not supported by what Joseph Smith's scribes and other witnesses said. On the contrary, the eyewitnesses reported that Joseph read the English text as it appeared, word for word, in the seer stone, sometimes called "the interpreters," which he placed in his hat, his face over the hat's opening to shut out the light. Those who reported this include Emma Hale Smith (Joseph's wife), Isaac Hale (Joseph's father-in-law), Michael Morse (brother-in-law), Martin Harris, and Joseph Knight Sr.[3] Morse said that he watched Joseph on several occasions: "The mode of procedure consisted in Joseph's placing the Seer Stone in the crown of a hat, then putting his face into the hat, so as to entirely cover his face, resting his elbows upon his knees, and then dictating, word after word, while the scribe ... wrote it down."[4] (See fig. 2.)

The Book of Mormon was dictated first in Harmony, Pennsylvania, then in Fayette, New York, where it was completed. In Fayette, David Whitmer and Elizabeth A. Whitmer (later the wife of Oliver Cowdery) observed the dictation process and reported that Joseph used a seer stone placed in his hat, the same as previously reported.[5] In other words, the method was consistent throughout the project and it did not constitute what we would normally consider to be a translation. With his face covered, Joseph was unable to see the source document, the golden plates, even if the plates were nearby; more than often they were not.

---

read like Hebrew, from right to left, this implies that he used the plates while translating the Book of Mormon. Dean C. Jessee, ed., *The Papers of Joseph Smith: Autobiographical and Historical Writings* (Salt Lake City: Deseret Book Co., 1989), 1:300.

2. See the *Ensign*, Dec. 1983, inside cover, 25; Jan. 1988, 4, 9; Nov. 1988, 35, 46; July 1993, 62; Jan. 1997, 38; Aug. 1997, 11; July 1999, 41.

3. Richard S. Van Wagoner and Steven C. Walker, "Joseph Smith: 'The Gift of Seeing,'" *Dialogue: A Journal of Mormon Thought* 15 (Summer 1982): 50-53.

4. Ibid., 52-53; Michael Morse, interview by William W. Blair, in Letter to the Editor, *Saints Herald*, 15 June 1879, 190-91.

5. Van Wagoner and Walker, "The Gift of Seeing," 51-52.

Fig. 2. Joseph Smith dictating to Martin Harris. Joseph used the same stone for translating the Book of Mormon and for treasure hunting. Illustration by Kurt Gray.

For a time Emma Smith acted as her husband's scribe. She said that she received dictation from him as he sat "with his face buried in his hat ... hour after hour with nothing between us." Occasionally, she said, the plates "lay on the table ... wrapped in a small linen table cloth," but she was never allowed to see them—a decision which caused her to "murmur" (See Doctrine and Covenants 25:4; hereafter D&C).[6]

David Whitmer confirmed that Joseph "did not use the plates in the translation"[7] and that "the plates were not before Joseph, while he translated, but seem to have been removed by the custodian an-

---

6. Joseph Smith III, "Last Testimony of Sister Emma," *Saints' Herald*, 1 Oct. 1879, 290.

7. "Mormonism," *Kansas City Daily Journal*, 5 June 1881, 1, rpt. in *Deseret Evening News*, 11 June 1881, 1; *Saints' Herald*, 1 July 1881, 198; *Latter-day Saints' Millennial Star*, 4 July 1881, 423.

gel."[8] Isaac Hale said that while Joseph was translating, the plates were "hid in the woods."[9] Martin Harris and Joseph Smith Sr., respectively, added that the plates were covered "in the box" and hid "in the mountains" while they were being translated.[10]

Shortly after becoming Joseph's full-time scribe in April 1829, Oliver Cowdery learned that just as the plates were not necessary for translation, other source documents could be read without being present. In a disagreement between the two men over whether John the Revelator was on earth or in heaven, Joseph, through a stone, "translated" the answer from "a record made on parchment by John and hidden up by himself" somewhere in the Middle East (D&C 7, headnote).

Thus the testimony from Joseph's closest associates, relatives, and scribes was that the golden plates were not directly used in the translation. No primary witness reported that Joseph used them in any way, as we otherwise might assume he would need to in "translating" them.

It would be relevant to note here that in the Book of Mormon, King Mosiah translated ancient records using seer stones or "interpreters"—"two stones" set in eye frames or spectacles (Mosiah 8:13; 28:13-16). In the Book of Mormon there is a specific prophecy that Joseph Smith would be able to read the Book of Mormon's Nephite record using Mosiah's interpreters. It foretells that Joseph will "read the words which I shall give unto thee" (2 Ne. 27:11, 20, 22, 24).

---

8. "The Golden Tablets," *Chicago Times*, 7 Aug. 1875, 1.

9. Affidavit of Isaac Hale, 20 Mar. 1834, *Susquehanna Register and Northern Pennsylvanian*, 1 May 1834, 1; newspaper in the Susquehanna County Historical Society, Montrose, Pennsylvania; rpt. in *Mormonism Unvailed*, ed. E. D. Howe (Painesville, OH: by the Author, 1834), 265.

10. Martin Harris, interview by John A. Clark, 1828, in *The Episcopal Recorder* (Philadelphia), 5 Sept. 1840, 94; qtd. in *Early Mormon Documents* 3+ vols., ed. Dan Vogel (Salt Lake City: Signature Books, 1996-), 2:266; Joseph Smith Sr., interview by Fayette Lapham, ca. 1830, in "The Mormons," *Historical Magazine* 7 (May 1870): 308; qtd. in Dan Vogel, ed., *Early Mormon Documents*, 1:464.

"The Lord had prepared spectacles for to read the Book," Joseph Smith explained.[11] In other words, neither Mosiah nor Joseph Smith could read the ancient scripts as a scholar would; rather, they read what they saw, provided for them in their own language, when they looked into the stones.

Converts to Mormonism in the early days understood that when Joseph looked in the seer stone, he was shown the English text; he was a reader rather than a translator. Martin Harris clerked for Joseph in 1828 and informed classical scholar Charles Anthon and Episcopal minister John A. Clark that Joseph saw the text in English. Joseph simply "read" the translation, Harris said. When Joseph looked "through his spectacles ... [he] would then write down or repeat what he saw, which, when repeated aloud, was written down by Harris."[12] Years later Harris described this to church member Edward Stevenson, who wrote: "By aid of the seer stone, sentences would appear and were read by the Prophet and written by Martin. ... If correctly written that sentence would disappear and another appear in its place."[13] David Whitmer announced that on the seer stone "appeared the writing. ... Joseph would read off the English to Oliver Cowdery."[14] Joseph Knight Sr., an early convert, explained: "Now the way he translated was he put the urim and thummim into his hat and Darkened his Eyes[,] then he would take a sentence and it would appear in Brite Roman Letters[,] then he would tell the writer and he would write it[,] then that would go away [and] the next Sentence would Come and so on."[15] In an 1830 court trial in New York, "Oliver Cowdery ... testified under oath, that said Smith found with the plates, from which he translated his book, two transparent stones. ...

11. Jessee, *Papers of Joseph Smith*, 1:9.
12. Charles Anthon, Letter to E. D. Howe, 17 Feb. 1834, in Howe, *Mormonism Unvailed*, 270-71; qtd. in Vogel, *Early Mormon Documents*, 2:268.
13. Qtd. in Van Wagoner and Walker, "The Gift of Seeing," 50.
14. Ibid., 51.
15. Ibid., 52.

Through these, he was able to read in English, the reformed Egyptian characters."[16]

Some writers have cited the revelations given to Oliver Cowdery in April 1829 as evidence that Joseph was more than a reader.[17] These sections explain how Oliver translated using his "gift," a "rod of nature" (divining rod), rather than Joseph's use of seer stones (6:25-28).[18] When Oliver was young, he was taught how to handle a divining rod and ask it questions in faith. This, when accompanied by the Spirit, caused the rod to move and meant that the answer was yes. If the rod did not move, the answer was no.[19] This process was more difficult than reading from a stone; it required patience. When Cowdery attempted to apply it to translation, he ultimately "did not continue" (D&C 9:3-5).

That Joseph claimed to be reading an ancient text within a stone soon caused trouble. Critics who sought to test this claim stole 116 pages of the Book of Mormon transcript, then apparently waited to see if Joseph "should bring forth the same words again." According to a revelation recorded in May 1829, the critics would say: "If he bringeth forth the same words, behold, we have the same words with us, and we have altered them; Therefore they will not agree, and we will say that he has lied in his words, and that he has no gift" (D&C 10:17-18, 31; Book of Mormon, 1830 edition, preface).[20]

---

16. A[bram]. W. Benton, "Mormonites," *Evangelical Magazine and Gospel Advocate*, 9 Apr. 1831, 120.

17. D&C 6, 8, 9; see Stephen D. Ricks, "Joseph Smith's Means and Methods of Translating the Book of Mormon" (paper prepared for the Foundation for Ancient Research & Mormon Studies, 1984), 4-5.

18. Cf. D&C 8:6-8 with the Book of Commandments 7:3 (1833) in Wilford C. Wood, *Joseph Smith Begins His Work: The Book of Commandments ...*, 2 vols. (Salt Lake City: by the Author, 1962).

19. Barnes Frisbie, *The History of Middletown, Vermont* (Rutland, VT: Tuttle and Co., 1867), 43-64, rptd. in the *Vermont Historical Gazetteer,* ed. Abby Maria Hemenway (Claremont, NH: Claremont Manufacturing Co., 1877), 3:810-12, 818-19; qtd. in Vogel, *Early Mormon Documents*, 1:603-05, 619-20.

20. For evidence that D&C 10 (current edition) was not written in "the

This is problematic. If these critics had "altered the words," as Joseph divined they had, and produced the original manuscript to discredit him, the alterations in a different handwriting would have been readily apparent. Aside from that, there is an assumption that was unchallenged by Joseph Smith that a second translation would be identical to the first. This confirms the view that the English text existed in some kind of unalterable, spiritual form rather than that someone had to think through difficult conceptual issues and idioms, always resulting in variants in any translation.

Joseph avoided this test altogether by translating a different version of the same story from a different set of plates, said to have been attached to the original plates. Interestingly, from this time on, whenever Joseph spoke of translation, he emphasized that he translated by "the gift and power of God," which was a more general statement (see 11 June 1829 copyright title page and Testimony of Three Witnesses, both in the Book of Mormon). These more general statements after June 1829 did not conflict with his earlier explanations but did not rule out the possibility that he had been a reader. Thus David Whitmer, Martin Harris, Joseph Knight Sr., Oliver Cowdery, and others could say that they understood Joseph to say that he read from the stone.[21]

The question is whether or not Joseph could indeed read text from a stone or whether the stone was a device to enhance concentration or a prop for the benefit of onlookers. Previously he was em-

summer of 1828," but rather in "May 1829" as it originally appeared in the 1833 Book of Commandments, see Max H. Parkin, "A Preliminary Analysis of the Dating of Section 10," *The Seventh Annual Sidney B. Sperry Symposium* (Provo, UT: Brigham Young University, 1979), 68-74; Stanley R. Larson, "A Study of Some Textual Variations in the Book of Mormon Comparing the Original and the Printer's Manuscripts and the 1830, the 1837, and the 1840 Editions" (master's thesis, Brigham Young University, 1974), 17-18n15; and Richard P. Howard, *Restoration Scriptures: A Study of Their Textual Development,* 2nd ed. (Independence MO: Herald Publishing House, 1995), 152.

21. Van Wagoner and Walker, "The Gift of Seeing," 52, 54.

ployed as a scryer for treasure hunters and was brought to court three times for stone-gazing.[22] The fact that he and his colleagues never obtained any riches by this method may argue against the efficacy of the endeavor. Of interest is the testimony given in the July 1830 trial, heard before Justice Joseph Chamberlain of Bainbridge, New York. The proceedings were reported by A. W. Benton, a young medical doctor who lived in South Bainbridge:

> During the trial it was shown that the Book of Mormon was brought to light by the same magic power by which he [Joseph] pretended to tell fortunes, discover hidden treasures &c ... Addison Austin was next called upon, who testified, that [he was] ... with Smith alone, and [that Austin] asked [Smith] to tell him honestly whether he could see this money or not. Smith hesitated some time, but finally replied, "[T]o be candid, between you and me, I cannot, any more than you or any body else; but any way to get a living."[23]

The same information was also conveyed under oath at Joseph's second July 1830 trial in front of Justice Joel K. Noble of Colesville, New York. Noble wrote: "Jo. was asked by witness [Austin] if he could see or tel[l] more than others[.] Jo. said he could not and says any thing for a living. I now and then Get a sh[i]lling."[24] Isaac Hale, Alva Hale, and Peter Ingersoll each signed affidavits stating that Joseph said the same to them.[25]

We don't know how accurately these statements may reflect something that might have been said in a certain context. For instance, if Joseph attempted to explain the spiritual rather than me-

22. H. Michael Marquardt and Wesley P. Walters, *Inventing Mormonism: Tradition and the Historical Record* (San Francisco: Smith Research Associates, 1994), 70-75, 174-78.

23. A[bram]. W. Benton, "Mormonites," *Evangelical Magazine*, 9 Apr. 1831, 120.

24. Joel K. Noble, Letter to Jonathan B. Turner, 8 Mar. 1842, in the Jonathan B. Turner Collection, Illinois State Historical Library, Springfield.

25. Affidavits of Alva and Isaac Hale, 20 Mar. 1834, in the *Susquehanna Register*, 1 May 1834, 1.

chanical aspect of seer stones, people may have misunderstood him. In any case, Peter Ingersoll, whose Palmyra property adjoined the Smiths on the north, reported what he overheard Joseph say. Sometime after Joseph and Emma eloped in January 1827, Ingersoll helped them return to Emma's parents' home in Harmony, Pennsylvania, to collect her furniture and other belongings. Ingersoll said he witnessed a very emotional scene:

> His father-in-law (Mr. Hale) addressed Joseph, in a flood of tears: "You have stolen my daughter and married her. I had much rather have followed her to her grave. You spend your time in digging for money—pretend to see in a stone, and thus try to deceive people." Joseph wept, and acknowledged he could not see in a stone now, nor never could; He then promised to give up his old habits of digging for money and looking into stones.[26]

Another possibility is that Joseph told his early followers that he could read documents from a stone because it was easy for them to conceptualize. They already believed that scryers could find hidden treasures that way. The "interpreters," later called the urim and thummim, had a sense of biblical authority to them. On the other hand, the Old Testament urim and thummim seem to have been two objects that were thrown like a pair of dice and then observed for God's "yes" or "no" answer; there is no evidence that they were used to translate languages.[27] Again, it is interesting that after the lost manuscript incident, Joseph became more vague in his explanation to others about how he translated.

Although Joseph said he was a reader rather than a literal translator of the Book of Mormon, it has become clear that he was also a participant in the book's creation. He made textual alterations in 1837, changing passages that described the Father and the Son as one

26. Affidavit of Peter Ingersoll, 2 Dec. 1833, in Howe, *Mormonism Unvailed*, 234-35; qtd. in Vogel, *Early Mormon Documents*, 2:42-43.

27. *The Interpreter's Dictionary of the Bible*, 4 vols. (New York: Abingdon Press, 1962), 4:739-40.

God to a description of them as distinct and separate beings.[28] He did not view the original text as inviolate, in other words. Otherwise the corrected text would either reflect a previous error upon God or upon the translator for changing God's words as read from the stone. Perhaps Joseph placed his face in the hat and dictated to his scribe the revelatory "sudden strokes of ideas" that entered into his mind.[29]

Usually he did not mind if others observed him translating, but sometimes he separated himself from his scribe. Martin Harris reported that while he wrote for Joseph, "a thick curtain or blanket was suspended between them" and that Joseph was "behind a curtain," behind a "sheet," or that he "would sit in a different room, or up stairs."[30] Since the gold plates were not used during the translation, why the curtain? No nineteenth-century church member mentions that Joseph used notes or books, but scholars have determined that he consulted an open Bible, specifically a printing of the King James translation dating from 1769 or later, including its errors.[31]

---

28. Cf. the Book of Mormon (1982), 1 Ne. 11:16, 18, 21, 32; 13:40, with Wilford C. Wood, *Joseph Smith Begins His Work: Book of Mormon 1830 First Edition*, 2 vols. (Salt Lake City: by the Author, 1958), 1:25-26, 32. The godhead alterations were not continued beyond 1 Nephi.

29. Joseph Smith's 27 June 1839 discourse in Joseph Smith et al, *History of the Church of Jesus Christ of Latter-day Saints,* ed. B. H. Roberts, 7 vols. (Salt Lake City: Deseret Book Co., 1978 printing), 3:381.

30. Martin Harris, interview by John A. Clark, 1828, *The Visitor, or Monthly Instructor, for 1841* (London: Religious Tract Society, 1841) 63-64; qtd. in Vogel, *Early Mormon Documents*, 2:268; Howe, *Mormonism Unvailed*, 14; qtd. in Vogel, *Early Mormon Documents*, 2:285; qtd. in Charles Anthon, Letter to E. D. Howe, 17 Feb. 1834, ibid., 270-71; Abner Cole, "Gold Bible No. 6," *The Reflector* (Palmyra, NY), 19 Mar. 1831, 126; qtd. in Vogel, *Early Mormon Documents*, 2:248.

31. David P. Wright, "Joseph Smith's Interpretation of Isaiah in the Book of Mormon," *Dialogue* 31 (Winter 1998):181-206; Stan Larson, "The Historicity of the Matthean Sermon on the Mount in 3 Nephi," in *New Approaches to the Book of Mormon: Explorations in Critical Methodology,* ed. Brent Lee Metcalfe (Salt Lake City: Signature Books, 1993), 115-63.

The Bible

To continue the discussion of what Joseph meant by the word "translate," between 1830 and 1833 he worked on a translation of the Bible (the Joseph Smith Translation, abbreviated as JST), intending to eliminate or restore material "by the power of God."[32] He gave consideration to all the books from Genesis to Revelation, but most of the changes were confined to Genesis and Matthew. His added insights and a few deletions have provided us with a document that is often cited in the LDS church today. Unfortunately, none of the significant additions or deletions have been supported by the numerous Old and New Testament manuscript finds since 1833. The discovery of the Dead Sea Scrolls provided us with Hebrew manuscripts for all of the Old Testament (except Esther) that are a thousand years earlier than any previously known (100 B.C.). Manuscripts for New Testament texts now date to about A.D. 200. We could expect that with these many discoveries over the last 172 years, some important confirming evidence should be available for Joseph's alterations of the Bible. Such is not the case.[33]

Moreover, some of Joseph's doctrinal changes in the JST are at odds with current LDS beliefs. For example, KJV Luke 10:22 reads: "[N]o man knoweth who the Son is, but the Father; and who the Father is, but the Son, and he to whom the Son will reveal him." The

---

32. 1 Ne. 13:28, 39-40; Moses 1:41; 8th Article of Faith; Andrew F. Ehat and Lyndon W. Cook, eds., *The Words of Joseph Smith: The Contemporary Accounts of the Nauvoo Discourses of the Prophet Joseph* (Provo, UT: Religious Studies Center, 1980), 256.

33. Kevin L. Barney, "The Joseph Smith Translation and Ancient Texts of the Bible," in *The Word of God: Essays on Mormon Scriptures*, ed. Dan Vogel (Salt Lake City: Signature Books, 1990), 143-60; Richard L. Anderson, "Manuscript Discoveries of the New Testament in Perspective," in the *Fourteenth Annual Symposium on the Archaeology of the Scriptures* (Provo, UT: BYU Department of Extension Publications, 1963), 52-59; Robert J. Matthews, *A Plainer Translation: Joseph Smith's Translation of the Bible, A History and Commentary* (Provo, UT: BYU Press, 1975), 214-15, 236-37, 252-53.

JST reads: "[N]o man knoweth that the Son is the Father, and the Father is the Son, but him to whom the Son will reveal it." In 1 Timothy 2:4, Joseph expands the verse to clarify that the Father and Son "is one God." This view is consistent with Joseph's other scriptural writings of 1829-34 but not with his later thought.[34] All of these JST changes suggest that they were personal insights rather than authoritative statements or reflections of the intent of the original authors.

The Book of Abraham

On 27 November 1967, eleven pieces of Egyptian papyri originally purchased by Joseph Smith were recovered from the Metropolitan Museum of Art in New York City. Among them were Facsimile 1 and Papyrus 11, both important to Joseph Smith in his translation of Abraham 1 through 2:18 in the Pearl of Great Price. Egyptologists discovered that Facsimile 1, Papyri 10 and 11, and Facsimile 3 belonged to the same original scroll, written for a deceased man named Hor. The original Facsimile 1 has the altar scene which has long been printed as part of the Pearl of Great Price and, flanking the picture, five lines of hieroglyphics. When translated, these lines reveal the titles of Hor, his parentage, and that he is the deceased man lying on the altar (figs. 3-4). The adjoining papyrus, number 11, again gives Hor's name, the name of Taikhibit his mother, and instructions for wrapping his mummy (fig. 5). Joseph Smith used this papyrus as his source for Abraham 1 through 2:18.[35] The next adjoining papyrus,

---

34. See Thomas G. Alexander, "The Reconstruction of Mormon Doctrine: From Joseph Smith to Progressive Theology," *Sunstone* 5 (July-Aug. 1980): 24-28; revised as "The Reconstruction of Mormon Doctrine," in *Line Upon Line: Essays on Mormon Doctrine*, ed. Gary James Bergera (Salt Lake City: Signature Books, 1989), 53-57; Boyd Kirkland, "The Development of the Mormon Doctrine of God," in *Line Upon Line*, 35-39; Dan Vogel, "The Earliest Mormon Concept of God," in *Line Upon Line*, 21-33.

35. Klaus Baer, "The Breathing Permit of Hor: A Translation of the Apparent Source of the Book of Abraham," *Dialogue* 3 (Autumn 1968): 109-34; Klaus Baer, Letter to Howard Gelling [James D. Still], 6 June 1982, James D. Still Mormon History Collection (1591/3:2), Manuscripts Division, Marriott Library, University of Utah, Salt Lake City.

Fig. 3. Facsimile No. I from the Book of Abraham, as printed in the *Times and Seasons*, I Mar. 1842, 703.

number 10, again identifies Hor as he progresses through the Egyptian funeral rites (fig. 6), culminating with Facsimile No. 3. Here Hor's name appears at the top and bottom of the illustration showing him in a judgement scene with Osiris and other familiar Egyptian gods associated with these rites (fig. 7).

According to scholars, the scroll was written during the first century B.C. The papyri do not deal with Abraham.[36] In fact, Abraham's

---

36. Charles M. Larson, *By His Own Hand upon Papyrus: A New Look at the Joseph Smith Papyri* (Grand Rapids, MI: Institute for Religious Research, 1992); for translations by Egyptologists Parker and Baer, see H. Michael Marquardt, *The Book of Abraham Papyrus Found* (Salt Lake City: Modern Microfilm, 1981); and *The Book of Abraham Revisited* (Salt Lake City: Utah Lighthouse Ministry, 1983).

Fig. 4. Joseph Smith Papyrus 1, written for a first-century B.C. deceased person named Hor, a priest for Amon-Ra at Thebes in Egypt. The image in the circle is the Egyptian hieroglyph for the name of Hor. His father's name, "Osorwer" and his mother's name, "Taikhibit," also appear in this fragment. Notice how the fragment connects with the one in fig. 5.

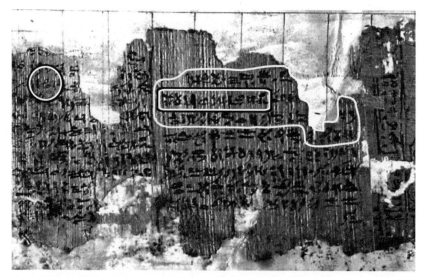

Fig. 5. Joseph Smith Papyrus 11. Areas enclosed within the white line are the portions which Joseph Smith used to produce the English text found in Abraham 1-2:18. The circle and oval highlight the names of Hor (left) and his mother, Taikhibit (right), written in hieratic script.

Fig. 6. Joseph Smith Papyrus 10 continues to the left of papyrus 11 (fig. 5). Hor's name appears three times in Egyptian hieratic.

Fig. 7. Facsimile No. 3 from the Book of Abraham. Images in circles translate "Osiris Hor justified."

Facsimile No. 3 (fig. 7)	Papyrus No. 10 (fig. 6)	Papyrus No. 11 (fig. 5)	Papyrus No. 1 (fig. 4)

The order in which the papyri appear in the original scroll. Spaces between the papyri indicate where small portions of the scroll are missing.

name does not appear anywhere in this narrative.[37] In 1967 most Latter-day Saints anticipated that Joseph's translation of the Book of Abraham would be confirmed. The documents were turned over to Hugh Nibley of Brigham Young University, and between January 1968 and May 1970, he produced a lengthy series of articles on Egyptian culture and related topics in the church magazine, the *Improvement Era*, although no translations of the papyri appeared in the *Era*.[38] Nor did Nibley correct the clear identification of Hor, not Abraham, in Facsimile 1, Papyri 10 and 11, and Facsimile 3.[39] Clearly, the first place to look for the interpretation of Facsimiles 1 and 3 is in the writing directly around these pictures. Nibley ignored this writing and instead focused on Egyptian temple ritual, assembling culturally and spatially unrelated Abrahamic legends over several thousand years of history to demonstrate that the Book of Abraham had the support of some ancient traditions.[40]

In reality, Joseph Smith apparently used other sources in "translating" the Book of Abraham. In 1835, the year he produced the opening chapters of Abraham, his counselor Oliver Cowdery, in the *Messenger and Advocate*, mentioned Josephus three times in interpreting the pictures from the "Joseph of Egypt" scroll.[41] In the *Antiquities of the Jews*, Josephus wrote about how Noah, who had trouble with his son Ham, "cursed his posterity," whereas the lineage of Abra-

---

37. Some of Joseph Smith's statements about Abraham in the papyri are cited in Jay M. Todd, *The Saga of the Book of Abraham* (Salt Lake City: Deseret Book Co., 1969), 196, 211, 221, 237, 256-57.

38. Hugh Nibley, "A New Look at the Pearl of Great Price," *Improvement Era*, Jan. 1968-May 1970.

39. Hugh Nibley, *The Message of the Joseph Smith Papyri: An Egyptian Endowment* (Salt Lake City: Deseret Book Co., 1975), 1-3, 19-23.

40. Ibid., 57-253; Edward H. Ashment, "Reducing Dissonance: The Book of Abraham as a Case Study," in *The Word of God*, 221-35; and Edward H. Ashment, "The Facsimiles of the Book of Abraham," *Sunstone* 4 (Dec. 1979): 33-51.

41. Oliver Cowdery, "Egyptian Mummies," *Messenger and Advocate* 2 (Dec. 1835): 236.

ham and others "escaped that curse."[42] Joseph Smith expanded this original curse (Gen. 9:20-27) to include denial of priesthood ordination to blacks (Abr. 1:21-26). LDS scholar Lester Bush, with these Abraham verses in mind, commented: "Mormon scripture [The Book of Abraham] and the contemporary pro slavery arguments are striking."[43] Josephus further identified Abraham as a resident of Chaldea and "a person of great sagacity" who "began to have higher notions of virtue than others had, and he determined to renew and to change the opinion all men happened then to have concerning God." Abraham's preaching was not welcome. They "raised a tumult against him ... and by the assistance of God, he came and lived in the land of Canaan."[44] While in Canaan, a land promised to his posterity, Abraham encountered a famine. This brought him and his wife Sarah to Egypt, where he successfully pretended to be his wife's brother. The pharaoh eventually allowed him to "enter into conversation with the most learned among the Egyptians; from which conversation his virtue and his reputation became more conspicuous than they had been before. ... He communicated to them arithmetic, and delivered to them the science of astronomy; for before Abram came into Egypt they were unacquainted with those parts of learning ..."[45]

This sketch by Josephus, which was available to Joseph Smith (fig. 8), explains why, upon examining Facsimile 1 of the Hor papyrus, Joseph might have assumed that Abraham was being sacrificed for preaching against heathen gods but escaped with God's assistance. Viewing the other end of the scroll, Joseph further saw (Facsimile 3) Abraham teaching astronomy in Pharaoh's court just as Josephus's

---

42. William Whiston, trans., *The Works of Flavius Josephus: New Updated Edition* (Peabody, MA: Hendrickson Publishers, 1987), 1:6:37.

43. Lester Bush, "A Commentary on Stephen G. Taggart's 'Mormonism's Negro Policy: Social and Historical Origins,'" *Dialogue* 4 (Winter 1969): 93, 93n35.

44. *Josephus*, 1:7:38. Adam Clarke and Matthew Henry, popular commentators of the day, told a traditional account about Abraham being delivered by God when idol worshipers cast him into a fire.

45. *Josephus*, 1:8:39.

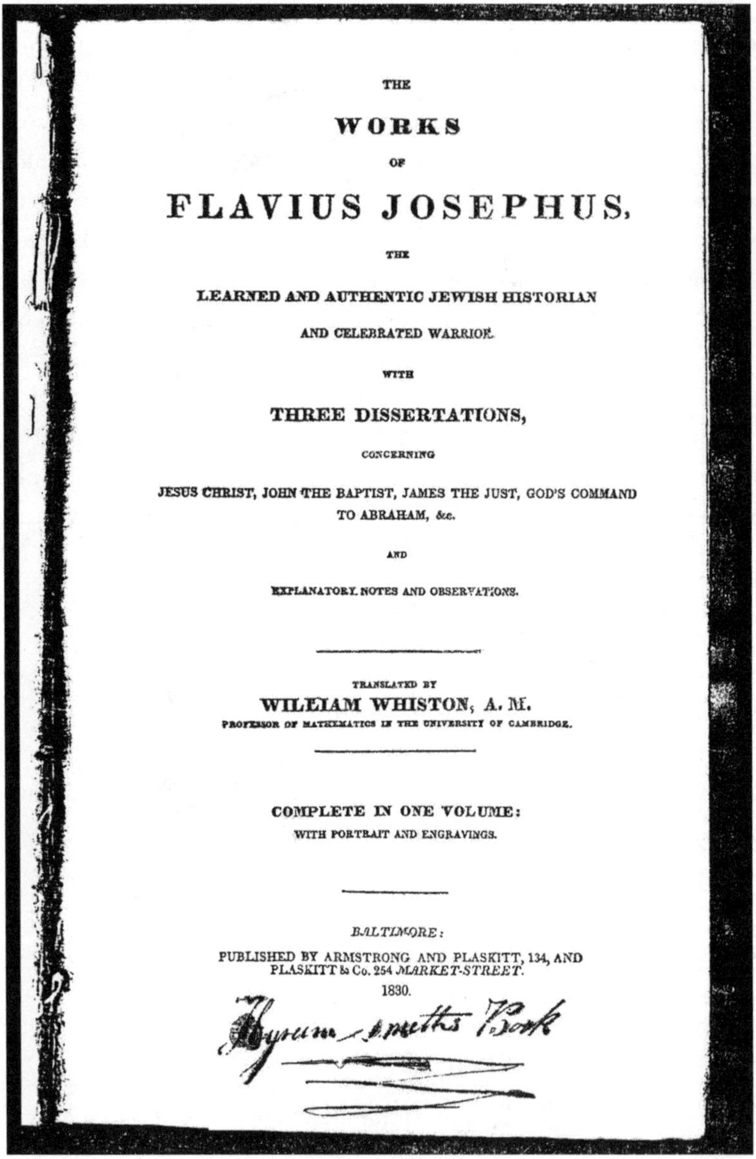

THE

WORKS

OF

FLAVIUS JOSEPHUS,

THE

LEARNED AND AUTHENTIC JEWISH HISTORIAN

AND CELEBRATED WARRIOR.

WITH

THREE DISSERTATIONS,

CONCERNING

JESUS CHRIST, JOHN THE BAPTIST, JAMES THE JUST, GOD'S COMMAND
TO ABRAHAM, &c.

AND

EXPLANATORY NOTES AND OBSERVATIONS.

———

TRANSLATED BY

WILLIAM WHISTON, A. M.
PROFESSOR OF MATHEMATICS IN THE UNIVERSITY OF CAMBRIDGE.

———

COMPLETE IN ONE VOLUME:
WITH PORTRAIT AND ENGRAVINGS.

———

BALTIMORE:
PUBLISHED BY ARMSTRONG AND PLASKITT, 134, AND
PLASKITT & Co. 254 MARKET-STREET.
1830.

Hyrum smiths Book

Fig. 8. Hyrum Smith's signature on the flyleaf of this 1830 edition of *The Works of Flavius Josephus*, LDS church archives.

narrative portrays. (For other parallels, see the appendix to this chapter.)

The Abraham material available in Joseph Smith's own environment provided a reasonable source for his interpretation of the two pictures and the Egyptian writing between them. Joseph himself believed that his source for interpreting the Hor scroll was a divine gift to intuit the meaning of Egyptian characters by the spirit of revelation. Facsimile 3 (see figs. 2, 4, and 5) clearly demonstrates that he believed that these Egyptian characters supported his spiritual impressions (fig. 9). Unfortunately, his interpretations have been shown by Egyptologists today to be a misreading of the papyri.[46]

The primary source for chapters 2, 4, and 5 of Abraham is Genesis 1, 2, 11 (vv. 28-29), and 12. Sixty-six out of seventy-seven verses in this section of Abraham (86 percent) are quotations or close paraphrases of KJV wording.[47] The few Hebrew names and words in the Abraham text reflect Joseph's study under the Hebrew scholar Joshua Seixas in Kirtland, Ohio, during the winter of 1835-36.[48] The differences between these Genesis and Abraham chapters appear to be Joseph's "targumizing" (interpreting or paraphrasing) of the Bible.

Chapters 4 and 5 of Abraham reflect Joseph's changing theology

---

46. Robert K. Ritner, "The 'Breathing Permit of Hor' Thirty-four Years Later," *Dialogue* 33 (Winter 2000): 97-119, esp. note 119; Stephen E. Thompson, "Egyptology and the Book of Abraham," *Dialogue* 28 (Spring 1995): 143-60 (Thompson, an LDS Egyptologist at Brown University, enumerates the anachronisms in the Book of Abraham); Marquardt, *Book of Abraham Revisited*, 106-8.

47. Abr. 2:1-2=Gen. 11:28-29; Abr. 2:3=Gen. 12:1; Abr. 2:9=Gen. 12:2; Abr. 2:11=Gen. 12:3; Abr. 2:14-15, 18=Gen. 12:4-6; Abr. 2:19-23 =Gen. 12:7-12; Abr. 2:25=Gen. 12:13; Abr. 4:1-2=Gen. 1:1-2; Abr. 4:3-5 =Gen. 1:3-5; Abr. 4:6-8=Gen. 1:6-8; Abr. 4:9-11=Gen. 1:9-11; Abr. 4:12-13=Gen. 1:12-13; Abr. 4:14-19=Gen. 1:14-19; Abr. 4:20-23=Gen. 1:20-23; Abr. 4:24-31=Gen. 1:24-31; Abr. 5:1-7=Gen. 2:1-7; Abr. 5:8-10 =Gen. 2:8-10; Abr. 5:11-13=Gen. 2:15-17; Abr. 5:14=Gen. 2:18; Abr. 5:15-19=Gen. 2:21 25; Abr. 5:20-21=Gen. 2:19-20.

48. Louis C. Zucker, "Joseph Smith as a Student of Hebrew," *Dialogue* 3 (Summer 1968): 50-54.

Isis	Osiris	Offering stand	Maat	Hor	Anubis
2	1	3	4	5	6

EXPLANATION OF CUT

1. Abraham sitting upon Pharaoh's throne, by the politeness of the king; with a crown upon his head, representing the priesthood; as emblematical of the grand presidency in heaven; with the sceptre of justice, and judgment in his hand.

2. King Pharaoh; whose name is given in the characters above his head.

3. Signifies Abraham, in Egypt; referring to Abraham, as given in the 9th No. of the Times & Seasons.

4. Prince of Pharaoh, King of Egypt; as written above the hand.

5. Shulem; one of the kings principal waiters; as represented by the characters above his hand.

6. Olimlah; a slave belonging to the prince.

Abraham is reasoning upon the principles of astronomy, in the kings Court.

Fig. 9. Joseph Smith's explanation of Facsimile No. 3 in the *Times and Seasons*, 16 May 1842, 783-84. Above the facsimile, I have indicated who the characters are according to the Egyptian text.

on the godhead. From 1820 to 1834 he believed that there is one God, as seen in the Book of Mormon, the testimony of the three witnesses, the Book of Commandments 24:13-18, the Book of Moses, the JST, and the 1832 account of his first vision. By 1835 he had come to believe that two personages formed the godhead, as taught in the Doctrine and Covenants 20:28 (cf. Book of Commandments 24:18), the Lectures on Faith (5), and the 1835 and 1838 accounts of his first vision. From 1839 on, he preached a plurality of gods, as seen in Abraham 4 and 5 and the LDS temple ceremony.[49] His evolving concept of God suggests that he imposed his own changing view onto the Abrahamic period as well as onto other periods of history. The implication is that the material in these chapters is not "[a] translation of some ancient Records," as the heading of the Book of Abraham claims, but rather nineteenth-century sources.

The astronomical phrases and concepts in the Abraham texts were also common in Joseph Smith's environment. For example, in 1816 Thomas Taylor published a two–volume work called *The Six Books of Proclus on the Theology of Plato*. Volume 2 (pp.140-46) contains phrases and ideas similar to the astronomical concepts in Abraham 3 and Facsimile No. 2. In these six pages, Taylor calls the planets "governors" and uses the terms "fixed stars and planets" and "grand key." Both works refer to the sun as a planet receiving its light and power from a higher sphere rather than generating its own light through hydrogen-helium fusion (cf. Fac. 2, fig. 5).[50] LDS scholar R.

---

49. Joseph first clearly taught the plurality of gods in March 1839 (D&C 121:32). See also Alexander, "The Reconstruction of Mormon Doctrine," in Bergera, ed., *Line Upon Line*, 53-57; Kirkland, "The Development of the Mormon Doctrine of God," in *Line Upon Line*, 35-39; and Jessee, *Papers of Joseph Smith*, 1:6, 272; 2:69.

50. Thomas Taylor, *The Six Books of Proclus on the Theology of Plato* (London: 1816), 2:140-46. See also Clarence F. Packard, *The Mystery Religions of Freemasonry, Paganism, Mormonism* (Bountiful UT: 1965), 205-23, for other comparisons between Taylor's work and the Book of Abraham. See especially the following: (1) on the plurality of gods, "there is one God, the king and father of all things, and many Gods, sons of God, ruling together

Grant Athay, a research astronomer and director of the University of Colorado Observatory, has written, "At the time that the Book of Abraham was translated ... the energy source of the sun was un-known," and "the concept of one star influencing another was also a common concept of the time."[51] Further reflecting nineteenth-century cosmology, Taylor (cf. Abraham 3:4-10) describes the progression of time among the universal bodies. Like Abraham 3:16-19, certain people of Joseph Smith's day also believed in progressive orders of orbs and the intelligences that inhabited them. According to Athay:

> They believed that the surface of the sun was solid, and that it was inhabited by human beings. In fact, they believed that it was inhabited by man. They also believed that all the planets in the solar system were inhabited by man, and the moon as well ... [T]he concept of multiple-world systems, multiple dwellings of man ... was a rather common topic of that time.[52]

Klaus Hansen, an LDS scholar, has written: "The progressive aspect of Joseph's theology, as well as its cosmology, while in a general way compatible with antebellum thought, bears some remarkable resemblances to Thomas Dick's *Philosophy of a Future State*, a second edition of which had been published in 1830." Joseph Smith owned a copy of this work, and Oliver Cowdery in December 1836 quoted

---

with him" (p. 206; cf. Abr. 4 and 5); (2) on unbegotten intellects, "But intellects which ride as it were in souls as in a vehicle, cannot be called the works of the father; for they were not generated" (pp. 210-11; cf. Abr. 3:18); (3) on man's potential to become the equal of the gods, "if these [intellects] ... participate of life through me [God] they will become the equal of the Gods" (p. 211; cf. Abr. 3:22-26); and (4) on the council of the gods, "But Jove to Themis gives command to call the Gods to council" (p. 212; cf. Abr. 4:1).

51. R. Grant Athay, "Astronomy in the Book of Abraham," *Book of Abraham Symposium* (Salt Lake City: University of Utah Institute of Religion, 3 Apr. 1970), ix, 60-61.

52. Ibid., 60. For many primary citations on the cosmology of the early nineteenth-century, see Dan Vogel and Brent Lee Metcalfe, "Joseph Smith's Scriptural Cosmology," in *The Word of God*, 187-219.

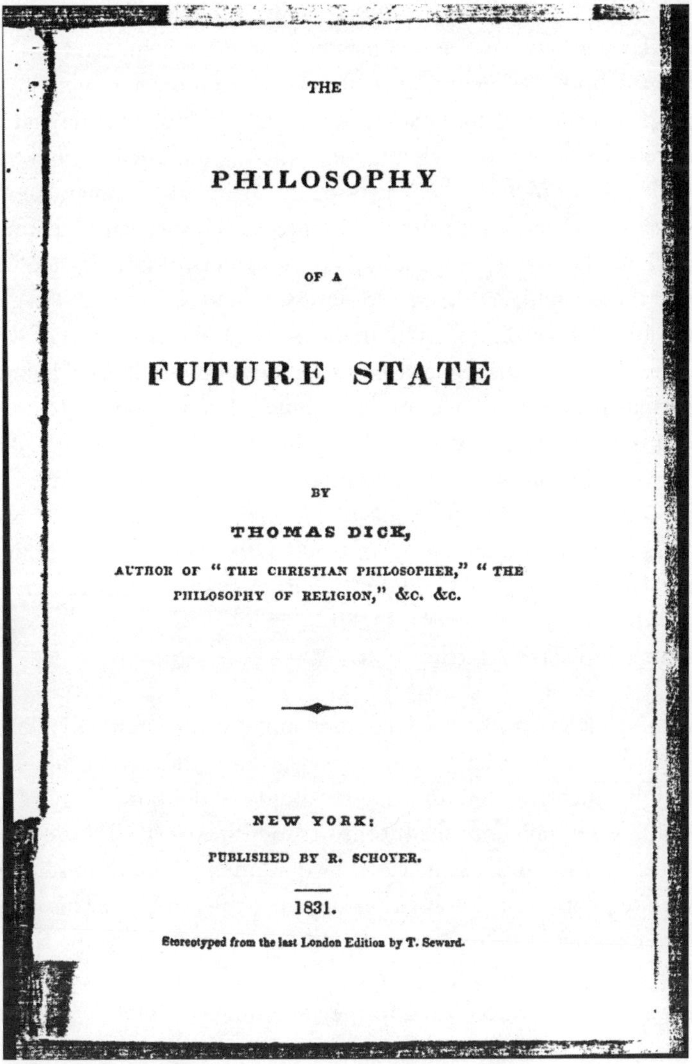

THE

PHILOSOPHY

OF A

FUTURE STATE

BY

THOMAS DICK,

AUTHOR OF " THE CHRISTIAN PHILOSOPHER," " THE
PHILOSOPHY OF RELIGION," &c. &c.

———◆———

NEW YORK:

PUBLISHED BY R. SCHOYER.

————

1831.

Stereotyped from the last London Edition by T. Seward.

Fig. 10. Joseph Smith owned a copy of Thomas Dick's *Philosophy of a Future State*. Several editions were published before 1835.

some lengthy excerpts from it in the *Messenger and Advocate*[53] (fig. 10). Hansen continues:

> Some very striking parallels to Smith's theology suggest that the similarities between the two may be more than coincidental. Dick's lengthy book, an ambitious treatise on astronomy and metaphysics, proposed the idea that matter is eternal and indestructible and rejected the notion of a creation ex nihilo. Much of the book dealt with the infinity of the universe, made up of innumerable stars spread out over immeasurable distances. Dick speculated that many of these stars were peopled by "various orders of intelligences" and that these intelligences were "progressive beings" in various stages of evolution toward perfection. In the Book of Abraham, part of which consists of a treatise on astronomy and cosmology, eternal beings of various orders and stages of development likewise populate numerous stars. They, too, are called "intelligences." Dick speculated that "the systems of the universe revolve around a common centre ... the throne of God." In the Book of Abraham, one star named Kolob "was nearest unto the throne of God." Other stars, in ever diminishing order, were placed in increasing distances from this center.

Hansen observed further that:

> According to the Book of Abraham, the patriarch had a knowledge of the times of various planets, "until thou come nigh unto Kolob which Kolob is after the reckoning of the Lord's time; which Kolob is set nigh unto the throne of God, to govern all those planets which belong to the same order as that upon which thou standest." One revolution of Kolob "was a day unto the Lord, after his manner of reckoning, it being one thousand years according to the time appointed unto that whereon thou standest. This is the reckoning of the Lord's time, according to the reckoning of Kolob." God's time

---

53. Oliver Cowdery, "Extract ... from 'Dick's Philosophy of a Future State,'" *Messenger and Advocate* 3 (Dec. 1836): 423-25; Kenneth W. Godfrey, "A Note on the Nauvoo Library and Literary Institute," *BYU Studies* 14 (Spring 1974): 387.

thus conformed perfectly to the laws of Galilean relativity and Newtonian mechanics.[54]

What we find in Abraham 3 and the official scriptures of the LDS church regarding science reflects a Newtonian world concept. The Catholic church's Ptolemaic cosmology was displaced by the new Copernican and Newtonian world model, just as the nineteenth-century, canonized, Newtonian world view is challenged by Einstein's twentieth-century science. Keith Norman, a Mormon scholar, has written that for the LDS church, "it is no longer possible to pretend there is no conflict." He continues:

> Scientific cosmology began its leap forward just when Mormon doctrine was becoming stabilized. The revolution in twentieth–century physics precipitated by Einstein dethroned Newtonian physics as the ultimate explanation of the way the universe works. Relativity theory and quantum mechanics, combined with advances in astronomy, have established a vastly different picture of how the universe began, how it is structured and operates, and the nature of matter and energy. ... This new scientific cosmology pose[s] a serious challenge to the Mormon version of the universe.[55]

Many of the astronomical and cosmological ideas found in both Joseph Smith's environment and in the Book of Abraham have become out of vogue, and some of these Newtonian concepts are scientific relics. The evidence suggests that the Book of Abraham reflects concepts of Joseph Smith's time and place rather than those of an ancient world.

The Book of Joseph

When Joseph acquired two rolls of Egyptian papyri from Michael Chandler in July 1835, he said that "one of the rolls contained

---

54. Klaus J. Hansen, *Mormonism and the American Experience* (Chicago: University of Chicago Press, 1981), 79-80, 110.

55. Keith E. Norman, "Mormon Cosmology: Can It Survive the Big Bang?" *Sunstone* 10 (1986): 19-23.

the writings of Abraham, another the writings of Joseph of Egypt."[56] William W. Phelps, his scribe, wrote in 1835: "As no one could translate these writings, they were presented to President Smith. He soon knew what they were and said they, the 'rolls of papyrus,' contained the sacred record kept of Joseph in Pharaoh's Court in Egypt, and the teachings of Father Abraham."[57]

LDS apostle Orson Pratt and church historian John Whitmer described how Joseph determined that the two scrolls before him were the writings of Joseph and Abraham of antiquity. Pratt recalled:

> Mr. Chandler presented to him the ancient characters, asking him if he could translate them. The prophet took them and repaired to his room and inquired of the Lord concerning them. The Lord told him they were sacred records, containing the inspired writings of Abraham when he was in Egypt, and also those of Joseph, while he was in Egypt ... The Prophet Joseph having learned the value of the ancient writings was very anxious to obtain them, and expressed himself wishful to purchase them.[58]

Whitmer wrote that "Joseph the Seer saw these Record[s] and by the revelation of Jesus Christ could translate these records, which gave an account of our forefathers, much of which was written by Joseph of Egypt."[59]

Albert Brown, a Kirtland church member, wrote to his father on 1 November 1835 that some of the papyri contained:

> the history of Josef while in egypt ... These records were bought by the Church and also the Mummis and are now in Kirtland. They

---

56. Smith, *History of the Church*, 2:236.

57. Leah Y. Phelps, "Letters of Faith from Kirtland," *Improvement Era* 45 (Aug. 1942): 529; also in Bruce A. Van Orden, ed., "Writing to Zion: The William W. Phelps Kirtland Letters (1835-1836)," *BYU Studies* 33 (1993): 554.

58. Orson Pratt, 25 Aug. 1878, in the *Journal of Discourses*, 26 vols. (London and Liverpool: LDS Booksellers Depot, 1854-86), 20:65.

59. Bruce N. Westergren, ed., *From Historian to Dissident: The Book of John Whitmer* (Salt Lake City: Signature Books, 1995), 167.

Fig. 11. Detail from Joseph Smith Papyrus 4. Some of the characters were rendered in red on the original papyrus.

bought the Mummis for the sake of the record and paid 2400 hundred dollars for them. Many of the learned ... have been able to tell but very little about them and yet Joseph without any of the wisdom of this world can read them and know what they are.[60]

Oliver Cowdery gave an excellent description in the church periodical, the *Messenger and Advocate*, of the pictures on "Joseph's record":

The representation of the god-head—three, yet in one [fig. 11] ... The serpent, represented as walking, or formed in a manner to be

---

60. Albert Brown, Letter to James Brown, 1 Nov. 1835, in Christopher C. Lund, "A Letter Regarding the Acquisition of the Book of Abraham," *BYU Studies* 20 (Spring 1980): 403.

Fig. 12. Joseph Smith Papyrus 5. Some of the characters were rendered in red on the original papyrus.

able to walk, standing in front of, and near a female figure ... Enoch's
Pillar, as mentioned in Josephus, is upon the same roll ... [fig. 12]
The inner end of the same roll, (Joseph's record) presents a represen-
tation of the judgment.

Cowdery further identified the Book of Joseph in this article when he
wrote: "Upon the subject of the Egyptian records, or rather the
writings of Abraham and Joseph, I may say a few words. This record
is beautifully written on papyrus with black, and a small part, red ink
or paint, in perfect preservation."[61]

When eleven pieces of the lost Egyptian papyri collection were
rediscovered and acquired in 1967, it was easy to identify the source
of the Book of Joseph. The Abraham roll does not have red ink on it,
is not well preserved, and is easily identifiable because of Facsimile 1.
In comparison, the second roll is beautifully written, well preserved,
and has characters in red ink throughout. Of these eleven papyri,
numbers 2 and 4-8 belong to this second roll. The latter five have red
ink characters, and numbers 4-5 were clearly described by Cowdery
in the *Messenger and Advocate*.[62] Egyptologists have determined that
these papyri were originally connected together before Joseph Smith
had them cut into individual pieces.[63]

Papyri 2 and 4-8 were originally owned by Ta–Shert–Min, daugh-
ter of Nes–Khensu, whose Egyptian funerary rites were preparing her
to be received into the presence of Osiris, according to the modern
translations.[64] This raises a question not only about Joseph Smith's in-

---

61. Oliver Cowdery, "Egyptian Mummies," *Messenger and Advocate* 2
(Dec. 1835): 234, 236.

62. See the two colored rolls of papyrus after page 32 in Larson, *By His
Own Hand upon Papyrus*.

63. Baer, "The Breathing Permit of Hor," 111, 111n3; Richard A.
Parker, "The Joseph Smith Papyri: A Preliminary Report," *Dialogue* 3 (Summer 1968): 86-88.

64. John A. Wilson, "The Joseph Smith Egyptian Papyri: Translations
and Interpretations," *Dialogue* 3 (Summer 1968): 73-84; Stan Larson, *Quest
for the Gold Plates: Thomas Stuart Ferguson's Archaeological Search for the
Book of Mormon* (Salt Lake City: Freethinkers Press in association with Smith
Research Associates, 1996), 110-12.

terpretation of the scrolls but also about the "Reformed" Egyptian characters he said he copied from the gold plates in 1827-29. Prior to purchasing the papyri, Smith showed Chandler "a number of characters like those upon the writings of Mr. C[handler's papyri] which were previously copied from the plates, containing the history of the Nephites, or Book of Mormon."[65] If the plates were available today and if their writing were in translatable Egyptian, we can only wonder what they might contain.

Kinderhook Plates

On 23 April 1843, six brass "plates" were recovered by a group of men from an earth mound near Kinderhook, Pike County, Illinois, and were brought six days later to Nauvoo for Joseph Smith to translate. Charlotte Haven, a Nauvoo resident, wrote on 2 May to her family:

> Mr. Joshua Moore ... last Saturday [29 April] ... brought with him half a dozen thin pieces of brass, apparently very old, in the form of a bell about five or six inches long. They had on them scratches that looked like writing, and strange figures like symbolic characters. They were recently found, he said, in a mound a few miles below Quincy. When he showed them to Joseph [Smith], the latter said that the figures or writing on them was similar to that in which the Book of Mormon was written, and if Mr. Moore could leave them, he thought that by the help of revelation he would be able to translate them.[66]

On 1 May 1843 Joseph Smith's trusted clerk, William Clayton, married Joseph to Lucy Walker.[67] On the same date, Clayton re-

---

65. Oliver Cowdery, "Egyptian Mummies," *Messenger and Advocate* 2 (Dec. 1835): 235.

66. Charlotte Haven, "Letter to My Friends," 2 May 1843, in "A Girl's Letters from Nauvoo," *Overland Monthly* 16 (Dec. 1890): 629-31.

67. Joseph Smith mentioned Clayton among those who "carefully kept my history" in Smith, *History of the Church*, 6:409.

corded Joseph's declaration that the Kinderhook plates were genuine and that he had translated part of them. Clayton wrote:

> I have seen 6 brass plates which were found in Adams County by some persons who were digging in a mound ... They are covered with ancient characters of language containing from 30 to 40 on each side of the plates. Prest J. [Joseph] has translated a portion and says they contain the history of the person with whom they were found and he was a descendant of Ham through the loins of Pharaoh king of Egypt, and that he received his kingdom from the ruler of heaven and earth.[68]

Apostle Parley P. Pratt wrote from Nauvoo to a cousin six days later:

> [S]ix plates having the appearance of Brass have lately been dug out of a mound by a gentleman in Pike Co. Illinois. they are small and filled with engravings in Egyptian language and contain the genealogy of one of the ancient Jaredites back to Ham the son of Noah ... the gentlemen who found them were un-connected with the church, but have brought them to Joseph Smith for examination and translation. [A] large number of Citizens here have seen them and compared the Characters with those on the Egyptian papyri which is now in this city.[69]

Joseph Smith thought enough of "the history" of this Jaredite descendant of "Ham" to direct LDS member Reuben Hedlock to make woodcuts of the plates for future publication.[70] By 24 June the church was advertising that "[t]he contents of the Plates, together with a Fac-Simile of the same, will be published in the 'Times and Seasons,'

---

68. James B. Allen, *Trials of Discipleship: The Story of William Clayton, a Mormon* (Urbana: University of Illinois Press, 1987), 117.

69. Parley P. Pratt, Letter to John Van Cott, 7 May 1843, archives, Historical Department, Church of Jesus Christ of Latter-day Saints, Salt Lake City.

70. For facsimiles of these plates and a defense of their genuineness, see Smith, *History of the Church*, 5:372-79.

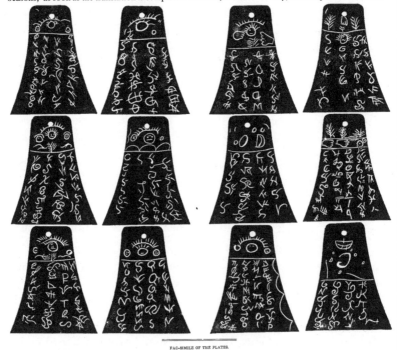

The contents of the Plates, together with a Fac-Simile of the same, will be published in the 'Times and Seasons,' as soon as the translation is completed. Nauvoo, Hancock county, Illinois. June 24th, 1843.

Fig. 13. The first facsimiles of the Kinderhook plates, front and back views, appeared in this broadside published 24 June 1843 by the *Nauvoo Neighbor*.

as soon as the translation is completed"[71] (fig. 13). The Kinderhook hoax began to unravel in 1855 when W. P. Harris, a witness who had helped unearth the plates, wrote:

> Some years since, I was present with a number at or near Kinder-hook, and helped to dig at the time the plates were found ... The plates were found in the pit by Mr. Fayette Grubb. I washed and cleaned the plates and subsequently made an honest affidavit to the same. But since that time, Bridge Whitton said to me that he cut and prepared the plates and he (B. Whitton) and R. Wiley engraved them themselves, and that there was nitric acid put upon them the night before ... to rust the iron ring and band. And that they were carried to the mound, rubbed in the dirt and carefully dropped into the pit where they were found.[72]

In June 1879 Wilbur Fugate—another of the original group who recovered the plates—confessed that the plates were fabricated. Fugate stated that the plates were:

> a humbug, gotten up by Robert Wiley, Bridge Whitton and myself ... Whitton cut them out of some pieces of copper; Wiley and I made the hieroglyphics by making impressions on beeswax and filling them with acid and putting it on the plates. When they were finished we put them together with rust made of nitric acid, old iron and lead, and bound them with a piece of hoop iron, covering them completely with the rust ... Wiley went to the Mound where he had previously dug to the depth of about eight feet, there being a flat rock that sounded hollow beneath, and put them under it.[73]

---

71. A copy of this broadside, "Discovery of the Brass Plates," is located in the H. Michael Marquardt Collection (900/77:17), Manuscripts Division, Marriott Library.

72. W. P. Harris, letter to W. C. Flagg, 25 April 1855, in "A Hoax: Reminiscences of an Old Kinderhook Mystery," *Journal of the Illinois State Historical Society* 5 (July 1912): 271-73. The letter was not published until 1912.

73. Wilbur Fugate, letter to James T. Cobb, 30 June 1879, in Welby W. Ricks, "The Kinderhook Plates," *Improvement Era* 65 (Sept. 1962): 656,

Some Latter-day Saints have wondered if the Harris and Fugate statements are credible and have pointed to the fact that the artifacts have not been available for independent testing. In 1920 one of the plates came into the possession of the Chicago Historical Society.[74] Dr. D. Lynn Johnson, a Northwestern University materials engineer and a Latter-day Saint, conducted some sophisticated electronic and chemical tests on the tablet in 1980 (fig. 14) and concluded: "The plate owned by the Chicago Historical Society, and known as the Kinderhook Plate, is made from a brass alloy consistent with the technology of the middle 19th Century. The characters on the plate were formed by etching with acid, probably nitric acid."[75] This confirms the statements by Harris and Fugate about how the tablets were made and aged in April 1843.

A Greek Psalter

Henry Caswall's experience with Joseph Smith at Nauvoo on 18-19 April 1842 expresses the frustration of an increasing number of LDS students with Joseph's ability to translate ancient documents. Caswall was a visiting minister from England who was shown the Egyptian papyri. He decided to test Joseph's credibility by presenting him with a known, ancient Greek psalter for his examination. Caswall, who probably exaggerates Joseph's frontier grammar and idiom, said:

> He asked me if I had any idea of its meaning. I replied, that I believed it to be a Greek Psalter; but that I should like to hear his opinion. "No," he said; "it ain't Greek at all; except, perhaps, a few words ... This book is very valuable. It is a dictionary of Egyptian

658. See also Fugate to Cobb, 8 April 1878, in the A. T. Schroeder Collection, State Historical Society of Wisconsin, Madison.

74. Stanley B. Kimball, "Kinderhook Plates Brought to Joseph Smith Appear to Be a Nineteenth-Century Hoax," *Ensign* 11 (Aug. 1981): 68.

75. D. Lynn Johnson, "Analysis of the Kinderhook Plate Owned by the Chicago Historical Society," 10 pp., Nov. 1980, copy in the Marquardt Collection (23:6).

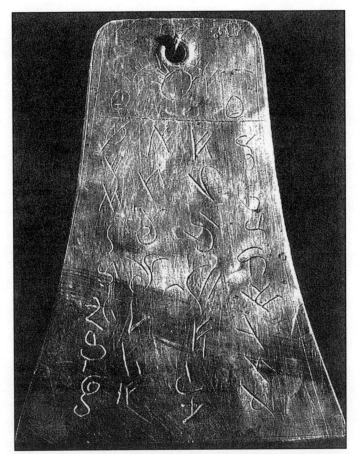

Fig. 14. This Kinderhook plate is located at the Chicago Historical Society. Notice that it is the first plate on the top row of the graphic that appeared in the *Nauvoo Neighbor* (see fig. 13). This is also the plate that was tested by D. Lynn Johnson in 1980.

hieroglyphics." Pointing to the capital letters at the commencement of each verse, he said: "Them figures is Egyptian hieroglyphics; and them which follows, is the interpretation of the hieroglyphics, written in the reformed Egyptian. Them characters is like the letters that was engraven on the golden plates."

Caswall told this incident to Dr. Willard Richards, a Mormon apostle, to which

the Mormon doctor said, "Sometimes Mr. Smith speaks as a prophet, and sometimes as a mere man. If he gave a wrong opinion respecting the book, he spoke as a mere man." I said, "Whether he
spoke as a prophet or as a mere man, he has committed himself, for
he has said what is not true. If he spoke as a prophet, therefore, he is
a false prophet. If he spoke as a mere man, he cannot be trusted, for
he spoke positively and like an oracle respecting that of which he
knew nothing."[76]

While it is true that we have only Caswall's view of this incident,
it is consistent with Joseph's pattern of rather quickly determining
the value and content of unknown documents that were presented to
him.

My conclusion is that a large body of evidence demonstrates that
Joseph mistranslated a number of documents. I know of no substan-
tial evidence to support his claim to have ever literally translated any
document, leaving me to appreciate his writings at face value rather
than because of their antiquity. With this perspective, when I read the
Book of Mormon or Pearl of Great Price, I harbor the suspicion that
they represent a nineteenth-century encounter with God rather than
an ancient epic. This is enlightening on a spiritual level but of no
value in trying to learn more about ancient America or the Middle
East. In the subsequent three chapters, I will explore what influences
may have been at work as Joseph dictated the Book of Mormon.

---

76. Henry Caswall, *The City of the Mormons: Or Three Days at Nauvoo
in 1842* (London, 1842), 35-36, 43. Caswall's representation of poor grammar is uncharacteristic of Joseph in the 1840s.

Appendix

Abraham in Nineteenth-Century Commentaries (1809-11) and the Book of Abraham (1835)[77]

Abraham Lived among Idolaters

Abraham himself also, most agree, was bred up in the same idolatry. (Symon Patrick et al., *A Critical Commentary and Paraphrase on the Old and New Testament*, 1809, on Josh. 24:2.)

My fathers, having turned from their righteousness ... unto the worshipping of the gods of the heathen ... (Abr. 1:5)

Abraham's Father (Terah) Was an Idolater

Terah was an idolater, living in a country from whence, as many think, idolatry first came (ibid.).

[M]y father was led away by their idolatry (Abr. 1:27); my father turned again unto his idolatry (Abr. 2:5).

Terah Was a Priest

The Jews, in Schalsch Hakkabala, say he was a priest (ibid.).

I will ... put upon thee [Abraham] ... the Priesthood of thy Father (Abr. 1:18).

Abraham's Countrymen Knew Astronomy

Those who dwelt in Ur were either priests or astronomers, Dan ii, 10, and also idolaters, Josh xxiv. 2, 3, 14, 15. (Adam Clarke, *The Holy Bible ... Commentary and Critical Notes ...* [New York: Ezra Sargeant, 1811], on Gen. 11:31.)

[A] knowledge ... of the planets, and of the stars, as they were made known unto the fathers, have I kept even unto this day (Abr. 1:31).

---

77. Adapted from Wesley P. Walters, "Well Known Jewish Legends about Abraham," photocopy in my possession, used by permission.

Abraham Was Threatened and Divinely Delivered

If we may credit the tradition ... Abraham was cast into such a fire by this idolatrous people, because he would not worship their idols (ibid., on Dan. 3:6).

My fathers ... hearkened not unto my voice, but endeavored to take away my life (Abr. 1:5, 7); the priests laid violence upon me, that they might slay me also (Abr. 1:12).

[T]his tradition of the Jews [says Abraham was cast into the fire] for refusing to worship idols, and out of which he was delivered. (Matthew Henry, *An Exposition of the Old and New Testaments ...* [London, 1811], on Dan. 3:19ff.)

[T]he angel of his presence stood by me, and immediately unloosed my bands (Abr. 1:15).

Abraham's Converts Followed Him to Canaan

And all the souls they had gotten ... [a] Chaldee paraphrase ... [that means] the proselytes they had won to God. (Patrick, *A Critical Commentary*, on Gen. 12:5.)

I, Abraham, departed ... and the souls we had won in Haran (Abr. 2:14-15).

Abraham Wrote a Book

Abraham instructed the men ... concerning which he wrote a book ... and left it to his son Isaac (ibid.).

[H]aving been myself a follower of righteousness ... they ... hearkened not unto my voice (Abr. 1:2, 7); the Book of Abraham, written by his own hand (heading; cf. Abr. 1:31).

2.
Authorship of the Book of Mormon

One of the official publications of the Latter-day Saint church is Elder James E. Talmage's *The Articles of Faith*. On the Book of Mormon, Elder Talmage advises: "This book is entitled to the most thorough and impartial examination. Not only does the Book of Mormon merit such consideration, it claims, even demands the same."[1] Early twentieth-century apostle John A. Widtsoe added, "To Latter-day Saints there can be no objection to the careful and critical study of the scriptures, ancient or modern, provided only that it be an honest study—a search for truth."[2] Their contemporary, J. Reuben Clark, a counselor in the First Presidency, expressed the same attitude in a provocative epigram. He stated that "If we have the truth, [it] cannot be harmed by investigation. If we have not the truth, it ought to be harmed."[3] Thus the church has encouraged a "thorough and impartial examination" of the Book of Mormon, including questions regarding its authorship.

---

1. James E. Talmage, *The Articles of Faith* (Salt Lake City: The Church of Jesus Christ of Latter-day Saints, 1982), 273.

2. John A. Widtsoe, *In Search of Truth: Comments on the Gospel and Modern Thought* (Salt Lake City: Deseret Book Co., 1963), 80.

3. D. Michael Quinn, *J. Reuben Clark: The Church Years* (Provo, UT: Brigham Young University Press, 1983), 24.

One of the most persistent beliefs regarding the Book of Mormon's authorship is that Joseph Smith was intellectually incapable of writing it. This invites an exploration of the creative mind and the secular and religious education of the prophet.

Elder B. H. Roberts, president of the First Council of Seventy, conducted an extensive investigation in the early 1920s to determine if the twenty-two-year-old Joseph was capable of writing the Book of Mormon. He determined that Joseph was "uneducated but brilliant" and that he exhibited a degree of "genius."[4] In fact, the distinguishing characteristic of Joseph's mind was "a vivid, and strong, and creative imagination." Roberts continued: "That Joseph Smith possessed such a gift of mind there can be no question." He gives examples from Joseph's life to demonstrate this.[5]

Looking at the Book of Mormon, Roberts wrote, one detects a creative influence at work. For instance, where the Book of Mormon speaks of miracles, they seem reminiscent of those we read about in the Bible, only that they are more spectacular—"surpassing the miracles of the Bible."[6] Where there are wars, they are epic in scale. Roberts wondered if this is real history or if the accounts are meant to be read as inspirational tales. He wrote:

> As an illustration of the amazingly miraculous events connected with Nephite wars, reference is made to the performances of a corps of 2,000—ultimately 2,060—young men, "striplings," who fought through what could appropriately be called the Thirteen Years War, since it lasted that long—73 B.C. to 60 B.C. These "striplings" fought in many battles, *yet none of them were killed* ... Often they saved the day at critical periods of battle, and though many of them were wounded, yet none were slain, to the amazement of both armies. On one occasion two hundred of the 2,060 "fainted because of

---

4. B. H. Roberts, *Studies of the Book of Mormon*, ed. Brigham D. Madsen (Urbana: University of Illinois Press, 1985), 10, 247 (hereafter *Studies*).
5. Ibid., 243, 247.
6. Ibid., 262-63.

loss of blood. ... Nevertheless according to the goodness of God ... not one soul of them did perish." "Yea," and speaking of this same particular battle, "*neither was there one soul among them who had not received many wounds! ...*"

"Is it history?" Roberts asked, or the product of "a pious but immature mind?"[7]

At the commencement of the Thirteen Years War (73 B.C.), the same scenario is described for the adult troops (Alma 49:23). After several extensive encounters with the enemy, the narrative records, "more than a thousand of the Lamanites were slain; while, on the other hand, there was not a single soul of the Nephites which was slain." Again, this seemed implausible to Roberts.

There are also similarities in the histories of the two major civilizations within the Book of Mormon, the Nephites and Jaredites. Roberts wrote about the extreme fates these two civilizations faced and concluded:

> In all this war of extinction, and destruction there is only one important variation, and that is that in the case of the Jaredites, the annihilation was complete for both sides down to the last man; in the case of the Nephites and Lamanites only the Nephites were wholly annihilated; ... And now, I doubt not, at the conclusion of this review of the Nephite and Jaredite wars of extinction [both of which coincidentally centered around the same militarily insignificant hill in Joseph Smith's New York neighborhood], some will be lead to exclaim—and I will set it down for them—"Is all this sober history inspired written and true, representing things that actually happened? Or is it a wonder-tale of an immature mind, unconscious of what a test he is laying on human credulity when asking men to accept his narrative as solemn history?"[8]

When Joseph Smith was presented with a partial skeleton found in 1834, he declared that God had told him the man's name was

---

7. Ibid., 272-73; emphasis in the original. See also Alma 53, 56-57.
8. Ibid., 279-83.

Zelph and that he had been a godly "white" Lamanite. Zelph was killed, he said, while serving under Onandagus, a Nephite general who was known across North America.[9] When shown the forged Kinderhook Plates, Joseph reported that they contained the history of an ancient Jaredite whose genealogy extended back to Ham, son of Noah. Joseph also gave many other vivid descriptions of secular and spiritual heroes from the past and their treasures hidden in the hills of New York and Pennsylvania. Elder Roberts concluded that, given such examples, we should consider the possibility that it would have been within Joseph's reach "to create a book such as the Book of Mormon is."[10]

Joseph's secular education began in 1812 when he was about seven years old. His mother, Lucy, recalled: "As our children had, in a great measure, been debarred from the privilege of schools, we began to make every arrangement to attend to this important duty. We established our second son Hyrum [age thirteen] in an academy at Hanover; and the rest, that were of sufficient age, we were sending to a common school that was quite convenient."[11]

Sending Hyrum to a private academy reveals how important education was to the Smith family. He eventually taught school in Manchester.[12] By 1828 he was one of the trustees of the school and was responsible for hiring teachers. Lucy informs us that her husband,

---

9. Joseph Smith Jr. et al., *History of the Church of Jesus Christ of Latter-day Saints*, ed. B. H. Roberts (Salt Lake City: Deseret Book Co., 1978 printing), 2:79-80.

10. Roberts, *Studies*, 243-50.

11. Lucy Mack Smith, *History of Joseph Smith by His Mother, Lucy Mack Smith* (Salt Lake City: Bookcraft, 1958), 51.

12. Mrs. S. F. Anderick said Hyrum was her school teacher. She recalled: "I attended when he [Hyrum] taught school in the log school-house east of uncle's [Earl Wilcox]. He also taught in the Stafford District." Affidavit of S. F. Anderick, 21 Dec. 1887, in Arthur B. Deming, ed., *Naked Truths about Mormonism* 1 (Oakland, CA., Jan. 1988): 2; original publication in the Yale University Library; qtd. in *Early Mormon Documents*, 3+ vols., ed. Dan Vogel (Salt Lake City: Signature Books, 1996-), 2:208.

Joseph Smith Sr., was a school teacher, as well.[13] William Smith wrote of his father: "[H]is occupation in early life was that of a School teacher[.] he was a man well letter[e]d in the Common branches of our english Studies."[14] This became important to Joseph Jr. when his parents began teaching school in their home in Manchester. John Stafford, a nearby neighbor and later surgeon, said: "Joe was quite illiterate. After they began to have school at their house, he improved greatly ... [They also] studied the Bible."[15] Because of Joseph Sr.'s education, as limited as it might have been by more elite, urban standards, young Joseph nevertheless benefitted from his father's interest in learning and from observations his father probably made on topics of the day. Joseph irregularly attended public schools. At age twenty he briefly returned to formal public schooling.[16] Orson Pratt summarized Joseph's education: "He could read without much difficulty, and write with a very imperfect hand; and had a very limited understanding of the ground rules of arithmetic."[17] This describes what passed as schooling for most rural people in the nineteenth century.

From the beginning, people tended to view Joseph as a bright but

---

13. Lucy Smith, *History of Joseph Smith*, 46, 138.

14. William Smith, "Notes Written on 'Chambers Life of Joseph Smith,' by William Smith," ca. 1875, typescript, 20, archives, Historical Department, The Church of Jesus Christ of Latter-day Saints, Salt Lake City; qtd. in Vogel, ed., *Early Mormon Documents*, 1:489.

15. John Stafford, interview by William H. Kelley, 1881, in William H. Kelley Papers, Library-Archives, Reorganized Church of Jesus Christ of Latter Day Saints, Independence, Missouri. These notes were published in "The Hill Cumorah and the Book of Mormon," *Saints' Herald*, 1 June 1881, 167; qtd. in Vogel, *Early Mormon Documents*, 2:122.

16. H. Michael Marquardt and Wesley P. Walters, *Inventing Mormonism: Tradition and the Historical Record* (San Francisco: Smith Research Associates, 1994), 44. Speaking of his formal education, Joseph Smith wrote, "I was mearly instructid in reading and writing and the ground rules of Arithmatic which constuted my whole literary acquirements." Dean C. Jessee, ed., *The Papers of Joseph Smith: Autobiographical and Historical Writings* (Salt Lake City: Deseret Book Co., 1989), 1:5.

17. Orson Pratt, *A[n] Interesting Account of Several Remarkable Visions* (Edinburgh: Ballantyne and Hughes, 1840), 3.

unschooled farm boy. Critics stressed his lack of formal education and poor spelling and penmanship. But spelling was not standardized until after Noah Webster's dictionary was published in 1828, and Joseph's penmanship was in fact quite good (fig. 15). Yet, from Eber D. Howe's 1834 *Mormonism Unvailed* [sic] to Fawn Brodie's 1945 *No Man Knows My History*, the overwhelming belief was that he was incapable of writing the Book of Mormon and that someone must have written it for him. Within the church, the portrait of a bright but ignorant farm boy placed the Book of Mormon in a miraculous light.

Thus we have an image of Joseph Smith as one "not learned" (see Isa. 29:12). While this accurately describes his formal education, it misstates his knowledge of the Bible, of evangelical Protestantism, and of American antiquities within his environment. He wrote in his 1832 history that his parents were thorough in "instructing me in the christian religion" and that, from age twelve on, he became a serious Bible student by "searching the scriptures."[18] John Reed, a friend of his, observed: "I early discovered [him] ... often speaking of those things which professed Christians believe in."[19] Joseph attended religious meetings in his youth "as often as occasion would permit," was "awakened" by Reverend George Lane's "discourses on the scriptures," and became "somewhat partial to the Methodist sect."[20] Another early acquaintance remembered his participation in the Methodist church, stating that Joseph became "a very passable exhorter" at the evening meetings and that he "used to help us solve some portentous questions of moral or political ethics, in our juvenile debating club."[21] Apostle Parley P. Pratt noted about Joseph's preaching that

---

18. Jessee, *Papers of Joseph Smith*, 1:3, 5.

19. John Reed, "Remarks of John S. Reed, Esq., as Delivered before the [IL] State Convention," *Times and Seasons,* 1 June 1844, 549.

20. JS—History 1:8; Oliver Cowdery, "Letter III," *Latter Day Saints' Messenger and Advocate* 1 (Dec. 1834): 42; qtd. in Vogel, *Early Mormon Documents*, 2:424.

21. O[rsamus]. Turner, *History of the Pioneer Settlement of Phelps and Gorham's Purchase* (Rochester, NY: William Alling, 1851), 214; qtd. in Vogel, ed., *Early Mormon Documents*, 3:49-50. See also Calvin N. Smith, "Joseph Smith as a Public Speaker," *Improvement Era* 69 (Apr. 1966): 277.

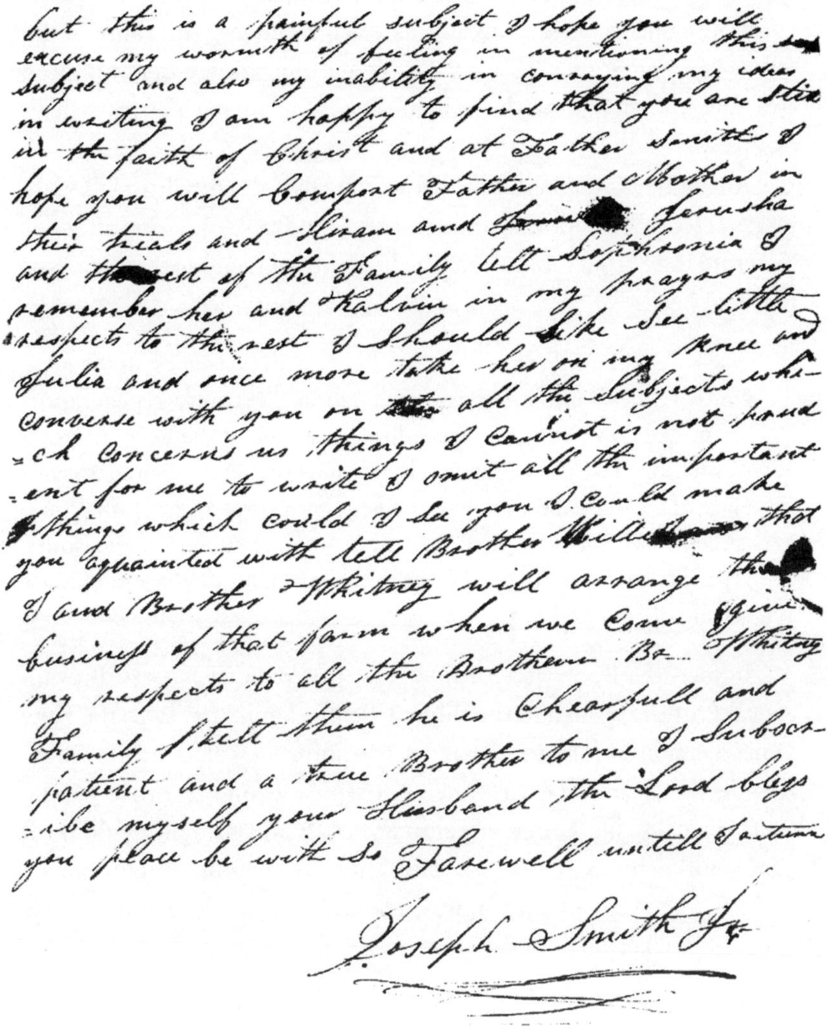

but this is a painful subject I hope you will
excuse my warmth of feeling in mentioning this
subject and also my inability in conveying my ideas
in writing I am happy to find that you are still
in the faith of Christ and at Father Smiths I
hope you will comfort Father and Mother in
their trials and Hiram and _____ Jerusha
and the rest of the Family tell Sophronia I
remember her and Kalvin in my prayrs my
respects to the rest I should like See little
Julia and once more take her on my knee and
converse with you on ___ all the Subjects which concerns us things I cannot is not pru-
ent for me to write I omit all the important
things which could I see you I could make
you acquainted with tell Brother Williams that
I and Brother Whitney will arrange the
business of that farm when we come give
my respects to all the Brotheren Br. Whitney
Family I tell them he is Chearfull and
patient and a true Brother to me I Subscr-
ibe myself your Husband the Lord bless
you peace be with So Farewell untill I return

Joseph Smith Jr

Fig. 15. Some of Joseph Smith's earliest extant handwriting is in this letter to his wife, Emma, 6 June 1832; Chicago Historical Society.

"none listened to him that were ever weary with his discourse."[22] Perhaps the most important statement of Joseph's religious education was written by himself in 1832. He related that during his formative years, he came to possess an "intimate acquaintance with those of different denominations."[23] While his formal education was not impressive, his knowledge of the religious opinion of the day was fairly extensive.

Alexander Campbell, founder of the Disciples of Christ, thought he detected contemporary influences in the Book of Mormon when he wrote in February 1831 that the book answered almost every issue that had been

> discussed in New York for the last ten years. He decides all the great controversies—infant baptism, ordination, the trinity, regeneration, repentance, justification, the fall of man, the atonement, transubstantiation, fasting, penance, church government, religious experience, the call to the ministry, the general resurrection, eternal punishment, who may baptize, and even the question of freemasonry, republican government, and the rights of man. All these topics are repeatedly alluded to.[24]

In fact, the Book of Mormon reflects a keen awareness of evangelical Protestantism and the Bible. Joseph's familiarity with the King James version before the Book of Mormon was dictated to Oliver Cowdery is clear when scrutinizing Joseph's second recorded revelation, given for his father in February 1829 and printed as Book of Commandments 3 (D&C 4). This short revelation contains many Old and New Testament phrases, identified below by biblical references in brackets. The revelation reads:

Now, behold, a marvelous work [Isa. 29:14] is about to come forth

---

22. Parley P. Pratt Jr., ed., *Autobiography of Parley Parker Pratt* (Salt Lake City: Deseret Book Co., 1970 printing), 46.

23. Jessee, *Papers of Joseph Smith*, 1:5.

24. Alexander Campbell, *Delusions: An Analysis of the Book of Mormon* (Boston: Waitt and Dow's Press, 1832), 19.

among the children of men [Ps. 12:1], therefore, O ye that embark in the service of God [Ezra 6:18], see that ye serve him with all your heart [Deut. 11:13], might, mind and strength [Luke 10:27], that ye may stand blameless before God at the last day: Therefore, if ye have desires to serve God, ye are called to the work, for behold, the field is white already to harvest [John 4:35], and lo, he that thrusteth in his sickle [Rev. 14:16] with his might, the same layeth up in store [1 Tim. 6:19] that he perish not [Jonah 1:6], but bringeth salvation to his soul, and faith, hope, charity [1 Cor. 13:13] and love, with an eye single to the glory of God, qualifies him for the work. Remember temperance, patience, humility, diligence [2 Pet. 1:5-6], &., ask and ye shall receive [John 16:24], knock and it shall be opened unto you [Matt. 7:7]: Amen.[25]

In the Doctrine and Covenants we learn that the "language" Joseph Smith used in dictating revelations was his own (1:24). He learned biblical language in his youth and seems to have applied it in these situations. Other people of that era knew the Bible equally well. Pomeroy Tucker, who was acquainted with Martin Harris and seemed to like him, said Harris could "repeat from memory nearly every text of the Bible from beginning to end, giving the chapter and verse in each case."[26] LDS apostle Orson Hyde claimed similar abilities. As a young man he "memorized the Bible, and when any one quoted one verse, I could quote the next. I have memorized it in English, German, and Hebrew."[27]

Some writers suggest that Elizabethan English was commonly used in Joseph Smith's community and that he absorbed it as he grew

25. Book of Commandments 3:1-2 (1833) in Wilford C. Wood, *Joseph Smith Begins His Work: The Book of Commandments* ..., 2 vols. (Salt Lake City: by the Author, 1962); cf. D&C 4. For additional biblical wording, see Ps. 21:10; Rom. 9:4; Heb. 9:6; Josh. 22:5; Rev. 14:19; Jonah 3:9; and Luke 11:9.

26. Pomeroy Tucker, *Origin, Rise, and Progress of Mormonism* (New York: D. Appleton & Co., 1867), 40; qtd. in Vogel, *Early Mormon Documents,* 3:109.

27. Orson Hyde, 6 Oct. 1854, *Journal of Discourses,* 26 vols. (London and Liverpool: LDS Booksellers Depot, 1854-86), 2:81.

up, but there is no supporting evidence for this. Letters from Joseph to Oliver Cowdery in 1829 and to his wife Emma and others do not reveal that he used biblical phrasing in daily life. Here is a plausible example of how Joseph may have used his biblical knowledge. The story of Jesus raising Lazarus from the dead in John 11 arguably serves as a source for Alma 19. Note the common phrases, which I have placed in italics, and the seven common motifs in both stories. In Alma, about 90 B.C., Lamoni is dying and his wife

> *sent* and desired that he [Ammon] should come ... and some say ... *he stinketh* ... He is not dead, [Ammon said,] but *sleepeth* ... [and] he *shall rise again* ... Ammon *said unto her: Believest thou this? And she said unto him* ... *I believe* ... [And] *he arose* ... (Alma 19: 2, 5, 8-9, 12).

Lazarus, in about A.D. 33, is dying and his sisters

> *sent* unto him ... [Jesus saith,] This sickness is not unto death, ... [for] Lazarus *sleepeth* ... [Then] Jesus saith unto her, Thy brother *shall rise again* ... Jesus *said unto her* ... *Believest thou this? She saith unto him*, Yea, Lord: *I believe* ... [but] by this time *he stinketh* ... [Jesus spoke a]nd he that was dead *came forth* ... (John 11: 3-4, 11, 23, 26-27, 39, 44).

The phrase "he stinketh" appears once in the Bible and once in the Book of Mormon. The words "he stinketh" and "sleepeth" are found together only in these two chapters. The seven-word phrase "Believest thou this? She saith unto him" appears only in John and Alma.

Within the story of Lazarus we can see potential evidence of a thorough knowledge of the Bible. The identifying and unique phrases of the Lazarus story appear with slight modifications in Alma. In the flow of this dictated narrative, the names of Ammon, the queen, and Lamoni are integrated into this language pattern. Beginning in Alma 19:12, the narrative moves to another form that is recognizable from Joseph's intellectual environment, in this case borrowing wording and themes from the Protestant evangelical conversion experience that was common to the early nineteenth century. This intermixing of evangelical phrases and themes into a complicated plot is impressive and will be examined in more detail in chapter four.

Another example of a biblical story that is expanded in the Book of Mormon is Alma 32 where Jesus' parable of the sower (Matt. 13) serves as a source of language. Both of these narratives compare the word of God to a seed. Motifs are developed in the same chronological order in both chapters and in no others, suggesting dependency of one on the other. A unique commentary appears in the Book of Mormon between the Matthean motifs:[28]

Matthew 13:3-8	Alma 32:28-43
[A] sower went forth to sow (3) ["The seed is the word of God," Luke 8:11] ... [S]ome seeds fell by the wayside (4) ... [Some] sprung up (5) ... [But] when the sun was up[, some] ... were scorched; and because they had no root, they withered away (6) ... [But some] brought forth fruit (8) ...	Now, we will compare the word unto a seed (28) ... [I]f ye do not cast it out by your unbelief (28) ... [it] sprouteth ... up (29-36) ... [But] when the heat of the sun cometh[, it] ... scorcheth it, because it hath no root[, and] it withers away (37-40) ... [But some seeds] bring forth fruit (41-43) ...

Joseph said the Book of Mormon was translated "by the gift and power of God," coming "forth out of the treasure of the heart ... thus bringing forth out of the heart, things new and old."[29] The evidence indicates that the Book of Mormon is in fact an amalgamation of ideas that were inspired by Joseph's own environment (new) and themes from the Bible (old).

Quite a number of "things ... old" appear in the Book of Mor-

---

28. While the New Testament texts are concise, the Book of Mormon, as a dictated text, is wordy and often redundant, as observed in Alma 32. Sometimes the same speech, with almost identical wording, is repeated, as in the speeches of Ammon and Aaron before their respective kings in Alma 18:24-42 and Alma 22:7-18.

29. Joseph Smith, "To the Elders of the Church of the Latter Day Saints," *Messenger and Advocate* 2 (Dec. 1835): 229.

mon. The story of Alma the younger seems to draw from the New Testament story of the apostle Paul as a model. Consider the following comparisons:

1. Both men were wicked before their dramatic conversion (Mosiah 27:8; 1 Tim. 1:12-13).

2. Both traveled about persecuting and seeking to destroy the church of God (Alma 36:6, 14; 1 Cor. 15:9; Acts 22:4).

3. Both were persecuting the church when they saw a heavenly vision (Mosiah 27:10-11; Acts 26:11-13).

4. Their companions fell to the earth and were unable to understand the voice that spoke (Mosiah 27:12; Acts 22:9; 26:14).

5. Both were asked in vision why they persecuted the Lord (Mosiah 27:13; Acts 9:4; 22:7).

6. Both were struck dumb/blind, became helpless, and were assisted by their companions. They went without food before converting (Mosiah 27:19, 23-24; Acts 9:8-9, 18).

7. Both preached the gospel and both performed the same miracle (Mosiah 27:32; Alma 15:11; Acts 9:20; 14:10).

8. While preaching, they supported themselves by their own labors (Alma 30:32; 1 Cor. 4:12).

9. They were put in prison. After they prayed, an earthquake resulted in their bands being loosed (Alma 14:22, 26-28; Acts 16:23, 25-26).

10. Both used the same phrases in their preaching.[30]

To expand on point number ten, much of the language of Alma the younger's speech in Alma 12-13 is reminiscent of Hebrews 3-4, as the following comparisons demonstrate:

---

30. Mosiah 27:26=1 Cor. 5:17; Alma 5:42=Rom. 6:23; Alma 7:15= Heb. 12:1; Alma 7:24=1 Cor. 13:13; Alma 12:27=Heb. 9:27; Alma 13:15 =Heb 7:1-2; Alma 13:28=1 Cor. 10:13; Alma 15:6=Rom. 1:16; Alma 32:21=Heb. 11:1; Alma 40:3=1 Cor. 15:51; Alma 40:14=Heb. 10:27; Alma 41:4=1 Cor. 15:53-54; Alma 41:11=Eph. 2:12; and Alma 42:6 =Heb 9:27. Joseph Smith and his contemporaries assumed that Paul wrote Hebrews.

Hebrews 3:7-13	Alma 12:33-36
The Holy Ghost *saith*, ... To day *if ye will* hear his voice, (7) *Harden not your hearts*, as in the provocation (8) ... So *I sware in my wrath, They shall not enter into my rest.* (11) Take heed, *brethren*, lest there be in any of you an evil *heart* of unbelief ... But exhort one another daily, while it is called To day; lest any of you be *hardened* (12-13) ...	But God did call on men, ... *saying: If ye will* repent, and *harden not your hearts*, (33) ... behold, *I swear in my wrath* that *he shall not enter into my rest* (35). And now, my *brethren*, ... if ye will *harden* your *hearts* ye shall not enter into the rest of the Lord; therefore your iniquity provoketh him that he sendeth down his wrath upon you as in the first provocation (36) ...

In the next verse, the same point-for-point sequence is again repeated:

Hebrews 3:15-18	Alma 12:37
To day if ye will hear his voice, *harden not your hearts*, as in the *provocation.* For some, when they had heard, did *provoke* (15-16) ... that they should not *enter into his rest* (18) ...	And *now,* my brethren, ... let us ... *harden not our hearts,* that we *provoke* not the Lord our God to pull down his wrath upon us; ... but let us *enter into the rest of God* (37) ...

These motifs are present elsewhere in Hebrews 3-4 and Alma 12-13. They seem to indicate some borrowing from Paul's discourse.[31]

---

31. For "today," cf. Hebrews 4:7b, 8=Alma 12:24; 13:21, 27; "hardening hearts," Hebrews 4:7b=Alma 12:10b, 11, 13b; 13:4; provoking God's wrath and entering into God's rest, Hebrews 3:19; 4:1, 3, 5, 6b, 8, 9, 10, 11=Alma 13:6, 12, 13, 16, 29. For other reasons why Alma 12-13 is dependent upon Hebrews 3-4, see David P. Wright, "'In Plain Terms that We May Understand': Joseph Smith's Transformation of Hebrews in Alma 12-13," in *New Approaches to the Book of Mormon: Explorations in Critical Methodology*, ed. Brent Lee Metcalfe (Salt Lake City: Signature Books, 1993), 178-84, 204-11, 218-20.

For Alma's speech in chapter 13, the biography of Melchizedek in Hebrews 7 appears to be an influence:[32]

Hebrews 7:1-4	Alma 13:7, 15, 17-19
For *this Melchisedec, king of Salem, priest of* the most high *God* (1) ... *[t]o whom* also *Abraham gave a tenth part of all;* first being by interpretation King of righteousness, and after that also *King of Salem,* which is, King *of peace;* (2) Without *father,* without mother, without descent, *having neither beginning of days, nor end of life; but made like* unto *the Son* of God; *abideth* a priest *continually.* (3) Now consider how *great* this man was (4) ...	Now *this Melchizedek* was a *king* over the land *of Salem*; and ... received the office of the high *priesthood* ... of God (17-18). *[T]o whom Abraham* paid tithes; yea, ... *one-tenth part of all* ... Melchizedek ... was called the prince *of peace,* for he was the *king of Salem*; and he did reign under his *father* ... [N]one were *greater* (15, 18-19). This high priesthood *being after* the order of *his Son* ... *being without beginning of days or end of years,* being prepared *from eternity to all eternity* (7) ...

We know that Paul's life, phrasing, and motifs form a powerful and popular narrative in the New Testament. Along with Paul's impressive style, notice the sequence of ideas in Hebrews 11 in comparison with Ether 12:[33]

Paul on Faith	Moroni on Faith
1. "Now faith is the substance of things hoped for, the evidence of things not seen." (1)	1. "[F]aith is things which are hoped for and not seen; wherefore, dispute not because ye see not, ..." (6)
2. The following list of biblical characters demonstrated faith in God: Abel, Abraham, Barak, David, Enoch, Gideon, Isaac, Jacob,	2. The following list of Book of Mormon characters showed faith in Christ: Alma, Ammon, Amulek, Jared's brother, Jesus'

---

32. Ibid., 165-78, and esp. 204-16.
33. Ibid., 195-96, 204-11, 221-23.

Jephthae, Joseph, Moses, Noah, Rahab, Samson, Samuel, Sara, the Israelites at Jericho, and the prophets. (3-33)

3. "Who through faith ... obtained promises, ..." (33)

disciples, Lehi, Moroni's ancestors, Nephi, other Nephites, the three Nephites, "they of old," and those who received the law of Moses. (7-31)

3. "And it is by faith that my fathers have obtained the promise ..." (22)[34]

Paul's writings continue to influence this section of Ether where Moroni delivers a sermon on "faith, hope and charity" (12:28), a phrase found in Paul's first letter to the Corinthians (13:3):

Paul on Hope

1. Jesus made a surety of a better testament. (Heb. 7:22).
2. Which hope we have as an anchor of the soul, both sure and steadfast, ... (Heb. 6:19)

3. [A] place which he should after receive for an inheritance, ... (Heb. 11:8)

Moroni on Hope

1. [I]n God [we] might with surety hope for a better world ...
2. [W]hich hope ... maketh an anchor to the souls of men, which would make them sure and steadfast, ...

3. [W]herefore man must hope, or he cannot receive an inheritance in the place ... (Eth. 12:4,

Paul on Charity

[If I] have not charity, I am nothing ... Charity suffereth long, and is kind; charity envieth not; charity vaunteth not itself, is not puffed up. Doth not behave itself unseemly, seeketh not her own, is not easily provoked, thinketh no

Moroni on Charity

[I]f he have not charity he is nothing ... [C]harity suffereth long, and is kind, and envieth not, and is not puffed up, seeketh not her own, is not easily provoked, thinketh no evil,

---

34. This phrase appears only in Hebrews in the KJV and is closest to Ether 12:17, 21-22 in the Book of Mormon. It also appears in 2 Nephi 1:9, 3:5, and 10:2, as "obtained a promise" but without the corresponding "through/by faith"; Moroni (7:41) says: "faith in him according to the promise."

evil; Rejoiceth not in iniquity, but rejoiceth in the truth; Beareth all things, believeth all things, hopeth all things, endureth all things. Charity never faileth. (1 Cor. 13:2, 4-8)	and rejoiceth not in iniquity but rejoiceth in the truth, beareth all things, believeth all things, hopeth all things, endureth all things ... [C]harity never faileth ... (Moroni 7:44-46)

The influence of Paul's writings continue up through the closing chapter of the Book of Mormon:

1 Corinthians 12	Moroni 10
[T]here are diversities of gifts, but the same Spirit. And there are differences of administrations ... but it is the same God which worketh all in all. But the manifestation of the Spirit is given to every man to profit withal. For to one is given by the Spirit the word of wisdom; to another the word of knowledge by the same Spirit; To another faith by the same Spirit; to another the gifts of healing by the same Spirit; To another the working of miracles; to another prophecy; to another discerning spirits; to another divers kinds of tongues; to another the interpretation of tongues: But all these [come] ... to every man severally as he will (4-11).	[T]he gifts of God ... are many; and they come from the same God. And there are different ways that these gifts are administered; but it is the same God who worketh all in all; and they are given by the manifestations of the Spirit of God unto men, to profit them. For behold, to one is given by the Spirit ... the word of wisdom; And to another ... the word of knowledge by the same Spirit; And to another, exceeding great faith; and to another, the gifts of healing by the same Spirit; And again, to another, that he may work mighty miracles; And again, to another, that he may prophesy ... to another ... ministering spirits ... to another, the interpretation of languages and of divers kinds of tongues. And all these gifts come ... unto every man severally, according as he will (8-17).

We may assume that God reveals similar concepts to different people at different times and that such similarities in theme are to be expected. The lingering question is whether such concepts could be expected to be found in identical sequences of ideas, phrases, and sentences. Consider the story of Judith in the Apocrypha compared to the decapitation of Laban in the Book of Mormon:

1. In this story Judith/Nephi are servants of God. They encounter Holofernes/Laban who wants to destroy God's people (Judith 7:1; 8:7; 1 Ne. 3:25). Interestingly, "Laban" is a name that appears in Judith's narrative (8:26).

2. Judith/Nephi leave/enter the city secretly by night. They find Holofernes/Laban upon the bed/ground, asleep and drunk with wine (Judith 13:2; 1 Ne. 4:4-5, 7).

3. Both take Holofernes/Laban by the hair and with his own sword cut off his head (Judith 13:6-8; 1 Ne. 4:9, 18).

4. Judith/Nephi then take some of Holofernes/Laban's possessions. When they rejoin their people, there is great rejoicing in their success (Judith 13:12; 14:9; 15:11; 1 Ne. 4:19, 38; 5:9).

5. Both groups celebrate by offering burnt offerings to the Lord (Judith 16:18; 1 Ne. 5:9).

Elsewhere in the Book of Mormon, one wonders if the twelve apostles of Jesus could be the model for the Nephite twelve disciples. For instance, the New Testament apostles include men with three duplicate sets of names: Simon Peter, Simon the Canaanite, James the son of Alphaeus, James the son of Zebedee, Judas the brother of James, and Judas Iscariot (Luke 6:13-16; Matt. 10:2-4; Mark 3:16-19; 1:13). The American twelve similarly include three sets of duplicate names: two men named Jonas, two named Mathoni (Mathoni and Mathonihah), and two named Kumen (Kumen and Kumenonhi) (see 3 Ne. 19:4). The Old World twelve include three sets of brothers: Andrew and Simon, James and John, and Judas and James. Among the American twelve are two sets of brothers and a father and son: Mathoni and Mathonihah, Nephi and Timothy, and Timothy's son Jonas. These parallels suggest a close relationship with the New Testament text. In chapter three, I will further examine themes in 3 Nephi.

For now, let us turn our attention to the American antiquities that formed such an immediate and compelling topic of study and discussion in young Joseph's environment. Dan Vogel's *Indian Origins and the Book of Mormon* demonstrates how extensively ideas concerning American antiquities were discussed in Joseph's era and how relevant these nineteenth-century views are to the Book of Mormon. For example, the most popular notion at the time was that Native Americans descended from Israelites. Genetically, it is now accepted that Indians are of Siberian and Mongolian extraction and that they migrated from Asia across the Bering Strait. Besides sharing distinctive genes, the corresponding morphological similarities are striking: "the characteristic eyefold, the pigmented spot which appears at the base of the spine of infants, and the shovel shape of the incisor. These traits have been found in varying proportions among every Indian group studied."[35]

During the last ten years, scientists from various research organizations, including biologists from Brigham Young University, have tested the DNA of over 7,000 American Indians. These tests cover about 130 tribes scattered throughout North, Central, and South America. This research has revealed that in excess of 99 percent of the ancestors of living Native American women arrived on the American continent from Asia over 12,000 years ago. About 90 percent of the men have Y-chromosome DNA from the same place of origin. Lesser DNA lineages originate in Africa or Europe, most likely Spain, but not from the Middle East.[36]

---

35. Dan Vogel, *Indian Origins and the Book of Mormon: Religious Solutions from Columbus to Joseph Smith* (Salt Lake City: Signature Books, 1986), 51-52, 69-72.

36. Theodore G. Schurr, "Mitochondrial DNA and the Peopling of the New World," *American Scientist* 88 (May-June 2000): 246-53; Simon Southerton to Grant Palmer, 16 Oct. 2000. Southerton, a Mormon geneticist with

The LDS position that Israelites "are the principal ancestors of the American Indians" is no longer probable even if a possibility still exists for the yet uncharted 1-2 percent of Indian DNA.[37] In addition, there is no evidence that ancient Americans practiced Hebrew or Christian rituals or held corresponding beliefs. No clearly identified Hebrew or Egyptian writing has been discovered in the New World dating before Columbus. Furthermore, linguists have determined from historical patterns the rate at which languages evolve. Given that rate, the Book of Mormon provides far too short a time (1,400 years) for the complete disappearance of the Nephite-Lamanite language. No indigenous American language has a demonstrable Hebraic or Egyptian origin.[38] If these non-Hebrew characteristics—genetic, biological, historical, and linguistic traits—are so prevalent, where and why did the idea of a Hebrew origin develop, and what implications does this hold for the Book of Mormon?

The tradition of appropriating biblical themes and imagery and applying them to America began with the Puritans. In the Bible, the Puritans found a view of themselves not as refugees but as partners with God on "an errand in the wilderness" to build the "latter-day church of God," the "New Jerusalem" on "Mount Zion." In Joseph Smith's day, this trend continued. Far from being a sleight, it was considered a high compliment and an act of inclusiveness to number Native Americans among the holy remnants of God's chosen people. By

Canberra Laboratories, is writing a book on the DNA genealogies of American Indians. See also Thomas W. Murphy, "Lamanite Genesis, Genealogy, and Genetics" *American Apocrypha: Essays on the Book of Mormon*, eds. Dan Vogel and Brent Lee Metcalfe (Salt Lake City: Signature Books, 2002), 47-77.

37. See Book of Mormon, xii, "A Brief Explanation about the Book of Mormon."

38. Thomas Stuart Ferguson, "Written Symposium on the Book of Mormon Geography: Response of Thomas S. Ferguson to the Norman and Sorenson Papers," 12 Mar. 1975, printed and updated in Stan Larson, *Quest for the Gold Plates: Thomas Stuart Ferguson's Archaeological Search for the Book of Mormon* (Salt Lake City: Freethinker Press, in association with Smith Research Associates, 1996), 175-268; Roberts, *Studies,* 91-94.

borrowing biblical metaphor, the people of Joseph's day interpreted the world around them and expressed their ideals and aspirations. They saw themselves as inheritors, by adoption, of God's prophetic promises just like the Puritans who believed that in America, God "hath discovered new things unto his anointed."[39]

Among the "things new" that Joseph Smith brought to his interpretation of the Bible was the view, already popular in nineteenth-century publications, that American Indians were of Israelite or Hebrew origin. One of these publications was Reverend Ethan Smith's 1823 *View of the Hebrews* (fig. 16). Among those who have seen this book as an inspiration for some of the basic structural material on which the Book of Mormon hangs is church authority B. H. Roberts. Elder Roberts recognized the utility of having a ground plan to work from to contextualize theological issues, and he therefore decided to investigate the possible connection between the two books. He concluded that there was "a great probability" that the Smith family had read or possessed a knowledge of *View of the Hebrews*. The book was written, published, and widely distributed in New England and New York where the Smith family lived, two editions rapidly selling out.[40] Roberts believed that if the Smiths did not purchase a copy, it could

---

39. Perry Miller, *The New England Mind: From Colony to Province* (Cambridge, MA: Harvard University Press, 1953), 187-88; Cotton Mather, *Psalterium Americanum: The Book of Psalms* (Boston: B. Eliot and partners, 1718); Sacvan Bercovitch, "How the Puritans Discovered America," *In the Puritan Grain*, Rivista di studi anglo-americani series no. 3, ed. Alfredo Rizzardi (Brescia: Paideia Editrice, 1983), 7-21; qtd. *www. facli.unibo.it.* A more contemporary example would be the use that Rastafarians make of the Bible in viewing America as the great "wilderness," Jamaica as "Babylon," and Ethiopia as "heaven." "Judah's Lion hath prevailed," Rastafarians write about Haile Selassie, king of Ethiopia. He is "the vine of David's tree" and "Zion's King." His followers are "true prophets," "the stone hewed out of the mountain without hands." Leonard Barrett, *The Rastafarians* (Boston: Beacon Press, 1977), xiii, 105, 231.

40. Roberts, *Studies*, 28-29, 151-54. A second edition of *View of the Hebrews* was published in 1825.

VIEW OF THE HEBREWS;

OR THE

TRIBES OF ISRAEL IN AMERICA.

EXHIBITING

CHAP. I. THE DESTRUCTION OF JERUSALEM. CHAP. II. THE CER-
TAIN RESTORATION OF JUDAH AND ISRAEL. CHAP. III. THE
PRESENT STATE OF JUDAH AND ISRAEL. CHAP. IV. AN
ADDRESS OF THE PROPHET ISAIAH TO THE UNITED
STATES RELATIVE TO THEIR RESTORATION.

SECOND EDITION, IMPROVED AND ENLARGED.

By Ethan Smith,
PASTOR OF A CHURCH IN POULTNEY (VT.)

" These be the days of vengeance."
" Yet a remnant shall return."
" He shall assemble the outcasts of Israel; and gather together the
dispersed of Judah."

PUBLISHED AND PRINTED BY SMITH & SHUTE,
POULTNEY. (VT.)
....
1825.

Fig. 16. Ethan Smith's *View of the Hebrews*. B. H. Roberts felt there was "a great
probability" that the Smith family had read or possessed a copy of this book.

easily have been supplied by Oliver Cowdery, Smith's cousin and scribe. Cowdery lived in the same small town as the author, Reverend Smith, who was the Cowdery family's Congregationalist pastor from 1821 to 1826.[41]

Roberts believed that if Joseph Smith's family had not read the volume, they would have had a good knowledge of its contents because of the intense and widespread public interest in Indian origins, customs, religion, traditions, and antiquities. Ethan Smith gathered ideas and materials on these subjects from over forty knowledgeable authorities and wove them into a narrative. The book's popularity was so widespread that its contents would have been "common knowledge," discussed at informal gatherings where people met to talk.[42]

There is no direct connection between *View of the Hebrews* and the Book of Mormon. *View of the Hebrews* represents a body of nineteenth-century thought and is not an early version of the Book of Mormon. But the parallels between the two books are instructive in understanding the environment in which the Book of Mormon emerged. Below are several of Roberts's summaries from his extensive study of Ethan Smith's book (fig. 17):

Israelites in Ancient America
[*View of the Hebrews*] not only suggests, but pleads on every page for Israelitish origin of the American Indians.

It deals with the destruction of Jerusalem and the scattering of Israel, as the Book of Mormon does.

It deals with the future gathering of Israel, and the restoration of the Ten Tribes, as the Book of Mormon does.

It emphasizes and uses much of the material from the prophecies of Isaiah, including whole chapters, as the Book of Mormon does.

It makes a special appeal to the Gentiles of the New World—

---

41. *Studies*, 27; also "Poultney Church Records," bk. 3, Poultney Vermont, 1793-1828, Poultney Historical Society.

42. *Studies*, 151-61.

Fig. 17. B. H. Roberts
(1857-1933), taken about 1922
when Roberts produced his
"Study of the Book of Mormon."

having in mind more especially the people of the United States—to become the nursing fathers and mothers unto Israel in the New World—even as the Book of Mormon does, holding out great promises to the great Gentile nation that shall occupy America, if it acquiesces in the divine program (*Studies*, 240).

Migrations to Ancient America

[*View of the Hebrews*] holds that the peopling of the New World was by migrations from the Old, the same as does the Book of Mormon. It takes its migrating people into a country where "never man dwelt," just as the Book of Mormon takes its Jaredite colony into "that quarter where there never had man been."

In both cases the journey was to the northward; in both cases the colony entered into the valley of a great river; they both encountered "seas" of "many waters" in the course of their journey; in both cases the journey was a long one. The motive in both cases was the same—a religious one; *Ethan* is prominently connected with the recording of the matter in the one case, and *Ether* in the other (240-41).

Two Classes of People

Ethan Smith's book supposes that his lost tribes divide into two classes, the one fostering the arts that make for civilization, the other followed the wild hunting and indolent life that ultimately led to barbarism, which is just what happens to the Book of Mormon peoples.

"Long and dismal" wars break out between Ethan Smith's civilized division and his barbarous division. The same occurs between Nephite and Lamanite, divisions drawn on the same lines of civilized and barbarous in the Book of Mormon.

The savage division utterly exterminates the civilized in Ethan Smith's book; the Lamanites, the barbarous division of the Book of Mormon, utterly destroy the civilized division—the Nephites.

Ethan Smith's book assumes for the ancient civilized people a culture of mechanic arts; of written language; of the knowledge and use of iron and other metals; and of navigation. The Book of Mormon does the same for its civilized peoples (241).

One Race

Ethan Smith's book assumes unity of race for the inhabitants of America—the Hebrew race, *and no other.* The Book of Mormon does the same for its civilized people.

Ethan Smith's book assumes that this race (save perhaps, the Eskimo of the extreme north) occupied the whole extent of the American continents. The Book of Mormon does the same for its peoples.

It assumes the Indian tongue to have had one source, the Hebrew; the Book of Mormon makes the same assumption for the language of its peoples (241).

Urim and Thummim and a Lost Book

Ethan Smith's book describes an instrument among the mound finds comprising a breast plate with two white buckhorn buttons attached, "in imitation of the precious stones of the Urim," says Ethan Smith. Joseph Smith used some such instrument in translating the Book of Mormon, called urim and thummim.

Ethan Smith's book admits the existence of idolatry and human sacrifice; the Book of Mormon does the same.

Ethan Smith's book extols generosity to the poor and denounces pride, as traits of the American Indian; the Book of Mormon does the same for its peoples. Ethan Smith's book denounces polygamy, the Book of Mormon under certain conditions does the same as to David and Solomon's practices.

Ethan Smith's book quotes Indian traditions of a "Lost Book of God" and the promise of its restoration to the Indians, with a return of their lost favor with the Great Spirit. This is in keeping with the lost sacred records to the savage Lamanites of the Book of Mormon.

Ethan Smith's sacred book was buried with some "high priest," "keeper of the sacred tradition;" the Book of Mormon sacred records were hidden or buried by Moroni, a character that corresponds to this Indian tradition in the Hill Cumorah (241-42).

Military Fortifications

Ethan Smith's book describes extensive military fortifications linking cities together over wide areas of Ohio and Mississippi valleys, with military observatory or "watch towers" overlooking them; the Book of Mormon describes extensive fortifications erected throughout large areas with military "watch towers" here and there overlooking them.

Ethan Smith's book also describes sacred towers or "high places," in some instances devoted to true worship, in other cases to idolatrous practices; the Book of Mormon also has its prayer or sacred towers (242).

Government

Part of Ethan Smith's ancient inhabitants effect a change from monarchal governments to republican forms of government; Book of Mormon peoples do the same.

In Ethan Smith's republics the civil and ecclesiastical power is united in the same person; this was a practice also with the Book of Mormon people.

Some of Ethan Smith's peoples believed in the constant struggle between the good and the bad principle, by which the world is governed; Lehi, first of [the] Nephite prophets, taught the existence of a necessary opposition in all things—righteousness opposed to wickedness—good to bad; life to death, and so following (242).

The Gospel and a Christ Type

Ethan Smith's book speaks of the gospel having been preached in the ancient America; the Book of Mormon clearly portrays a knowledge of the gospel had among the Nephites.

Ethan Smith gives, in considerable detail, the story of the Mexican culture-hero Quetzalcoatl—who in so many things is reminiscent of the Christ; the Book of Mormon brings the risen Messiah to the New World, gives him a ministry, disciples and a church (242).

In short, according to President Roberts, the Book of Mormon's view of American antiquities is in harmony with the thinking that was prevalent in Joseph Smith's environment. Archaeological discoveries of the day presented an ideal backdrop for explaining a lost race of people. The Book of Mormon also demonstrated an understanding of the Bible and of evangelical Protestantism.

It is important to understand the impulse behind the Book of Mormon's creation. We know from his 1832 history that Joseph Smith had an unusual concern about sin in the 1820s: "I discovered that they [Christians] did not adorn their profession by a holy walk and Godly conversation agreeable to what I found contained in that sacred depository [the Bible. T]his was a grief to my Soul ... [Because of] the wicke[d]ness and abominations and the darkness which pervaded the minds of mankind[,] my mind became exceedingly distressed ..."[43]

His spiritual angst is further seen in a letter to Emma in 1832:

This day I have been walking through the most splended part of the City of New Y[ork] ... [T]heir iniquities shall be visited upon their heads and their works shall be burned up with unquenchable fire[. T]he inequity of the people is printed in every countiance and nothing but the dress of the people makes them look fair and butiful[; A]ll is deformity[. T]heir is something in every countiance that is disagreable with few exceptions ... [A]fter beholding all that I had any

43. Jessee, *Papers of Joseph Smith*, 1:5.

desire to behold[,] I returned to my room to meditate and calm my mind ...[44]

What Joseph perceived as wickedness and spiritual alienation caused him deep distress. The Book of Mormon would help remedy the agnosticism and confusion that people of the day felt over religion. As found on the Book of Mormon's title page, it was intended to convince "Jew and Gentile that Jesus is the Christ." It was to promote piety by enhancing belief in the Bible. Mormon 7:9 states explicitly: "For behold, this is written for the intent that ye may believe [the Bible]." The Book of Mormon called a hypocritical Christian world to repentance. And perhaps more than any other volume except the Bible, it successfully motivated people to confront their sins and come to Christ.

The Book of Mormon also unified Joseph's immediate family, religiously and otherwise, including some projected economic consequences. During the 1824-25 Palmyra revival, the Smith family had become divided. Mother Lucy pleaded with her husband, but he refused to attend church after two or three meetings.[45] Joseph Jr. said he wept when he baptized his parents in April 1830 and thereby reunited the family.[46] He later told his brother William, "I brought salvation to my father's house, as an instrument in the hands of God, when they were in a miserable situation."[47] Economically, the family was in dire straits. Lucy said that when Joseph brought the plates home in September 1827, "There was not a shilling in the house."[48] Hiram Page wrote in 1848 that he, Oliver Cowdery, Joseph Knight Sr., and Josiah Stowell received a revelation from Joseph Smith in

---

44. Dean C. Jessee, comp. and ed., *The Personal Writings of Joseph Smith* (Salt Lake City: Deseret Book Co., 1984), 252-53.

45. Lucy Smith, *History of Joseph Smith*, 90.

46. Dean C. Jessee, ed., "Joseph Knight's Recollection of Early Mormon History," *BYU Studies* 17 (Autumn 1976): 37.

47. Dean C. Jessee, ed., *The Papers of Joseph Smith* (Salt Lake City: Deseret Book Co., 1992), 2:118.

48. Lucy Smith, *History of Joseph Smith*, 104.

1829-30 to go to Canada and sell the copyright of the Book of Mormon for "8,000 dollars." After expenses, the money was to go to the Smith family. The men tried but failed.[49]

The following is a plausible scenario for how the Book of Mormon came to be. After Joseph's marriage to Emma Hale in January 1827, he promised his father-in-law that he would give up treasure hunting. Influenced by the revival fervor and by his mother's piety, his mind began to fill with impressions that blended his familiarity with Indian lore and his conviction of biblical promises. Perhaps the outline of a book began to form sometime before Martin Harris became his scribe in April 1828. He had already experimented with seer stones, and perhaps he thought that through greater faith and concentration, God would open to his mind a vision of the secrets of the artifacts being discovered in upstate New York. The dictation proceeded, and after Martin lost the first 116 pages of transcription in mid-1828, this may have been fortuitous. An apprenticeship had been served, and the vision that was unfolding in Joseph's mind may have become more clear. The dictation probably progressed haltingly at first, perhaps as a kind of stream-of-consciousness narrative. Before Oliver Cowdery became his new scribe in April 1829, the prophet had had nine months to ponder the details of the plots and subplots and to flesh out the time line. Given his familiarity with the Bible and with American antiquities, it would have become progressively easier for him to put form to the vision. He dictated the final manuscript in about ninety days.[50] Over the next eight months, before the book was published in March 1830, he had the opportunity to make textual refinements.[51]

---

49. Hiram Page to William E. McLellin, 2 Feb. 1848, in RLDS Library-Archives; see also David Whitmer, *An Address to All Believers in Christ* (Richmond, MO: by the Author, 1887), 30-31.

50. John W. Welch, "How Long Did It Take Joseph Smith to Translate the Book of Mormon?" *Ensign* 18 (Jan. 1988): 46-47.

51. Royal Skousen, "Piecing Together the Original Manuscript," *BYU Today* 46 (May 1992): 22.

He thus had three years to develop, write, and refine the book—six years from the time he told his family about the project.

The next two chapters will continue to explore Joseph's blending of "things new and old" into a syncretic whole, with emphasis on his interpretation of the Bible as it impacted the theology and prose of the Book of Mormon.

3.

The Bible in the Book of Mormon

Krister Stendahl, at the time dean of the Harvard Divinity School, wrote of the Bible's influence on the Book of Mormon:

> The biblical material behind the Book of Mormon strikes me as being in the form of the KJV [King James Version]. ... I have applied standard methods of historical critics, redaction criticism, and genre criticism. From such perspectives it seems very clear that the Book of Mormon belongs to and shows many of the typical signs of the Targums [interpretations or paraphrasings] and the pseudepigraphic recasting of biblical material. The targumic tendencies are those of clarifying and actualizing translations, usually by expansion and more specific application to the need and situation of the community. The pseudepigraphic, both apocalyptic and didactic, tend to fill out the gaps in our knowledge about sacred events, truths, and predictions ... It is obvious to me that the Book of Mormon stands within both of these traditions if considered as a phenomenon of religious texts.[1]

---

1. Krister Stendahl, "The Sermon on the Mount and Third Nephi," in *Reflections on Mormonism, Judaeo-Christian Parallels,* ed. Truman G. Madsen (Provo, UT: Brigham Young University Religious Studies Center, 1978), 149, 152.

The following five examples exemplify Stendahl's observations.

Main Characters

The most important books within the Book of Mormon are arguably 1, 2, and 3 Nephi because they prophesy about and record the fulfilled promises of Christ's coming. Hints of biblical models appear in these books, including even the name Nephi.[2] Interwoven among this material is a narrative in 1 and 2 Nephi seemingly identifying Lehi and Nephi, the two principal figures in these two books, with aspects of the lives of Joseph Smith Sr. and Joseph Smith Jr. Lehi also seems to have characteristics of Jacob of old, while in Nephi's persona we can detect echoes of Joseph of Egypt and Moses.

For example, Joseph Sr. had a dream in 1811, recalled by his wife as his "1st vision," which is remarkably similar to Lehi's first vision in 1 Nephi. In these visions, both Lehi and Joseph Sr. are visited by a personage who provides them with a box or book, the contents of which enables them to understand God's salvation. They are jubilant at first but soon encounter opposition and flee for their lives. They both awake from their vision trembling.[3]

---

2. "Nephi" appears in 2 Maccabees 1:36 of the Apocrypha (KJV); see also 1 Chronicles 5:19. Of the 330 names in the Book of Mormon (Isaiah extracts excluded), 161 are found in the Bible. Of these, 20 are pronounced the same but spelled phonetically. Another 60 appear to be formed either by rhyme or adaptation of biblical names. Thus 221, or about two-thirds, appear to be biblically inspired, mainly from the Old Testament. See Wesley P. Walters, "The Use of the Old Testament in the Book of Mormon" (M.A. thesis, Covenant Theological Seminary, St. Louis, Missouri, 1981), 17-19. Some Bible indexes in Joseph Smith's day had "An Alphabetical Table of the Proper Names in the Old and New Testaments: Together with the Meaning or Signification of the Words in Their Original Languages." Joseph purchased a Bible in October 1829 containing this index title. His Bible is in Library-Archives of the Community of Christ (RLDS), Independence, Missouri.

3. For the title, "1st vision of Joseph Smith Sr," see Lucy Mack Smith, Preliminary Manuscript (MS), "History of Lucy Smith." This manuscript was dictated to Martha Jane Coray in 1844-45 and is in the Historical Department archives of the Church of Jesus Christ of Latter-day Saints, Salt Lake City, Utah; published in Dan Vogel, ed., *Early Mormon Documents*, 3+ vols.

Lehi's dream about the tree of life is strikingly similar to another of Joseph Sr.'s 1811 dreams. The elder Smith said:

> I was traveling in an open, desolate field ... My guide ... said, "This is the desolate world" ... I came to a narrow path ... I beheld a beautiful stream of water ... I could see a rope, running along the bank of it ... [I saw] a tree such as I had never seen before. It was exceedingly handsome ... Its beautiful branches ... bore a kind of fruit ... as white as snow ... I drew near and began to eat of it, and I found it delicious beyond description ... [and thought that] I must bring my wife and children, that they may partake with me. Accordingly, I brought my family ... [and] we all commenced eating ... We were exceedingly happy, insomuch that our joy could not easily be expressed. While thus engaged, I beheld a spacious building ... [that] appeared to reach to the very heavens. It was full of ... people, who were very finely dressed ... [T]hey pointed the finger of scorn at us ... But their contumely [arrogance] we utterly disregarded ... [in preference to] the fruit that was so delicious. He [the guide] told me it was the pure love of God, shed abroad in the hearts of all those who love him ... "[L]ook yonder [he said], you have two more [children], and you must bring them also" ... I asked my guide what was the meaning of the spacious building which I saw. He replied, "[I]t is Babylon, it is Babylon, and it must fall."[4]

In comparing this dream of Joseph Sr. to Lehi's dream in the Book of Mormon, I detect twenty-five similar motifs and much the same phrasing. Possibly, there is some cross-pollination between Joseph Sr.'s dream and his wife Lucy's telling of it on the one hand and Lehi's dream on the other since Lucy wrote her autobiography after the Book of Mormon was published. But Lucy's memory is accurate

---

(Salt Lake City: Signature Books, 1996-), 1:255n52; and in Lucy Mack Smith, *History of Joseph Smith by His Mother, Lucy Mack Smith* (Salt Lake City: Bookcraft, 1958), 46-47 (hereafter *History of Joseph Smith*). Cf. this first vision with 1 Ne. 1:16, 11-12, 14-15, 19-20.

4. Lucy Smith, *History of Joseph Smith*, 48-50.

in other areas, and I assume that it is at least as accurate in this case. Lehi's dream in the Book of Mormon reads as follows:

[A] man ... bade me follow him ... I had traveled for the space of many hours ... I beheld a large and spacious field ... I beheld a tree, whose fruit was desirable to make one happy ... I did go forth and partake of the fruit ... [which] was most sweet, above all that I ever tasted. Yea, I beheld that the fruit thereof was white ... [I]t filled my soul with exceedingly great joy; wherefore, I began to be desirous that my family should partake of it also ... I beheld a river of water ... [and] they [his family] did come unto me and partake of the fruit also. And ... I saw them [sons Laman and Lemuel], but they would not come unto me and partake of the fruit ... I beheld a rod of iron, and it extended along the bank of the river ... I also beheld a strait and narrow path ... [and] a large and spacious field, as if it had been a world ... [I saw] a great and spacious building; and it stood as it were in the air, high above the earth. And it was filled with people ... and their manner of dress was exceedingly fine ... they did point the finger of scorn at me and those that were partaking of the fruit also; but we heeded them not (1 Ne. 8:5-6, 9-13, 16-20, 26-27, 33).

The narrator in 1 Nephi refers often to his father: "These are the words of my father" (8:34); "And all these things did my father see, and hear, and speak" (9:1); "I must speak somewhat of the things of my father" (10:1). In chapter 11, another reference is made to his father's dreams:

And the Spirit said unto me: Behold, what desirest thou? And I said: I desire to behold the things which my father saw. ... [T]he Spirit said unto me: Look! And I looked and beheld a tree; and it was like unto the tree which my father had seen; and the beauty thereof was far beyond, yea, exceeding of all beauty; and the whiteness thereof did exceed the whiteness of the driven snow. ... [An angel said,] Knowest thou the meaning of the tree which thy father saw? ... [I]t is the love of God, which sheddeth itself abroad in the hearts of the children of men ... And the multitude of the earth ... were in a large and spacious building ... and it fell, and the fall thereof was exceedingly great (2-3, 8, 21-22, 35-36).

These opening chapters of the Book of Mormon provide an example of how "things new and old" combine to provide a new meaning for a new audience. In the verses cited above, between these motifs, the narrator quotes passages from the KJV about the coming ministry of Jesus Christ.[5]

If Lucy was overly influenced by Lehi's tree of life dream in remembering her husband's dreams, this would be an exception to other, numerous parallels between Lehi and Joseph Sr. Both Lehi and Joseph Sr. consider their dreams to be divinely inspired, and they both report that they had many dreams.[6] Both Lehi and Joseph Sr. had six sons, two with the same names (Sam and Joseph). The fourth son in each case eventually assumed family leadership from his father. The chosen sons, like their fathers, were more visionary than others in the family. They were seemingly favored by their fathers. Furthermore, both sons are large in stature, better speakers than writers, afflicted by much suffering, and favored of God. Both have difficulty procuring metal plates. They both make a record of their own life and include at the beginning that they were "born of goodly parents."[7] The lamentation in 2 Nephi 4:17-35 fits well the lives of these two sons of Joseph Sr. and Lehi.

One difference is the hatred that Nephi's older brothers harbor towards him. Joseph's older brothers were supportive of him throughout their lives. But this motif identifies Nephi with Joseph of Egypt.

---

5. Cf. 1 Nephi 11 with the following New Testament passages: 11:7/ John 1:34; 11:13/Luke 1:26; 11:22/Rom. 5:5; 11:27/Luke 3:22; 11:30/ John 1:51; 11:31/Matt. 4:24; 11:33/John 12:32.

6. Cf. 1 Ne. 8:2, 26 with Lucy Smith, *History of Joseph Smith*, 47-48, 50, 68; see also Joseph Smith Jr., *History of the Church of Jesus Christ of Latter-day Saints*, ed. B. H. Roberts (Salt Lake City: Deseret Book Co., 1978 printing), 6:610. Cf. 1 Ne. 1:16 with *History of Joseph Smith*, 47-50, 64-68, for five of Joseph Sr.'s dream-visions.

7. 1 Ne. 1:1, 17; 2:16; 3-4; 2 Ne. 33:1. Dean C. Jessee, ed., *The Papers of Joseph Smith: Autobiographical and Historical Writings* (Salt Lake City: Deseret Book Co., 1989), 1:3. Note that Lehi's son Nephi made the plates with his "own hands."

Both have jealous, revengeful older brothers who want to kill them in the wilderness because of their visions and their claims to family leadership. Both Nephi and Joseph of Egypt are liberated in the end, their brothers eventually bowing to them and seeking their forgiveness, which they graciously grant.[8]

An aspect of Book of Mormon characters in general, also evident here, is that they do not strike most readers as three-dimensional. Morally, their views are black or white, and the idealized portrait of Nephi in particular lacks the complexities, weaknesses, and development over time of the Old and New Testament prophets. He does not have the normal number of blemishes or warts, in other words. Even though Nephi claims to have imperfections, the text reveals him to be near perfect and altogether larger than life.

Journey to a Promised Land

Stendahl's conclusion that the Book of Mormon "recast[s] ... biblical material" is best seen in the beginning of the book—the wilderness journey of Lehi's family to a promised land. This closely parallels ten chapters in Exodus as the following twenty chronological motifs illustrate:

1. The main character in both stories (Moses, Nephi) knows the Egyptian language, lives a life of luxury, and leaves it behind because their lives are threatened (Ex. 2:5-10, 15; 1 Ne. 1:2; 2:1, 4; also 3:24-25).
2. Each protagonist is portrayed as justifiably killing a man before becoming a prophet (Ex. 2:11-12; 1 Ne. 4:10-11, 18).
3. Both receive, through a divine vision, a warning to escape into the wilderness (Ex. 3:2, 8; 1 Ne. 1:4-6, 13).
4. God promises them (Moses/Lehi, Nephi) that they will lead their people to a promised land (Ex. 3:8, 10; 1 Ne. 2:19-20).
5. They camp by the Red Sea (Ex. 13:18; 1 Ne. 2:2, 5-6).

---

8. Gen. 37:1-28; 42:6; 45:1-7; cf. 1 Ne 2:19, 22; 7:8-9, 16-21.

6. They are provided divine means, a "pillar of a cloud" in one case and a "Liahona" in the other, to lead them (Ex. 13:21-22; 1 Ne. 16:10, 16; also see Alma 37:44). The liahona functions like a compass needle over a map, but it takes the shape of a "ball ... of fine brass ... And we did follow the directions of the ball" (1 Ne. 16:10, 16). This is reminiscent of the "holy," four-inch "balls ... [of] cast brass" mentioned in William Morgan's 1827 *Freemasonry Exposed:* "These globes or balls contain on their convex surface all the maps and charts of the celestial and terrestrial bodies" (cf. 1 Ne. 16:30, 16; see fig. 18).[9]

7. At the Red Sea, the people lose faith and begin to murmur (Ex. 14:11-12; 1 Ne. 2:11-12).

8. While camped at the Red Sea, God arranges to have an opponent slain (Pharaoh's horseman/Laban the record keeper) so that God's people will not perish (Ex. 14:27-30; 1 Ne. 4:2-3, 11-12, 18).

9. After traveling three or four days in the wilderness along the Red Sea, they call their camp Shur/Shazer (Ex. 15:22; 1 Ne. 16:6, 11-13). The Israelites travel along the Red Sea in the Sinai Peninsula, while the Nephites travel by the Red Sea in Arabia.[10]

10. They move several times, finally camping at an oasis with twelve "wells of water" and seventy "palm trees," or in the Book of Mormon, the "fertile parts" are mentioned for the first time (Ex. 15:22-25, 27; 16:1; 1 Ne. 16:14b-17). At the previous biblical camp of Marah, the bitter water is "made sweet" (Ex. 15:23-25). The Nephites are not allowed to cook but their food "become[s] sweet" (1 Ne. 17:12).

11. The Israelites murmur about their hardships, specifically about

---

9. William Morgan, *Freemasonry Exposed: Illustrations of Masonry by One of the Fraternity* (Batavia, NY: David C. Miller, 1827), 56-57, 104. Note the two brass balls on p. 104. It is interesting that Hyrum Smith belonged to Palmyra Lodge No. 112 during 1827-28. H. Michael Marquardt and Wesley P. Walters, *Inventing Mormonism: Tradition and the Historical Record* (San Francisco: Smith Research Associates, 1994), 123, 142n33.

10. See The Holy Bible (Salt Lake City: The Church of Jesus Christ of Latter-day Saints, 1981), map 3.

MASTERS CARPET

Fig. 18. "The Masters Carpet," published in 1820 by Jeremy Cross in the *Masonic Monitor*. The liahona appears to combine the pillar of a cloud in the Old Testament and the Masonic globes atop two columns.

---

hunger (Ex. 16:2-3; 1 Ne. 16:18-20). The Nephites murmur about hunger when Nephi's steel hunting bow breaks.

12. Directions from the cloud/liahona provide food in the form of manna and quail for the Israelites and "wild beasts" for the Nephites (Ex. 16:9-15; 1 Ne. 16:25-31).

13. Accusations erupt against the groups' leaders for bringing them into the wilderness. The people yearn to return home (Ex. 17:1-3, 7; 1 Ne. 16:33-36). They travel "many days" before again stopping to camp at Meribah/Nahom (see map). When Ishmael dies, the Nephites increase their complaints of "hunger, thirst, and fatigue." When Miriam, the sister of Moses, dies, this exacerbates Israelite complaints about having been brought into the wilderness to perish of thirst (1 Ne. 16:33-35; Ex. 17:1-7; Num. 20:1-13). Dathan and Abiram accuse Moses, as Laman and Lemuel do Nephi, of wanting to be "a prince over us," "a king and a ruler over us" (Num. 16:13; 1 Ne. 16:38).

14. The leaders' lives are now threatened because of the strife (Ex. 17:4; 1 Ne. 16:37).

15. God speaks to his people, and starvation is once again avoided (Ex. 17:5-7; 1 Ne. 16:35, 39).

16. The people, despite many miraculous interventions on their behalf, fail to remain repentant very long (Ex. 2-33, esp. 16:9-35; 17:1-7; 1 Ne. 1-18).

17. Because of their transgressions, the people continue to wander in the wilderness for many years (Num. 32:13; Ex. 16:35; Alma 37:41-42; 1 Ne. 17:4).

18. Moses ascends "the mount" to receive the "laws"; Nephi ascends "the mount" to learn "great things," after which Moses supervises construction of a tabernacle, Nephi a ship, prior to entering the promised land. They remain a considerable period of time before departing (Ex. 19:1-5, 20; 19-40; 1 Ne. 17:5-8; 18:1-3).

19. The people rebel by dancing and singing, and they begin to forget the Lord (Ex. 32:6-7, 17-19; 1 Ne. 18:9). In the Bible this event occurs while Moses is on the mountain. In 1 Nephi it occurs on the ocean voyage to their promised land.

20. God is displeased and threatens the people with destruction. However, the people repent and eventually reach their destination (Josh. 1; 1 Ne. 18:10-23).

It is remarkable that many of the Nephite ideas and events occur at the same point in the chronology and at similar places as in the Israelite wilderness experience. These twenty shared motifs suggest dependency on the Bible exodus story.

Prophecy in 1 and 2 Nephi

The second major focus in 1 Nephi is prophecy. It begins within the wilderness journey and continues through 2 Nephi, the primary sources being Isaiah and the four Gospels. The Isaiah prophecies occupy two chapters in 1 Nephi and half of 2 Nephi. The major themes are: (1) the coming and ministry of Christ, (2) the scattering of Israel and the eschatological events surrounding Israel's gathering, and (3) judgment upon the wicked and the millennial era of peace for the righteous. With hindsight, the Book of Mormon provides commentary upon these prophetic Isaiah themes by "clarifying ... by expansion and ... fill[ing] out the gaps in our knowledge about sacred events, truths and predictions," a process which fits Stendahl's description of targumic and pseudepigraphic literature.

Like Isaiah, Nephi and Jacob in the Book of Mormon have seen the Savior: "Wherefore, by the words of three, God hath said, I will establish my word ... [M]y soul delighteth in proving unto my people the truth of the coming of Christ" (2 Ne. 11:2-4). As Nephi and Jacob see the same prophecies as Isaiah, the narrator can add this further "proof" to convince a skeptical world.[11] The prophecies of Nephi, Ja-

---

11. On the coming and ministry of Christ, see: 1. Birth of Christ: *Isaiah* (2 Ne. 17:14; 19:6); *Nephi* (1 Ne. 11:13-21; 19:8; 26:3); *Jacob* (2 Ne. 6:9). 2. Ministry of Christ: *Isaiah* (Isa. 53:2-4 or Mosiah 14:2-4; 61:1-3); *Nephi* (1 Ne. 11:27-31); *Jacob* (2 Ne. 9:5). 3. Crucifixion of Christ: *Isaiah* (Isa. 53:4-12 or Mosiah 14:4-12); *Nephi* (1 Ne. 10:11; 11:33; 12:4; 19:10-14; 2 Ne. 25:12-13; 26:3, 24); *Jacob* (2 Ne. 6:9; 9:5; 10:3-5). 4. Resurrection of

cob, and others throughout the Book of Mormon are remarkable for their specificity. They are unmistakable, unconditional, and manifest boldness and certainty, specifying names, dates, places, and precise sequences of recognizable events down to Joseph Smith's own time. Moreover, they read more like history than prophesy. For example, the prophecies of the coming and ministry of Christ are written in the precise language of their fulfillment as found in the New Testament. In contrast, predictions of events beyond 1830, when the Book of Mormon was published, are vague, conditional, and subject to a variety of interpretation.

Jesus' Birth and Baptism

It is said that in ancient America the birth of the Messiah was known to the very year, even "six hundred years" prior to the event; that his name would be "Jesus Christ" (2 Ne. 25:19/Luke 1:31); and

---

Christ: *Isaiah* (Isa. 25:8; 26:19); *Nephi* (2 Ne. 2:8-9; 25:13; 26:1); *Jacob* (2 Ne. 9:6-7, 21-22).

On the scattering and gathering of Israel, see: 1. Israel scattered: *Isaiah* (2 Ne. 15:1-8; 18:4; 20:20-23); *Nephi* (1 Ne. 13:10-14; 22:4-5; 2 Ne. 25:15); *Jacob* (2 Ne. 6:10-11; 10:6, 21-22). 2. Coming forth of the Book of Mormon and the true gospel: *Isaiah* (Isa. 29:4, 11-12, 14, 18. cf. 2 Ne. 27:6-30. While 2 Ne. 27 was dictated in 1829, the Charles Anthon/Martin Harris incident occurred in February 1828. No Hebrew text supports this change to Isaiah. See David P. Wright, "Joseph Smith's Interpretation of Isaiah in the Book of Mormon," *Dialogue: A Journal of Mormon Thought* 31 [Winter 1998]:196-204); *Nephi* (1 Ne. 13:35, 40; 2 Ne. 25:17-18; 27:6-30); *Jacob* (6:1-3). 3. Gathering of Israel: *Isaiah* (2 Ne. 8:11; 11:11-12; 15:26-30; 20:20-23; 21:10-16); *Nephi* (1 Ne. 15:13-20; 22:11-12; 2 Ne. 25:16-18); *Jacob* (2 Ne. 6:11; 9:2; 10:7-9).

On judgments and a millennial era, see: 1. Acts, teachings, and destruction of ["the great and abominable church"] Babylon: *Isaiah* (1 Ne. 20:14, 20; 2 Ne. 23:4-23; 24:4-24); *Nephi* (1 Ne. 13:4-9, 24-40; 14:3-17; 22:13-15; 2 Ne. 26: 20-21; 28:3-32); *Jacob* (2 Ne. 6:12-15; 10:16). 2. Wicked to be destroyed by fire at Christ's coming: *Isaiah* (2 Ne. 12:12-22; 13; 14:3-4); *Nephi* (1 Ne. 22:13-17; 2 Ne. 30:9-10); *Jacob* (2 Ne. 6:14-15). 3. Millennium: *Isaiah* (2 Ne. 12:14; 19:6-7; 21:5-9; 22:1-6); *Nephi* (1 Ne. 22:24-26; 2 Ne. 30:12-18); *Jacob* (Jac. 1:6-7; 5:75). 4. Last Judgment: *Isaiah* (2 Ne. 21:1-5); *Nephi* (1 Ne. 15:33; 2 Ne. 25:18; 33:14-15); *Jacob* (2 Ne. 9:15, 46).

that his mother, "Mary," would live in "Nazareth" (1 Ne. 11:13/ Luke 1:26). Mary, it is said, would be "a virgin, a precious and chosen vessel, who shall be overshadowed and conceive by the power of the Holy Ghost, and bring forth a son, yea, even the Son of God" (Alma 7:10/Luke 1:27-28, 35).

Information concerning Jesus' baptism by John the Baptist borrows from the Gospel authors: "For there standeth one among you who ye know not; and he is mightier than I, whose shoe's latchet I am not worthy to unloose ... [H]e should baptize [Jesus] in Bethabara, beyond Jordan ... with water ... the Lamb of God, who should take away the sins of the world ... [and] ye shall bare record that it is the Son of God" (1 Ne. 10:8-10; 11:7/John 1:26-29, 34; Matt: 3:11). Jesus was to be baptized "to fulfill all righteousness ... [and then] the Holy Ghost descended upon him in the form of a dove" (2 Ne. 31:5, 8/Matt. 3:15-16; Luke 3:22).

Coming unto Jesus

Salvation comes through faith—indeed, "through faith on his name" (Mosiah 3:9/Acts 3:16). Jesus is "the straitness of the path, and the narrowness of the gate, by which they should enter." To those who follow him "cometh the baptism of fire and of the Holy Ghost." For those who reject him, it would be "better for you that ye had not known me ... [but] he that endureth to the end, the same shall be saved ... [T]here is none other way nor name given under heaven whereby man can be saved" (2 Ne. 31:9, 13-15, 21/Matt. 7:13-14; John 21:22; Matt. 3:11; 2 Pet. 2:21; Matt. 24:13; Acts 4:12).

Jesus' Ministry, Death, and Resurrection

Of Christ's ministry, it is prophesied that despite his good works, many will say he has "a devil" (Mosiah 3:9/John 8:48); that he will heal "multitudes of people who were sick, and who were afflicted with all manner of diseases, and with devils ... [and about] the twelve apostles of the Lamb; Behold they are they who shall judge the twelve tribes of Israel" (1 Ne. 11:31; 12:9/Matt 4:23-24; Rev. 21:14; Luke

22:30); also that one of these apostles, called "John," will write the Apocalypse (1 Ne. 14:22, 27/Rev. 1:1).

Christ's enemies will "scourge him ... they smite him ... they spit upon him, and ... [he will be betrayed] into the hands of wicked men ... to be crucified" (1 Ne. 19:9-10/Matt. 27:26, 30-31; 26:45). He will be "lifted up upon the cross" so that "he may draw all men unto him" (1 Ne. 11:33; 2 Ne. 26:24/John 12:32). He will sweat "blood" (Mosiah 3:7/Luke 22:44), and his enemies will "scourge him and crucify him" (2 Ne. 6:9/Matt. 20:19). Then "the earth and the rocks" will be "rent" (1 Ne. 12:4/Matt. 27:51), and after Jesus is "laid in a sepulchre" for "three days he shall rise" (2 Ne. 25:13/Luke 23:53; Matt 20:19).

These anachronistic details, which go far beyond Old Testament prophecy for the same period, recommend Isaiah and the four Gospels as a primary source for these writings.

Christ's Teachings in 3 Nephi

Stendahl's thesis is further illustrated in 3 Nephi where 246 verses out of 490 (11:3-28:14), 50 percent, contain recognizable KJV quotations or phrases.[12] Commentary accounts for the remaining verses.

---

12. *3 Nephi, chapter eleven*: 11:3=Matt. 3:17; 11:7=Matt. 17:5; 11:11 =John 1:29, 8:12, 18:11; 11:14=John 20:27; 11:25=Matt. 28:19; 11:27= John 14:10-11; 11:32=Acts 17:30; 11:33-34=Mark 16:16; 11:35=Matt. 3:11; 11:36, 27=John 10:30; 11:38=Luke 18:16-17; 11:39=John 7:16-17; 11:39=Matt. 16:18; 11:39-40=Matt. 7:24-27.

3 Nephi, chapters twelve through fourteen: 12:2=John 17:20, Matt. 3:11, Acts 2:38; 12:3-48=Matt. 5:3-48; 12:47=2 Cor. 5:17; 13:1-34= Matt. 6:1-34; 14:1-27=Matt. 7:1-27.

3 Nephi, chapters fifteen through seventeen: 15:1=John 6:39; 15:1= Matt. 7:24; 15:9=Matt. 10:22; 15:17, 21=John 10:16; 16:15=Matt. 5:13; 16:18-20=Isa. 52:8-10; 17:4=John 14:28; 17:10=Luke 7:38; 17:14= John 11:33; 17:21 =Mark 10:16.

3 Nephi, chapters eighteen through twenty-one: 18:7, 11=Luke 22:19-20; 18:12-13=Matt. 7:24-27, 16:18; 18:18=Luke 22:31; 18:20=John 16:23; 18:28-29=1 Cor. 11:27, 29; 19:18=John 20:28; 19:20, 23, 28-30= John 17:1, 6, 20-21, 9-10, 18:1; 20:16-17=Micah 5:8-9; 20:18-19=Micah

Even more significantly, there are no original motifs in 3 Nephi that are not already found in the Gospels. If Jesus visited ancient America, the 3 Nephi text is probably not an actual account of his appearances.

Christ is represented as saying during his first and second visits to the Nephites, "I command you that ye shall write these sayings" and "write the things which I have told you" (3 Ne. 16:4; 23:4). They do so (3 Ne. 19:8; 23:14), and Mormon includes Christ's sayings on the gold tablets that Moroni buries (3 Ne. 26:7). Joseph Smith tells us that he retrieved the gold plates in 1827 and translated them from re-formed Egyptian into English (Morm. 9:32). He thus had the very words of Christ available to him, but curiously chose not to use them for at least half the verses in 3 Nephi 11-28. This raises a question about the Book of Mormon's role as a second witness of Christ where half of the words and ideas represented as being uttered by Christ came from an Old World Bible text. By Joseph's own account, the King James Bible was corrupt,[13] not translated correctly (eighth Article of Faith), and produced without the original manuscripts. We are left with little to convince us. Although no eyewitness accounts mention that Joseph used a Bible during the translation, a blanket sometimes shielded Joseph from Martin Harris's view. Apparently there was no screening device during the time that Oliver Cowdery did the

---

4:12-13; 20:23-26=Acts 3:22-26; 20:32-35=Isa. 52:8-10; 20:36-38=Isa. 52:1-3; 20:39-45=Isa. 52:6-7, 11-15; 21:8=Isa. 52:15; 21:10=Isa. 52:14; 21:12-18, 21=Micah 5:8-15; 21:29=Isa. 52:12.

  3 Nephi, chapters twenty-two through twenty-five: 22:1-17=Isa. 54:1-17: 23:9, 11=Hel. 14:25; Matt. 27:52-53; 23:14=Luke 24:27; 24:1-18; 25:1-6= Mal. 4:1-6.

  3 Nephi, chapters twenty-six through twenty-eight: 26:3=2 Pet. 3:10, 12; 26:5=John 12:32; 26:5 =John 5:29; 26:18=2 Cor. 12:4; 26:19=Acts 2:44; 4:32; 27:2=Luke 24:36; 27:12=John 7:12; 27:14=John 12:32; 27:28=John 15:16; 27:29= Matt. 7:8; 27:32=Matt. 6:19; 27:33=Matt. 7:13-14; 28:8=1 Cor. 15:51-53; 28:15=2 Cor. 12:3; 28:13-14=2 Cor. 12:2, 4.

  13. Robert J. Matthews, A Plainer Translation: Joseph Smith's Translation of the Bible, a History and Commentary (Provo, UT: Brigham Young University Press, 1975), 4-6.

writing (see figure 19). Oliver was Joseph's main scribe day after day and perhaps the only one who really knew if a Bible was consulted. Oliver is silent on the matter. In fact, a Bible would have been needed only when quoting long passages; so again, Cowdery may be the only witness who knew about this, and he neglected to mention it.

A thesis composed by a Protestant minister shows that the Book of Mormon contains twenty-six full chapters from a 1769 edition of the KJV, in addition to quotations from other verses.[14] An LDS scholar's article on 3 Nephi 12-14, the Sermon at the Temple, demonstrates that Joseph's use of the KJV includes the modern errors which accumulated in the hand-written manuscripts and KJV over the centuries. Some of these are: "by them of old time" (Matt. 5:27/3 Ne. 12:27), "should be cast into hell" (Matt. 5:30/3 Ne. 12:30), "bless them that curse you, do good to them that hate you, and ... which despitefully use you" (Matt. 5:44/3 Ne. 12:44), and "for thine is the kingdom, and the power, and the glory, for ever, Amen" (Matt. 6:13/3 Ne. 13:13).[15] These and other phrases indicate that an ancient source was not used for this sermon, nor for the many other biblical quotations throughout the Book of Mormon. Yet, we still say that "the Plates of Brass [were] brought by the people of Lehi from Jerusalem in 600 B.C. ... Many quotations from these plates, citing Isaiah and other biblical and nonbiblical prophets, appear in the Book of Mormon."[16]

John W. Welch, an LDS scholar, suggests another explanation for how Joseph obtained the long KJV passages found in the Book of

---

14. Walters, "Use of the Old Testament." For hundreds of identical verse comparisons, see the computer study by Kenneth D. Jenkins and John L. Hilton, "Common Phrases between the King James Bible and the Book of Mormon," 3 vols., 1983, privately circulated.

15. Stan Larson, "The Historicity of the Matthean Sermon on the Mount in 3 Nephi," in *New Approaches to the Book of Mormon: Explorations in Critical Methodology,* ed. Brent Lee Metcalfe (Salt Lake City: Signature Books, 1993), 115-63.

16. "A Brief Explanation about the Book of Mormon," preface to the Book of Mormon.

Fig. 19. This scene borrows from a drawing of the table Cowdery used in the Whitmer cabin. The table appeared in *The Republic* (St. Louis, MO), 10 November 1895, [4]. As pictured here, Joseph Smith is dictating from the Bible. Illustration by Kurt Gray.

Mormon. He wrote, "God projected a text similar to the [KJV] Biblical text through Joseph Smith, or the power of God brought that text especially to his memory."[17] The problem with this is, if Joseph received these portions of the Book of Mormon by revelation, why would they include the modern mistakes as part of that revelation? Why would God reveal to Joseph Smith a faulty KJV text?

In other words, the textual evidence shows that the Bible was a primary source for the miracles, quotations, stories, names, and prophecies in the Book of Mormon, all of which provided a basis for Joseph's interpreting and targumizing. It is reasonable to conclude

---

17. John W. Welch, *The Sermon at the Temple and the Sermon on the Mount: A Latter-day Approach* (Salt Lake City: Deseret Book Co., 1990), 136.

that Joseph knew the Bible text intimately and used it extensively. LDS members have been slow to recognize this, while critics have recognized it from the beginning. Among the first to draw attention to this fact were ten anonymous Palmyra, New York, residents in a letter to the *Painesville Telegraph,* printed on 22 March 1831. They wrote:

> The book is chiefly garbled from the Old and New Testaments, the Apocryphy having contributed its share: names and phrases have been altered, and in many instances copied upwards [expanded?]. A quarto Bible now in this village, was borrowed and nearly worn out and defaced by their dirty handling. Some seven or eight of them spent many months in copying, Cowdery being principal scribe.[18]

The tone of the letter notwithstanding, its claim is worth considering. I will give a sampling of text borrowed from biblical sources, especially from the four Gospels, in ten chapters of 3 Nephi relating to Jesus' short ministry in America. These examples do not include the six full Bible chapters from Matthew, Isaiah, and Malachi found in 3 Nephi 12-14, 22, and 24-25 or the lengthy quotes from three other Bible chapters.[19] According to the Book of Mormon, these ten examples are statements that were uttered by Jesus in A.D. 34, predating the yet unwritten texts of Matthew, Mark, Luke, John, Peter, and Paul. These parallels lead to the conclusion that Joseph Smith obtained not only the quotations but the information generally from a King James translation for all eighteen chapters of Christ's visit in 3 Nephi. It is hard to imagine that these are Christ's unique words to the Nephites, recorded soon after he uttered them and then included on the plates Joseph received. Like the prophecies of 1 and 2 Nephi, the teaching ministry of Christ more likely came from the New Testament than from a Nephite record.

---

18. "Letter from Palmyra, NY," 12 Mar. 1831, *Painesville* [OH] *Telegraph,* 22 Mar. 1831, [2]; qtd. in Dan Vogel, ed., *Early Mormon Documents,* 3:9.

19. Cf. 3 Ne. 16:18-20 with Isa. 52:8-10; 3 Ne. 20:23-26 with Acts 3:22-26; 3 Ne. 21:12-18, 21 with Micah 5:8-15.

3 Nephi 9	John 1, 14; Rev. 22
I am in the Father, and the Father in me ... I came unto my own, and my own received me not ... And as many as have received me, to them have I given to become the sons of God; and even so will I to as many as shall believe on my name ... I am Alpha and Omega, the beginning and the end (15-18).	I am in the Father, and the Father in me ... He came unto his own, and his own received him not. But as many as received him, to them gave he power to become the sons of God, even to them that believe on his name ... I am Alpha and Omega, the beginning and the end, the first and the last (John 14:11; 1:11-12; Rev. 22:13).

3 Nephi 11	Mark 16
And whoso believeth in me, and is baptized, the same shall be saved ... And whoso believeth not in me ... shall be damned (33-34).	He that believeth and is baptized shall be saved; but he that believeth not shall be dammed (16).

3 Nephi 15	John 10
[O]ther sheep I have which are not of this fold; them also I must bring, and they shall hear my voice; and there shall be one fold and one shepherd (17).	And other sheep I have, which are not of this fold: them also I must bring, and they shall hear my voice; and there shall be one fold, and one shepherd (16).

3 Nephi 17	Luke 7, John 11, Mark 10
[They did] bow down at his feet, and did worship him; and as many as could come for the multitude did kiss his feet, insomuch that they did bathe his feet with their tears ... Jesus groaned within himself, and said ... I am troubled ... [H]e wept ... and he took their little children, one by one, and blessed them (10, 14, 21).	[She] stood at his feet behind him weeping, and began to wash his feet with tears ... and kissed his feet ... When Jesus therefore saw her weeping, ... he groaned in the spirit, and was troubled. And ... Jesus wept ... And he took them [children] up in his arms, put his hands upon them, and blessed them (Luke 7:38; John 11:33, 35; Mark 10:16).

3 Nephi 18

And if ye shall always
do these things
blessed are ye,
for ye are built upon
my rock.
But whoso among you shall
do more or less than these are not
built upon my rock, but are built
upon a sandy foundation; and
when the rain descends, and the
floods come, and the wind blow,
and beat upon them, they shall
fall ...
[Y]e shall not suffer anyone
knowingly to partake of my flesh
and blood unworthily,
when ye shall minister it.
For whoso eateth and drinketh
my flesh and blood unworthily
eateth and drinketh damnation to
his soul (12-13, 28-29).

Matthew 7; 1 Cor. 11

Therefore whosoever heareth
these sayings of mine, and doeth
them, ... [is like] a wise man,
which built his house upon a
rock ... And every one that
heareth these sayings ... and
doeth them not, ... [is like] a
foolish man, which built his
house upon the sand: And the
rain descended and the
floods came, and the winds blew,
and beat upon that house; and it
fell: and great was the fall of it ... .
But let a man examine himself,
and so let him eat of that bread,
and drink of that cup. For he
that eateth and drinketh unworthily, eateth and drinketh damnation to himself, not discerning
the Lord's body (Matt. 7:24-27;
1 Cor. 11:27-29).

3 Nephi 19

Father, I thank thee that thou hast
given the Holy Ghost unto these
whom I have chosen; and it is because of their belief in me that I
have chosen them out of the
world ... And now Father, I pray
unto thee for them, and also for
all those who shall believe on
their words, that they may believe
in me, that I may be in them as
thou, Father, art in me, that we
may be one ... Father, I pray not
for the world, but for those
whom thou hast given me out of

John 17, 18

Father, the hour is come ... I
have manifested thy name unto
the men which thou gavest me
out of the world: thine they
were, and thou gavest them to
me; ... Neither pray I for these
alone, but for them also which
shall believe on me through their
word; That they all may be one;
as thou, Father, art in me, and I
in thee, that they also may be
one in us ... I pray not for the
world, but for them which thou
hast given me ... I am glorified in

the world ... that I may be glorified in them. And when Jesus had spoken these words he came again unto his disciples (20, 23, 29-30).

them ... When Jesus had spoken these words, he went forth with his disciples (17:1, 6, 20-21, 9-10; 18:1).

Helaman 14; 3 Nephi 23

And many graves shall be opened, and shall yield up many of their dead; and many saints shall appear unto many (Hel. 14:25). ... there were many saints who should arise from the dead, and should appear unto many ... (3 Ne. 23:9).

Matthew 27

And the graves were opened; and many bodies of the saints which slept arose, And came out of the graves after his resurrection, and went into the holy city and appeared unto many (52-53).

3 Nephi 26

[T]he elements should melt with fervent heat, and the earth should be wrapt together as a scroll, and the heavens and the earth should pass away; And even unto the great and last day, when all people ... shall stand before God, to be judged of their works, whether they be good or whether they be evil. If they be good, to the resurrection of everlasting life; and if they be evil, to the resurrection of damnation. (3-5)

2 Peter 3, Rev. 20, John 5

[T]he heavens shall pass away with a great noise, and the elements shall melt with fervent heat, the earth also and the works that are therein shall be burned up ... And I saw the dead, small and great, stand before God ... and the dead were judged ... according to their works ... they that have done good, unto the resurrection of life; and they that have done evil, unto the resurrection of damnation (2 Pet. 3:10; Rev. 20:12; John 5:29).

3 Nephi 27

... that I might be lifted up upon the cross; ... that I might draw all men unto me ... whatsoever things ye shall ask the Father in

John 12, 15; Matthew 6, 7

And I, if I be lifted up from the earth, will draw all men unto me ... whatsoever ye shall ask of the Father in my name, he may give my name shall be given unto you. Therefore, ask, and ye shall receive; knock, and it shall be opened unto you; for he that asketh, receiveth; and unto him that knocketh, it shall be opened ... But behold, it sorroweth me because ... they will sell me for silver and gold, and for that which moth doth corrupt and which thieves can break through and steal ... Enter ye in at the strait gate; for strait is the gate and narrow is the way that leads to life, and few there be that find it; but wide is the gate, and broad the way which leads to death, and many there be that travel therein ... (14, 28-29, 32-33).

it you ... Ask, and it shall be given you; seek, and ye shall find; knock, and it shall be opened unto you: For everyone that asketh receiveth; and he that seeketh findeth; and to him that knocketh it shall be opened ... Lay not up for yourselves treasure upon earth, where moth and rust doth corrupt, and where thieves can break through and steal ... Enter ye in at the strait gate: for wide is the gate, and broad is the way, that leadeth to destruction, and many there be which go in thereat: Because strait is the gate, and narrow is the way, which leadeth unto life, and few there be that find it (John 12:32; 15:16; Matt. 6:19; 7:7-8, 13-14).

3 Nephi 28

[Y]e shall be changed in the twinkling of an eye from mortality to immortality ... [T]hey were caught up into heaven, and saw and heard unspeakable things. And it was forbidden them that they should utter ... [W]hether they were in the body or out of the body, they could not tell (8, 13-15).

1 Cor. 15; 2 Cor. 12

[W]e shall all be changed ... in the twinkling of an eye ... [T]his mortal must put on immortality ... [as] one caught up to the third heaven. And I knew such a man, (whether in the body, or out of the body, I cannot tell: God knoweth;) ... and heard unspeakable words, which it is not lawful for a man to utter (1 Cor. 15:51-53; 2 Cor. 12:2-4).

What is obvious about this section of the Book of Mormon is that it was borrowed from the KJV and placed in an ancient American context. In some cases, there are still rough edges. Jesus uses the Nephite monetary term "senine" rather than "farthing" (3 Ne. 12:26/

Matt. 5:26) and omits references to "scribes and Pharisees" (3 Ne. 12:20/Matt. 5:20) and to swearing oaths "by Jerusalem" (3 Ne. 12:35/Matt. 5:35). But the Book of Mormon retains references to "raca" and to being "in danger of the council" (3 Ne. 12:22/Matt. 5:22): "Whosoever shall say to his brother, Raca [a curse and term of hatred], shall be in danger of the council." Committing "raca" in Palestine resulted in being brought before the Jewish Sanhedrin or "council." As an Aramaic word, "raca" would not have been intelligible to a Nephite.

Jesus also told the Nephites, "Whosoever shall compel thee to go a mile, go with him twain." This refers to the Roman law that required a slave to carry a burden one mile when asked by a Roman citizen. It would presumably have had no meaning in the New World (3 Ne. 12:41/Matt. 5:41).

3 Nephi Miracles

A fifth area of comparison with the New Testament involves Jesus' miracles, repeated in the New World setting. As B. H. Roberts noted, they are both repeated and enhanced; they become more miraculous. Following are a few examples from 3 Nephi.

Jesus' birth

In Matthew, the sign of Jesus' birth is a "star in the east." In the Book of Mormon, the sign is "a new star [that shall] arise, such an one as ye never have beheld." The precise time of the anticipated birth is known only to Mary, Joseph, Zachariah, and Elizabeth in the Old World. But in 3 Nephi the entire Nephite civilization knows the exact day. Samuel the Lamanite, five years previously, predicts that the birth will be accompanied by three days of sunlight, "as though it was mid-day"—a sign not found in the Bible even though Central America and Bethlehem are both in the Northern Hemisphere (3 Ne. 1:18-21; Matt. 2:2; Hel. 14:2-5).

Parallel Ministry of Nephi and Jesus

Nephi's three-year ministry (3 Ne. 7-8) covers the same time period as Jesus' own mortal ministry, A.D. 31-33. Krister Stendahl's view of these chapters is that they "transpose the ministry of Jesus as seen in Nephi the prophet, into a ... man of miracles [acting] in the name of Jesus."[20] Nephi is portrayed in this manner:

> And he did minister many things unto them; and all of them cannot be written, and a part of them would not suffice, therefore they are not written in this book. And Nephi did minister with power and with great authority ... [T]hey were angry with him, even because he had greater power ... [A]ngels did minister unto him daily ... [H]e cast out devils and unclean spirits; and even his brother did he raise from the dead ... [H]e did also do many more miracles, in the sight of the people, in the name of Jesus. And [many] ... were healed of their sicknesses and their infirmities (3 Ne. 7:17-22).

The impression is that Nephi's ministry draws from the miraculous power and authority of Jesus' ministry during the same three years but in a different part of the world.

Jesus' Death and Resurrection

When Christ died, "the sun was darkened" for three hours and "the earth did quake, and the rocks rent." Nevertheless, this must have been a minor quake. No damage was reported, and Matthew was the only Gospel writer to mention it. But in 3 Nephi, the quake lasts a full three hours and causes tremendous destruction to lives, cities, and buildings. It mostly kills the wicked, sparing the righteous. The darkness lasts not three hours but three days. In addition, the entire civilization knows that Christ has died because the darkness was prophesied; in Jerusalem, this was not the case (3 Ne. 8-10; Matt. 27:45, 51, 54; Luke 23:45).

From the New Testament we learn that Jesus showed himself to a few chosen disciples and to a group of 500 men at once after his resurrection. His wounds were shown to his apostles and a few others. This occurred in a private setting. Only the apostle Thomas wished to

---

20. Stendahl, "The Sermon on the Mount and Third Nephi," 141.

touch the wounds. In 3 Nephi a crowd of 2,500 not only sees but touches the wounds (3 Ne. 11:14-16; 17:25; John 20:20, 24, 27; 1 Cor. 15:1-8).

Miracles and Blessings

During Jesus' three-year ministry, he performed healings, cast out evil spirits, controlled nature, and raised the dead. In 3 Nephi, Jesus again performs miracles in all these categories during a three-day period. He makes bread and wine from nothing, raises the dead, and heals "multitudes of people who were sick, and who were afflicted with all manner of diseases, and with devils and unclean spirits ..." (3 Ne. 17:7-9; 20:6-8; 26:15; 1 Ne. 11:31).

Jesus was known to bless little children. In 3 Nephi when he blesses the children, angels encircle them, prompting even babies to utter greater things than Jesus speaks, although these things were not allowed to be written down (3 Ne. 17:21-25; Matt. 19:13-15; 26:14, 16; Luke 18:15-16; Mark 10:13-16).

Jesus Feeding the Multitude

The Gospel writers described a hungry multitude of more than 5,000 with only five loaves and two fish among them. Jesus multiplied the loaves and fish and fed the people until they were full. In 3 Nephi, when it was time to institute the sacrament, "an exceedingly great number" had gathered. Jesus produced the bread and wine from nothing and the people partook of the sacrament until they were filled physically and spiritually (3 Ne. 19:1-3, 5; 20:2-9; Matt. 14:15-21; Mark 6:38-44; Luke 9:13-17; John 6:9-14).

Day of Pentecost

The Holy Ghost came upon the Twelve Apostles at a private residence in Jerusalem. It appeared as a strong wind and cloven tongues like fire that rested upon them. The Twelve were moved to speak in tongues. In 3 Nephi the Holy Ghost comes upon the twelve disciples in a public setting, witnessed by multitudes, and encircles them "as if it were by fire," as angels minister to them (3 Ne. 19:13-14; Acts 2:1-4).

Transfiguration of Peter, James, and John

In the Gospels, Jesus took Peter, James, and John to a high mountain. Here Jesus became brilliant and unearthly white. Moses and Elijah appeared, and the apostles heard the voice of the Father bearing record of his only begotten Son. In 3 Nephi the entire multitude witnessed the Nephite twelve turn "white, even as Jesus." They heard prayers by Jesus which "cannot be written, neither can they be uttered by man." The Nephite twelve saw and heard miraculous things which even Peter, James, and John had not witnessed: "So great faith have I never seen among all the Jews; wherefore I could not show unto them so great miracles, because of their unbelief. Verily I say unto you, there are none of them that have seen so great things as ye have seen; neither have they heard so great things as ye have heard" (3 Ne. 19:30-36; Matt. 17:1-5; Mark 9:2-7).

Jesus' Promise to John

Jesus told John that he would not die until Christ's return in glory. In 3 Nephi this promise is extended to three of the disciples who were "caught up into heaven, and saw and heard unspeakable things; And it was forbidden them that they should utter." To stress that they could not die, the record adds: "They were cast into prison ... And the prisons could not hold them ... And they were cast down into the earth ... [but] they could not dig pits sufficient to hold them. And thrice they were cast into a furnace and received no harm. And twice they were cast into a den of wild beasts ... and received no harm" (3 Ne. 28:4-22; John 21:20-24).

This confirming evidence of Stendahl's study seriously challenges the Book of Mormon as authentic ancient history. In 1, 2, and 3 Nephi we repeatedly see a profile of targumic and pseudepigraphic literature, Joseph Smith's means of persuading people to believe in Christ. Joseph used pseudepigraphy "in proving" and "convincing" humankind to come unto Christ, as stated on the title page of the Book of Mormon and elsewhere (1 Ne. 6:4; 2 Ne. 11:4).

4.

Evangelical Protestantism
in the Book of Mormon

While biblical material is evident in 1, 2, and 3 Nephi and else-where in the Book of Mormon, the inspiration for Jacob, Enos, Mosiah, and Alma seems to be partly drawn from Joseph Smith's own spiritual odyssey. Elements of his own life and experiences, his observations of circuit preachers and conversion in western New York, form a backdrop for the discourses and religious experiences of Abinadi, Alma, Ammon, Amulek, Benjamin, and others.

Reviews of the Book of Mormon in the 1830s detected this coloring from Joseph's own life. Alexander Campbell observed in 1831 that the book's author was "skilled in the controversies in New York."[1] Jason Whitman, editor of the Boston *Unitarian,* noted in January 1834 the popular western New York prejudices "against fine clothing," a paid "regular ministry," and "the institution of Masonry," which he believed were given "artful adaptations" in the Book of Mormon. He further reported that the book followed (1) "the camp-meeting ground" and (2) the evangelical "style of preaching," (3) "conversion," (4) and

---

1. Alexander Campbell, *Delusions: An Analysis of the Book of Mormon* (Boston: Waitt and Dow's Press, 1832), 19.

"dissent," and (5) that the "exhortations are strongly tinctured with the doctrines of modern [Protestant] Orthodoxy."[2]

Evangelical meetings in western New York in the 1820s were characterized by (1) camp settings; (2) preaching that interlaced paraphrased biblical passages with revival terminology designed to produce a powerful emotional impact; (3) a conversion pattern characterized by a conviction of sin, intense prayer for forgiveness, and a sweet calming assurance of being forgiven, often accompanied by trembling, tears, falling, and other physical manifestations; (4) denunciation of Deists, Unitarians, Universalists, and agnostics; and (5) vivid descriptions of the degenerate state of human beings. While all five of these elements formed a pattern that was typical in Joseph Smith's environment, one would not expect to find them packaged together in the discourses and experiences of ancient Americans. It is more believable that the Protestant Reformation, including its evolving doctrines and practices down to Joseph Smith's era, influenced these sections of the Book of Mormon.

The Methodist Camp Meeting Setting

We have not taken Joseph Smith seriously enough when he stated that he had an "intimate acquaintance" with evangelical religion and that he was "somewhat partial" to the Methodists.[3] Protestant concepts appear to abound in his discourses and experiences. For example, a Methodist camp meeting was held one mile from Palmyra, New York, on 7 June 1826—a pivotal time in Joseph Smith's life. Preparations for a camp meeting included leasing and consecrating the ground. Thus the "ground within the circle of the tents is considered sacred to the worship of God, and is our chapel."[4] The Methodists re-

---

2. Jason Whitman, "The Book of Mormon," *The Unitarian,* 1 Jan. 1834, 44, 47-49.

3. Dean C. Jessee, ed., *The Papers of Joseph Smith: Autobiographical and Historical Writings* (Salt Lake City: Deseret Book Co., 1989), 1:5, 270; JS—History, 1:8.

4. "Methodist Camp Meeting," *Christian Register,* 24 Sept. 1831, 1.

ferred to these "consecrated grounds" as their "house of God" or temple.[5] The Palmyra camp meeting reportedly attracted over 10,000 people. Families came from all parts of the 100-mile conference district and pitched their tents facing the raised "stand" where the preachers were seated, including one named Benjamin G. Paddock (fig. 20). This large crowd heard the "valedictory" or farewell speech of their beloved "Bishop M'Kendree [who] made his appearance among us for the last time." He was the Methodist leader who "had presided" over the area for many years. The people had such reverence for this "sainted" man "that all were melted, and … awed in his presence." In his emaciated and "feeble" condition, he spoke of his love for the people and then delivered a powerful message that covered "the whole process of personal salvation." Tremendous unity prevailed among the crowd, and "nearly every unconverted person on the ground" committed oneself to Christ. At the close of the meeting, the blessings and newly appointed "Stations of the Preachers" were made for the Ontario district.[6]

This is reminiscent of King Benjamin's speech to the Zarahemlans in the Book of Mormon, whose chronicler describes the setting:

> The people gathered themselves together throughout all the land, that they might go up to the temple to hear the [last] words which [their beloved] king Benjamin should speak unto them … [T]hey pitched their tents round about, every man according to his family … every man having his tent with the door thereof towards the temple … the multitude being so great that king Benjamin … caused a tower to be erected … [And he said from the platform,] I am about to go down to my grave … I can no longer be your teacher … For even at this time my whole frame doth tremble exceedingly while attempting to speak unto you (Mosiah 2:1, 5-7, 28-30).

---

5. Ibid.; George Peck, *Early Methodism within the Bounds of the Old Genesee Conference from 1788 to 1828* (New York: Carlton & Porter, 1860), 432.

6. Rev. Z. Paddock, *Memoir of Rev. Benjamin G. Paddock* (Cincinnati, 1875), 177-81; "Genesee Conference," *Methodist Magazine* 9 (Aug. 1826): 313; Peck, *Early Methodism,* 509.

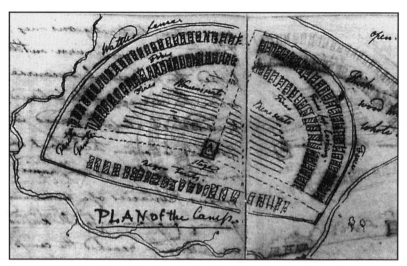

Fig. 20. Methodist "Plan of the Camp," sketch by Benjamin Henry Latrobe, 1809. Courtesy Maryland Historical Society.

The venerated King Benjamin, like Bishop M'Kendree, expresses his love for his people and gives a powerful farewell discourse on personal salvation. The response and unity are such "that there was not one soul, except it were little children, but who had entered into the covenant and had taken upon them the name of Christ." At meeting's end, Mosiah, Benjamin's son, "appointed priests to teach the people" (Mosiah 6:2-3). In Alma 17:18, Methodist phrasing is used: "Now Ammon being the chief among them, [blessed and appointed the sons of Mosiah] ... to their several stations." Alma 17-26 then gives a detailed recital of the sons' preaching with the following summary: "And they had been teaching the word of God for the space of fourteen years among the Lamanites, having had much success in bringing many to the knowledge of the truth; yea, by the power of their words many were brought before the altar of God, to call on his name and confess their sins before him" (17:4).

In evangelical meetings it was common for those who were moved by the preaching to break out in tears and fall to the ground. This was considered to be a state of "conviction." When a preacher

Fig. 21. A typical camp meeting, attributed to Alexander Rider, early 1800s. Notice the bench or "altar" in front of the pulpit.

looked up and saw those in the audience under "conviction" or "awakened to their awful state," he would invite them up to a bench in front of the pulpit, called the "altar" of God (fig. 21). There the penitents would pray and confess their sins, "crying aloud for mercy," seeking forgiveness from God.[7]

The Methodist Conversion Form

The Methodist way continues to be seen in the Zarahemla narrative. Mosiah 4:1-3 precisely observes the form popularized by the Methodists, as Brent Lee Metcalfe has observed:

> While it may be true that elements of religious conversions in Joseph Smith's environment derived from biblical predecessors, the congregation's response to Benjamin's homily follows an identical non-biblical form of spiritual regeneration developed in antebellum

---

7. Mark D. Thomas, "Revival Language in the Book of Mormon," *Sunstone* 8 (May-June 1983): 20.

revivals. ... This revivalistic conversion form can be illustrated from the Book of Mormon as follows:

1. *Revival Gathering* (Mosiah 2:1): The Zarahemlans gather at "the temple (in tents) to hear the words which king Benjamin should speak unto them."

2. *Guilt-Ridden Falling Exercise* (Mosiah 4:1-2a): When "king Benjamin had made an end of speaking ... he cast his eyes ... on the multitude, and behold they had fallen to the earth ... And they had viewed themselves in their own carnal state, even less than the dust of the earth."

3. *Petition for Spiritual Emancipation* (Mosiah 4:2b): And "they all cried aloud with one voice, saying: O have mercy, and apply the atoning blood of Christ that we may receive forgiveness of our sins, and our hearts may be purified ..."

4. *Absolution and Emotional Ecstasy* (Mosiah 4:3): After "they had spoken these words the Spirit of the Lord came upon them, and they were filled with joy, having received a remission of their sins, and having peace of conscience, because of the exceeding faith which they had in Jesus Christ ..."[8]

It should be noted that the falling exercise was not essential, but some kind of emotional manifestation was expected such as clapping, shouting, twitching, and dancing. Still, the falling exercise was common to both the Book of Mormon and nineteenth-century narratives. There are other variations, but Metcalfe's is a good outline for understanding the general pattern. Notice the conformity to these four points in the following examples:

Lucy Stoddard

In 1825 an itinerant Methodist preacher named George Lane (fig. 22), whom Joseph Smith mentioned in his autobiographical his-

---

8. Brent Lee Metcalfe, unpublished response to Blake T. Ostler, 1987, photocopy of typescript in my possession; used with permission. See Blake T. Ostler, "The Book of Mormon as a Modern Expansion of an Ancient Source," *Dialogue: A Journal of Mormon Thought* 20 (Spring 1987): 66-123.

Fig. 22. Reverend George Lane
(1784-1859) who influenced
Joseph Smith, from the
Methodist Magazine,
April 1826

tory, penned a vivid account commensurate with Mosiah 4:1-3. Lane wrote that young Lucy Stoddard of Palmyra was converted at:

[1] a [Methodist] prayer meeting ...

[2] The great deep of her heart was broken up; she saw clearly that she was a child of wrath, and in danger of hell. With this view of her sad condition, she fell prostrate at the feet of her offended sovereign,

[3] and in the bitterest anguish cried for mercy.

[4] In this situation, however, she was not suffered long to continue before she obtained a most satisfactory evidence of her acceptance with God through the merits of Jesus Christ. Her soul was unspeakably happy, and with great emphasis she exhorted others to come and share with her the inestimable blessing.[9]

---

9. George Lane, "Letter from Rev. George Lane," 25 Jan. 1825, *Methodist Magazine* 8 (Apr. 1825): 159.

The commonality of this conversion form, paralleling that of the Book of Mormon, inspired one author to express it poetically:

[1] Description of a Camp-Meeting Scene:—

[2] Crush'd beneath the weight of love, The trembling sinner prostrate falls;

[3] Implores the mercy from above, And loudly on compassion calls;

[4] Jesus in pity stoops to hear, and wipes away contrition's tear.[10]

Lorenzo Dow and Eleazer Sherman describe other common experiences typical of the Methodist conversion form. Both men later became Methodist preachers:

Lorenzo Dow

[1] One evening, a prayer-meeting [was] appointed ... [M]any present felt the power of God; saints were happy and sinners were weeping on every side ...

[2] [T]hey since have told me that I fell down several times ... my distress was so great, that I scarcely knew what position I was in. When I got home ... I then lay down to rest ... I awaked in endless misery.

[3] I strove to plead with God for mercy ... to break these chains ...

[4] I saw the Mediator step in, as it were, between the Father's justice and my soul, and these words were supplied to my mind with great power; "Son! thy sins which are many, are forgiven thee; thy faith hath saved thee, go in peace." The burden of sin and guilt and the fear of hell vanished ... I have now found Jesus and his religion ... [M]y soul was so filled

---

10. James Porter, *An Essay on Camp-Meetings* (New York: Lane and Scott, 1849), 37.

with peace and love and joy, that I could no more keep it to my self.[11]

Eleazer Sherman

[1] [After attending a] religious meeting ...

[2] I trembled in his presence ... [A]ll my sins were then in order before me ... I returned again to my sister's house, with a wounded heart ...

[3] [and cried out,] O be merciful to me a sinner ... and may I have repentance unto life ... [and] find the pardon of my sins ...

[4] I heard as it were a soft and pleasant voice saying to me, Behold the Lamb of God, that taketh away the sins of the world. And then was presented to my mortal view the dear Saviour, from his birth to his death ... I then viewed him on the mercy seat ... I found peace, and the glory of God filled my soul. I never enjoyed such exquisite happiness in all my life; my love extended to the whole world, and I felt ... [to] tell them what an inestimable blessing religion was.[12]

This conversion form is prevalent in the Book of Mormon. Examples of Metcalfe's outline are clear in the following:

Alma II

[1] [An angel] spake unto us, as it were the voice of thunder, ... [saying repent or] be destroyed (Alma 36:7, 9).

[2] I fell to the earth; and it was for the space of three days ... I could not open my mouth ... I was racked with eternal torment, for my soul was harrowed up to the greatest degree and racked with all my sins ... I was tormented with the pains of hell (10, 12-13).

---

11. Lorenzo Dow, *The Dealings of God, Man and the Devil, As Exemplified in the Life, Experience, and Travels of Lorenzo Dow* (Norwich, CT: Wm. Faulkner, 1833), 14-16.

12. Eleazer Sherman, *The Narrative of Eleazer Sherman* (Providence, RI: H. H. Brown, 1830), 1:11-21.

[3] I cried within my heart: O Jesus, thou son of God, have mercy on me, who am in the gall of bitterness, and am circled about by the everlasting chains of death (18).

[4] [When I arose,] I could remember my pains no more; yea, I was harrowed up by the memory of my sins no more. And oh, what joy, and what marvelous light I did behold; yea, my soul was filled with joy as exceeding as was my pain! ... Yea, methought I saw ... God sitting upon his throne, surrounded with numberless concourses of angels, in the attitude of singing and praising their God (19-22).

Zeezrom

[1] [Zeezrom heard Alma and Amulek preach] (Alma 10:31-12:46).

[2] [Zeezrom] began to tremble ... [H]is soul began to be harrowed up under a consciousness of his own guilt; yea, he began to be encircled about by the pains of hell. ... [And he] lay sick at Sidon, with a burning fever, which was caused by the great tribulations of his mind on account of his wickedness ... [A]nd his many other sins, did harrow up his mind until it did become exceedingly sore, having no deliverance; therefore he began to be scorched with a burning heat (Alma 11:46; 14:6; 15:3).

[3] [Confessing belief in] the power of Christ[, Zeezrom sought] redemption ... [And] Alma cried unto the Lord, saying: O Lord our God, have mercy on this man (15:6-10).

[4] And when Alma had said these words, Zeezrom leaped upon his feet ... And Alma baptized Zeezrom unto the Lord and he began from that time forth to preach unto the people (11-12).

Lamoni's Court

[1] [T]he king believed all his [Ammon's] words (Alma 18:36, 39-40).

[2] [And] he fell unto the earth, as if he were dead. ... [Soon the queen and court] had all fallen to the earth (18:42; 19:16).

[3] [Prior to this, Lamoni] began to cry unto the Lord saying: O Lord, have mercy; according to thy abundant mercy ... upon me, and my people (18:41).

[4] [Two days later the queen] arose and stood upon her feet, and cried with a loud voice, saying: O blessed Jesus, who has saved me from an awful hell! O blessed God, have mercy on this people! ... She clasped her hands, being filled with joy, speaking many words which were not understood (19:29-30).

[When the king arose, he said,] Blessed be the name of God ... I have seen my Redeemer ... and he shall redeem all mankind who believe on his name. Now, when he had said these words, his heart was swollen ... with joy. ... [The entire court declared] that their hearts had been changed; that they had no more desire to do evil ... that they had seen angels and had conversed with them; and thus they had told them things of God and of his righteousness (19:12-13, 33-34).

Lamoni's Father's Court

[1] [In nearly the identical words of Ammon, Aaron preached to Lamoni's father's court with the same result] (Alma 22:1-15).

[2] [Lamoni's father asks, W]hat shall I do that I may be born of God, having this wicked spirit rooted out of my breast ... that I may not be cast off at the last day? ... And now when the king had said these words, he was struck as if he were dead (15, 18).

[3] [Prior to this,] the king did bow down before the Lord, upon his knees ... and cried mightily, saying ... God, wilt thou make thyself known unto me, and I will give away all my sins (17-18).

[4] And the king stood forth, [forgiven of his sins,] to minister unto them, inasmuch that his whole household were converted unto the Lord (23).

A line-by-line comparison of revival conversions and Book of Mormon passages highlights how liberally the Book of Mormon borrows from evangelical usage. Compare the language of Alma and Enos with that of Darius Williams's biographer and Abel Thornton's autobiographical sketch. The passages I have selected emphasize Metcalfe's four steps to conversion. Both Williams and Thornton later became preachers.

Darius Williams

[1] [At a camp meeting under George Lane's direction,] Marmaduke Pierce preached a short but mighty sermon, and closed with a perfect storm. He addressed the wicked with tremendous power ... [T]he whole congregation shook like the forest in a mighty wind ...

[2] Darius Williams ... fell helpless in a prayer-meeting, and lay for two hours in his father's arms. ...

[3] [M]any cried aloud for mercy ...

[4] [Williams] declared that he had found peace. He afterward became a [Methodist] preacher.[13]

Alma II

[1] [The angel's] voice was as thunder, which shook the earth; and they knew that there was nothing save the power of God that could shake the earth and cause it to tremble as though it would part asunder.

[2] [Overcome, Alma] fell again to the earth ... and [was] carried helpless, even until he was laid before his father ... [for] two days.

[3] I did cry out unto the Lord Jesus Christ for mercy ...

[4] [A]nd I did find peace to my soul. [And he] began from this time forward to teach the people (Mosiah 27:18-19, 23, 32; Alma 38:8).

Abel Thornton

[1] The preaching sunk deep into my heart ...

[2] I wanted religion ...

Enos

[1] The words ... sunk deep into my heart.

[2] ... my soul hungered;

---

13. George Peck, *The Life and Times of Rev. George Peck, D.D.* (New York: Nelson & Phillips, 1874), 108-9.

[3] [Thus] the cry of my soul ... I continued to cry to the Lord ... [4] I heard a still small voice as it were whispering in my ears, saying, thy sins are forgiven.[14]

[3] I cried unto him ... [A]ll day long did I cry unto him ... [4] [T]here came a voice unto me, saying: Enos, thy sins are forgiven (Enos vv. 3-5).

Evangelical Preaching Approach, Style, and Impact

Once an individual was converted, according to this pattern, it was easy to become a traveling preacher because the Methodists were not as rigid as most other denominations. In antebellum America, Methodists did not require a diploma or formalized training to enter the ministry. Rather, like the sons of Mosiah and other Book of Mormon preachers, desire was the primary qualifier for entering the work.[15] Alma's life is reminiscent of the more successful Methodist camp meeting itinerants. After his conversion, "Alma did speak unto them, when they were assembled together in large bodies, and he went from one body to another, preaching unto the people repentance and faith on the Lord" (Mosiah 25:15; Alma 5:1; 8:4-5). This idea became popular and was especially successful shortly before Joseph Smith's birth. Few people attended church, so circuit-preachers, as they were called, took religion to the people (fig. 23). Itinerants were to receive a small annual remuneration, but many were never paid at all and maintained themselves by working with their own hands and receiving free shelter from the people they served.[16] Like the Book of Mormon preachers and itinerants, many Methodists, as well as Baptists, preached the gospel "without price."[17]

---

14. Abel Thornton, *The Life of Elder Abel Thornton* (Providence, RI: J. B. Yerrington, 1828), 17-18, 21.

15. Milton V. Backman Jr., *American Religions and the Rise of Mormonism* (Salt Lake City: Deseret Book Co., 1970), 283-85.

16. Backman, *American Religions,* 283-87; Nathan O. Hatch, *The Democratization of American Christianity* (New Haven: Yale University Press, 1989), 88.

17. Mosiah 18:24; 24:4-5; Alma 1:3, 20, 26; 30:32-35; Whitman, "The Book of Mormon," 47.

HARPER'S WEEKLY.

A JOURNAL OF CIVILIZATION

Vol. XI.—No. 563.]   NEW YORK, SATURDAY, OCTOBER 12, 1867.   [SINGLE COPIES TEN CENTS.
[$4.00 PER YEAR IN ADVANCE.

Entered according to Act of Congress, in the Year 1867, by Harper & Brothers, in the Clerk's Office of the District Court for the Southern District of New York.

THE CIRCUIT PREACHER.—Drawn by A. R. Waud.—[See Next Page.]

Fig. 23. "The Circuit Preacher," drawing by A. R. Waud, *Harper's Weekly*, 12 October 1867.

The manner of preaching was established by Methodist founder John Wesley himself. His biographer wrote:

> It was a peculiarity of Wesley, in his discourses, that in winding up his sermons, in pointing his exhortations and driving them home, he spoke as if he were addressing himself to an individual, so that every one to whom the condition which he described was applicable felt as if he were singled out; and the preacher's words were then like the eyes of a portrait which seem to look at every beholder.[18]

Methodists were admonished to preach "plain" and "pointed," something the Book of Mormon often mentions.[19] Presbyterian Charles G. Finney praised this preaching style:

> Look at the Methodists. Many of their ministers are unlearned, in the common sense of the term, many of them taken right from the shop or the farm, and yet they have gathered congregations, and pushed their way, and won souls everywhere. Wherever the Methodists have gone, their plain, pointed and simple, but warm and animated mode of preaching has always gathered congregations.[20]

When two Methodist itinerants traveled together, one preached and the other "exhorted." In this system, a sermon drew its points from a simple Bible text. The exhortation, given by another speaker, reemphasized the points the previous speaker had made and pled with the congregants to take the message seriously.[21] The Reverends Pierce and Lane followed this model at a camp meeting that George Peck reported on: "Marmaduke Pierce preached a short but mighty sermon, and ... [t]he exhortations of the presiding elder, George

---

18. Qtd. in Roberts, *Studies*, 313.
19. See 2 Ne. 25:20, 28; 31:2; Jac. 2:11; 4:13-14; 7:17-18; Enos 1:23; Mosiah 2:40; Alma 5:43; 13:23; 14:2; Peck, *Early Methodism*, 443.
20. Charles Grandison Finney, *Lectures on Revivals of Religion*, ed. William G. McLoughlin (Cambridge, MA, 1960), 273; first published in 1835. Finney preached in New York in the 1820s.
21. *The Doctrines and Discipline of the Methodist Episcopal Church* (New York: J. Emory and B. Waugh, 1828), 28, 43, 45, 64, 74.

Lane, were overwhelming. Sinners quailed under them."[22] Peck described the exhorter's role by using Joseph Towner as an example: "His gift was more for exhortation than preaching, and often under his powerful appeals the vast multitude would melt like wax before the fire."[23] As previously indicated, Joseph Smith was an exhorter at evening meetings and was acquainted with the role of making specific appeals to the audience to apply the preacher's message. Moroni 10 can be considered an example of this—an exhortation on the entire Book of Mormon. No fewer than eight times in the chapter, Moroni exhorts his readers to apply the lessons of the book. Similarly, Alma 33-34 shows Alma preaching and Amulek exhorting. After Alma speaks, Amulek reviews his sermon and then says in part: "And now, my beloved brethren, I desire that ye should remember these things ... Yea, and I also exhort you, my brethren, that ye be watchful unto prayer continually ... And now my beloved brethren, I would exhort you to have patience, and that ye bear with all manner of afflictions; that ye do not revile ..." (34:37-40).

These evangelical preachers could recite biblical passages from memory, although they often produced slight variations from the Bible. The Reverend Eleazer Sherman, quoted above, would modify verses from John and Acts and other passages in his sermons, as did the Reverend Benjamin Putnam, paraphrasing for example Luke, Acts, and Hebrews in an 1821 address.[24] It is also so for the Book of Mormon. From Jacob 1 through Alma 42, there are hundreds of King James passages, most of them slightly altered, sprinkled throughout the religious discourses and teachings of the preachers.[25] A prominent

---

22. Peck, *The Life and Times,* 108-9; also Peck, *Early Methodism,* 494.

23. Peck, *Early Methodism,* 442.

24. Eleazer Sherman, *A Discourse Addressed to Christians of All Denominations* (Providence, RI, 1829), 4-13; Benjamin Putnam, *Sketch of the Life of Elder Benj. Putnam* (Woodstock, VT: David Watson, 1821), 14-21. See also Dow, *The Dealings of God,* 9-17; Ray Potter, *Memoirs of the Life and Religious Experience of Ray Potter* (Providence, RI: H. H. Brown, 1829), 112-24.

25. Kenneth D. Jenkins and John L. Hilton, "Common Phrases between

example is Abinadi's slightly paraphrased recitation of the ten commandments, repeated later using still different words (Mosiah 12:33-36; 13:12-24).

Evangelical preaching was also characterized by the extemporaneous interlacing of biblical passages with descriptive evangelical terminology that was designed to awaken people emotionally to their sins and cause them to tremble, shed tears, and fall to the ground. The Reverends Lorenzo Dow, Ray Potter, Alfred Bennett, Eleazer Sherman, Abel Thornton, and George Whitefield serve as representative examples (fig. 24). Their evangelical phrases mingle with slightly modified Bible quotations. Notice the themes—sin and guilt, repentance and grace, absolution and ecstasy—that are so typical of the revival sermon, along with other trappings of this kind of preaching. After these examples, representative phrases from Book of Mormon passages will be listed for comparison.

Lorenzo Dow

awaken the mind ... midst of darkness ... unprepared to die ... everlasting misery ... What must I do? ... cry for mercy ... hard heart ... to sing my dear redeemers praise.[26]

Ray Potter

unprepared to meet God ... to tremble ... thick clouds of terrible darkness ... heavy chain ... dreadful state ... day of grace was gone ... midst of darkness ... I wrestled [in prayer] ... over a dreadful gulph ... into eternal burnings ... fill me with his love.[27]

---

the King James Bible and the Book of Mormon," 3 vols., 1983, privately circulated.

26. Dow, *The Dealings of God*, 10-16. Other terms used by Dow include "the pardoning love of God," "break these chains," "the day of grace is now passed," and "unprepared to meet God."

27. Potter, *Memoirs*, 112-20. Other terms used by Potter include "filled with horror," "must be damned," "without hope," "horrors of despair," "malice of heart," "happy state," "forever too late," and "vile wretch."

Fig. 24. Methodist preacher Lorenzo Dow and the "falling exercise," from Samuel G. Goodrich, *Recollections of a Lifetime* (New York, 1856), vol. I.

Alfred Bennett

being awakened ... pains of hell ... wicked heart ... O blessed Jesus ... overwhelmed with joy ... unspeakably happy ... Savior's image be pressed on your heart ... slumbering consciences ... eternal welfare of others ... awful terrors ... clouds of darkness round your soul ... filled with [His] love ... racked with pain.[28]

Eleazar Sherman

awful pains of death ... forever miserable ... temptations of this vain world ... O God have mercy on my soul ... what shall I do to be saved ... tremble in his presence ... a wounded heart ... crying for mercy ... trembling steps ... a thick cloud and such darkness ... unto tears ... exquisite happiness.[29]

Abel Thornton

life is a state of probation ... endless woe ... sunk deep in my heart ... hardness of heart ... cry to the Lord for mercy ... a great change in your heart ... his [Jesus'] arm extended to all ... trembling voice ... sing a new song, even praises to God ... children of wrath by nature.[30]

George Whitefield

nothing but fire and brimstone ... tormented in this flame ... awake, arise from their sleep ... Jesus stands ready with open arms to receive you ... what shall I do to be saved ... you rebels ... pangs in your death

---

28. H. Harvey, *A Discourse on the Life and Character of Rev. Alfred Bennett* (Homer, NY: Rufus A. Reed, 1851), 4-15. Other terms used by Bennett include "awful wickedness," "rebellious sinful worm," "joyful hope," "arrow of conviction to his soul," "unprepared for the call of death," "terrors of the second death," and "everlasting peace."

29. Sherman, *The Narrative of Eleazer Sherman*, 6-21. Other terms used by Sherman include "mind filled with horror," "perish forever," "not prepared for death," "serious awakenings," "piercing cries," "hardness of heart," "cut the rebel down," and "carnal pleasures."

30. Thornton, *The Life of Elder Abel Thornton*, 10-23. Other terms used by Thornton include "saved only by the merits of Jesus Christ," "perish everlastingly," "seeking the things of the world and the vanities thereof," "heart of opposition," "cut the sinner down," and "forever too late."

... poor creatures ... Methinks I see the Judge sitting on his throne ... damned forever ... til Christ be formed in your hearts ... wages [of] the devil ... a child of the devil ... place of torment.[31]

Interwoven among the modified biblical passages in the Book of Mormon (Jacob 1-Alma 42) are similar examples of literally hundreds of popular phrases from nineteenth-century frontier preaching. The following seven examples are a small sample:

Alma, Chapter 5

Mormon reports that he left this chapter unabridged from Alma the younger's transcription of 83 B.C. (Alma 5:2). Nevertheless, one can detect King James language in the chapter, along with some of the evangelical phrases of Joseph Smith's day:

awakened them out of a deep sleep ... midst of darkness ... encircled about by the bands of death, and the chains of hell ... a mighty change in your hearts ... to sing the song of redeeming love ... [unprepared] to die ... the arms of mercy are extended towards them ... a child of the devil ... wages of him [devil] ... setting your hearts upon the vain things of the world ...[32]

Jacob, Chapters 1-3, 6

Jacob uses exactly the same emotional, descriptive catchwords as the evangelical preachers of Joseph Smith's era to produce the same

---

31. George Whitefield, *Eighteen Sermons Preached by the Late Rev. George Whitefield,* ed. Andrew Gifford (Springfield, MA: Thomas Dickman, 1808), 90-93, 160-61, 230-32; qtd. in Roberts, *Studies,* 310-13. Other terms used by Whitefield include "vile selves," "an arrow steeped in the blood of Christ," "hardened indeed," "carnal relations," "be a new creature," "a universal change," "the devil works in me," and "the Lord may awaken you tonight."

32. Other examples of revival language in Alma 5 include "souls were illuminated by the light of the everlasting word," "everlasting destruction," "the image of God engraven upon your countenances," and "puffed up in the pride of your hearts." For biblical language, cf. Alma 5:15=1 Cor. 15:53; 5:24=Matt. 8:11; 5:42=Rom. 6:23; 5:48=John 1:14, 29; 5:50=Matt. 3:2; 5:52=Matt. 3:10; 5:54=Matt. 3:8; 5:57=2 Cor. 6:17.

guilt-ridden trembling, shedding of tears, and fainting. Like other Book of Mormon preachers, Jacob spoke in "plainness," using modified King James phrases and evangelical expressions:

> wicked hearts ... wounded soul ... the welfare of your souls ... pierced with deep wounds ... feast upon his love ... awake from the slumber of death ... pains of hell ... his arm of mercy is extended toward you ... awful guilt ... endless torment.[33]

Enos, 1:8-27

In Enos's prayer, evangelical phrases are prevalent:

> wrestle [in prayer] ... joy of the saints ... sunk deep into my heart ... welfare of my brethren ... cry unto God ... soul did rest ... evil nature ...[34]

Mosiah 2-5

Benjamin's sermons are well known. In the opening chapters of Mosiah, note the popular evangelical expressions:

> singing the praises of a just God ... his wages [devil] ... everlasting punishment ... shrink from the presence of the Lord ... awful situation ... happy state ... a state of misery ... torment is as a lake of fire and brimstone ... carnal state ... O have mercy ... unworthy creatures ... filled with the love of God ... wrought a mighty change in us, or in our hearts ...[35]

---

33. Other examples of revival language in Jacob 1-3, 6 include "come unto Christ," "rebel against God," "hard in hearts," "piercing eye of the Almighty," "pride of your hearts," and "smoke ascendeth up forever." For biblical language, cf. Jacob 1:4=1 Cor. 4:10; 1:7=1Cor. 8:9; 2:18=Matt. 6:33; 2:19=1 Cor. 15:19; 3:11=Rev. 21:8; 6:7=Matt. 3:10; 6:8=1Thes. 5:19.

34. Other revival language in Enos 1 includes the phrase "wrought upon by the power of God." For biblical language, cf. Enos 1:8=Matt. 9:22; 1:15=Matt. 21:22; 1:27=Matt. 25:34; 1:27=1 Cor. 15:53; 1:27=John 14:2.

35. Other examples of revival language in Mosiah 2-5 include "join the choirs above," "rebellion against God," "an enemy to God," "lively sense of his own guilt," "endless torment," "they had fallen to the earth," "your noth

Mosiah 15-16

Abinadi's speech has similar language:

> the bands of death ... tremble before God ... rebelled against God ... carnal, sensual, devilish ... carnal nature ... enemy to God ... endless damnation ... arms of mercy were extended towards them ... to tremble ...[36]

Alma 11-15, 34, 36

There are recognizable evangelical phrases in Amulek's and Alma's preaching:

> began to tremble ... hard hearts ... chains of hell ... awful state ... flame ascendeth up forever ... life a probationary state ... encircled about by the pains of hell ... cry unto him for mercy ... this life is the time for men to prepare to meet God ... become his [Devil's] subjects ... methought I saw God sitting upon his throne ... exceeding joy ... singing and praising their God ...[37]

---

ingness," "tasted of his love," "name [Christ] written always in your hearts." For biblical language, cf. Mosiah 2:14=Matt. 23:4; 2:15=1 Pet. 3:21; 2:21= Luke 17:10; 2:33=1 Cor. 11:29; 3:3=Luke 2:10; 3:9=John 1:11; 3:17= Acts 4:12; 3:18=John 5:20; 3:18=Matt. 18:3; 3:19=1 Cor. 2:14; 3:24=Rev. 20:13; 3:26=Rev. 16:19; 4:14=Acts 13:10; 4:21=Matt. 21:22; 5:13=Heb. 4:12; 5:15=1 Cor. 15:58.

36. For biblical language, cf. Mosiah 15:26=Rev. 20:6; 16:2=Matt. 8:12; 16:7-8=1 Cor. 15:55; 16:9=John 8:12; 16:10=1 Cor. 15:54; 16:11 =John 5:29.

37. Other examples of revival language in Alma 11-15, 34, 36 include "the bands of death," "snare of the adversary," "encircle you about with his chains," "captivity of Satan," "blindness of their minds," "harrowed up," "they fell to the earth," "pride of their hearts," "infinite atonement," "encircle them in the arms of safety," "Plan of redemption," "take upon you the name of Christ," "racked with eternal torment," "rebelled against my God," and "my soul did long to be there." For biblical language, cf. Alma 11:37= Eph. 5:5; 12:3=Acts 5:4; 12:7=Heb. 4:12; 12:8=Acts 24:15; 12:14=Rev. 6:16; 12:27=Heb. 9:27; 13:8=2 Tim. 1:9; 13:12=Rom. 15:16; 13:15= Heb. 7:1-2; 13:20=2 Pet. 3:16; 14:28=1 Cor. 10:13; 34:13=Matt. 5:18; 34:23=Acts 13:10; 34:29=Matt. 5:13; 34:31=2 Cor. 6:2; 34:37=Phillip. 2:12; 34:38=John 4:24.

Alma 18-19, 22-23, 26

Finally, observe the evangelical imagery in Ammon's and Aaron's sermons:

> cloud of darkness ... unto tears ... O blessed Jesus ... awful hell ... hearts had been changed ... the darkest abyss ... sing to his praise ... joy is full ... everlasting gulf of death and misery ... everlasting wo[e] ... carnal state ... what shall I do ... hardness of hearts ... laid down the weapons of their rebellion.[38]

These catch words, woven extemporaneously into sermons—especially those that depicted the terrifying fallen condition of humankind—caused audiences to respond emotionally.[39] The direct "plainness" of the message, the force of the language, and its emotional impact on its hearers caused George Peck to say of Valentine Cook's preaching that people fell "like the trees of the forest before a terrible tempest." Peck believed that "God was in the words [Cook] uttered." This characterization would be applicable to many of the Methodist evangelists.[40] Similarly, the Book of Mormon records that "by the power of their words many were brought before the altar of God to ... confess their sins" (Alma 17:4). Oliver Cowdery described the Reverend George Lane who "awakened" Joseph Smith: "Mr. Lane's manner of communication was peculiarly calculated to awaken the intellect of the hearer, and arouse the sinner."[41] All these preachers

---

38. Other examples of revival language in Alma 18-19, 22-23, 26 include "fell to the earth as if he were dead," "marvelous light of his goodness," "heart was swollen within him," "overpowered with joy," "O blessed God have mercy," "harrowed up," "to sing redeeming love," "chains of hell encircled them about with everlasting darkness," "the matchless bounty of his love," and "have snatched us [the devil]."

39. For further evidence that these evangelical phrases were common in Joseph Smith's era, see Mark D. Thomas, "Listening to a Voice from the Dust: The Book of Mormon as Rhetoric [1 Nephi-Words of Mormon]," 1988, photocopy in my possession; used by permission. See also Thomas, "Revival Language," 24-25n4.

40. Peck, *Early Methodism*, 72-120.

41. Oliver Cowdery, "Letter III," *Latter Day Saints' Messenger and Ad-*

sought to bring their audience to an awareness of their depraved situation, make them recognize their sinful state, and plead with God for mercy according to the Methodist conversion form.

The modern reader is unaware that he or she is reading revival literature in the Book of Mormon because it recasts and gives it a different setting. The advantage is that it removes the stigma often attached to evangelical meetings but allows the religious message to work upon readers' minds and emotions, bringing them to repentance and Christ. This is the wellspring of energy and warmth of the Book of Mormon—something that is felt by both member and convert. I think it will long be the book's primary value. The biblical and revival elements also help us understand how Joseph could dictate the Book of Mormon in such a short period of time.[42]

Along with the preaching style and impact of the early nineteenth-century circuit preachers, theology in the Book of Mormon is also reminiscent of evangelical teachings and doctrines of the day.

Evangelical Protestant Teaching Messages

Interestingly, the distinctive messages of evangelical preachers from the burned-over district, as the revival region was known, appear in the Book of Mormon. They include admonishments against treasure digging; against wearing costly apparel; warnings not to think oneself superior to Indians, but rather to Christianize them because they are Israelites; and an attack on Deism.[43] Other preaching targets from the period that appear as topics in the Book of Mormon are Catholics, the secret combination of Masonry, and a paid clergy.[44]

---

vocate 1 (Dec. 1834): 42; qtd. in *Early Mormon Documents*, ed. Dan Vogel, 3+ vols. (Salt Lake City: Signature Books, 1996-), 2:424.

42. John W. Welch, "How Long Did It Take Joseph Smith to Translate the Book of Mormon?" *Ensign* 18 (Jan. 1988): 46-47.

43. Whitman, "The Book of Mormon," 47; Roberts, *Studies*, 174-82; see Jac. 2:12-13; 3:3-4, 6, 9; 5; 6:1-2; 7:1-14.

44. Susan Curtis, "Early Nineteenth-Century America and the Book of Mormon," in *The Word of God: Essays on Mormon Scriptures*, ed. Dan Vogel (Salt Lake City: Signature Books, 1990), 89-92; Thomas, "Listening to a

A few other evangelical motifs in the Book of Mormon are the creation of a New Jerusalem in America, concern for the proper name of the church, the mode of baptism, the doctrine that little children do not require baptism, the nature of the godhead, and especially the Methodist doctrine that sin is inherent and that all unregenerate sinners will experience hell in the after life.[45] I will discuss four of these themes in more detail: the nature of man, the nature of God, the influence of Deism, and Universalism in the Book of Mormon.

The Nature of Man

LDS scholar Mark D. Thomas describes the human condition as taught by the Book of Mormon:

> The Book of Mormon "doctrine of man" is Methodist Arminianism except in minor details. The major points of agreement are that the "natural man" (or human nature after the fall from Eden) is completely corrupt and incapable of doing good. However, through the atonement the natural man is granted the light of Christ which restores human conscience and choice. Hence, all good comes from God. People are free to the extent that they accept this light of God's grace. But even with the light of Christ, human nature has the constant inclination toward evil. This is because the fall of Adam replaced the image of God with the image of Satan in mankind. The image of God can be restored through the conversion and sanctifica-

---

Voice from the Dust," chaps. 4:44-53, 5:19-28; Whitman, "The Book of Mormon," 47-48; Gordon S. Wood, "Evangelical America and Early Mormonism," *New York History* 61 (Oct. 1980): 374; 1 Ne. 13:4-9, 26-29; 14:9-23; 22:13; Morm. 8:32; 2 Ne. 26:22; Alma 37:27; Hel. 6:21-25; Eth. 8:20, 24; 2 Ne. 26:29; Mosiah 18:24; Alma 1:3, 16, 20, 26; 30:32-35.

45. Gerald Ham, "The Prophet and the Mummyjums: Isaac Bullard and the Vermont Pilgrims of 1817," *Wisconsin Magazine of History* 56 (Summer 1973): 290-99. Bullard took his followers from Vermont in search of "The Promised Land" in Missouri; Campbell, *Delusions,* 19; Thomas G. Alexander, "The Reconstruction of Mormon Doctrine: From Joseph Smith to Progressive Theology," *Sunstone* 5 (July-Aug. 1980): 24-33; 3 Ne. 20:22; 21:23-24; 27:3-11; 3 Ne. 19:8-13; Moro. 8:5-22.

tion process. Forgiveness of sin is granted in the conversion process. And sanctification (or perfect holiness) is achieved when a person overcomes the power and inclination of sin. Sanctification is possible in this life but one may still fall by sinning. The state of probation lasts until death, even for the sanctified.[46]

In the Book of Mormon, it is not just some people—or even many—who are evil, but all of humankind through the nature of the Fall. Abinadi said the Fall "was the cause of all mankind becoming carnal, sensual, devilish" (Mosiah 16:3). Alma recorded that because of Adam, "mankind ... had become carnal, sensual and devilish by nature" (Alma 42:9-10). The brother of Jared clarifies that "because of the fall our natures have become evil continually" (Eth. 3:2). Human beings, according to the Book of Mormon, are evil by nature, and "he that persists in his own carnal nature, and goes on in the ways of sin and rebellion against God, remaineth in his fallen state" (Mosiah 16:5; cf. 16:12; 26:4; 27:24-31; Hel. 12:4-7).

The constant use of expressions like "the natural man," "enemy to God," "carnal nature," "rebellion against God," and "hard heartedness" serve as frequent reminders of this uncomplimentary view of human nature held by evangelical preachers at the time the Book of Mormon appeared. Both evangelicals and the Book of Mormon view man as more sinful than good—not as a child of God but as God's "creature," thus emphasizing dependency upon God. King Benjamin contrasts "the goodness of God ... [with] your worthless and fallen state[,] ... the greatness of God, [with] your own nothingness" (Mosiah 4:5, 11; cf. 27:24-31).

This pessimistic view should explain to modern readers why people felt such incredible guilt, wretchedness, and wickedness about themselves in Joseph Smith's day. They believed that if they failed to repent and receive forgiveness through Christ's atonement, often referred to as the "plan of mercy," they automatically became subject to the "demands of justice" in the next life. This, they understood, con-

---

46. Mark D. Thomas to Grant H. Palmer, 1987, used with permission.

signed them to a deserved "never-ending torment" in hell, which Alma said endured as long "as the life of the soul" (Alma 42:15-16; cf. Mosiah 16:3-5; 27:24-31; 28:3-4). Preachers who "awakened" sinners to their awful condition felt they had succeeded when, like famous revivalist Charles G. Finney (and King Benjamin), they would see their audiences of thousands in tears, trembling, or fallen to the ground.[47] This brand of pentecostalism is a far cry from Joseph's doctrine in Nauvoo, Illinois, that human nature is inherently good, that we are children of God capable of achieving godhood. These two different concepts of human nature suggest that Joseph later changed his view on the topic.

The Godhead

The doctrine of the godhead in the Book of Mormon shows similar development. The LDS church today teaches that God the Father and Jesus Christ are two separate and distinct beings but the Book of Mormon does not. One would expect to find this foundational doctrine taught clearly and in "plainness" in this important second "witness for Christ." Yet this is not the case. In 2 Nephi 31:21 and in the "Testimony of Three Witnesses," we read of "the Father, and of the Son and of the Holy Ghost, which is one God." In Nephi's vision of Christ, an angel explains:

> Knowest thou the condescension of God? ... [T]he virgin which thou seest, is the mother of God, after the manner of the flesh ... [And he saw] the Lamb of God, yea even the Eternal Father ... that he was taken by the people; yea, the Everlasting God, was judged of the world; and I saw and bear record. And I, Nephi, saw that he was lifted up on the cross, and slain for the sins of the world ... [T]he Lamb of God is the Eternal Father and the Savior of the world.[48]

---

47. Charles G. Finney, *Charles G. Finney: An Autobiography* (Westwood, NJ: Revell), 69, 103, 136; Mosiah 4:1.

48. See Wilford C. Wood, *Joseph Smith Begins His Work: Book of Mormon 1830 First Edition*, 2 vols. (Salt Lake City: by the Author, 1958), 1:25-26, 32; cf. 1 Ne. 11:16, 18, 21, 32; 13:40, 1981 ed.

The prophet Abinadi informs us "that Christ was the God, the Father of all things" and "that God should come down among the children of men, and take upon him flesh and blood"; also "that God himself should come down among the children of men, and take upon him the form of man" (Mosiah 7:27; 13:34). Abinadi further states: "I would that ye should understand that God himself shall come down among the children of men, and shall redeem his people. And because he dwelleth in the flesh he shall be called the Son of God, and having subjected the flesh to the will of the Father, being the Father and the Son ... And they are one God, yea, the very Eternal Father of heaven and of earth" (Mosiah 15:1-4).

Mosiah 16:15 summarizes Abinadi's doctrine: "Teach them that redemption cometh through Christ the Lord, who is the very Eternal Father." We also learn in Alma that the Father and the Son are the same God: "Now Zeezrom said: Is there more than one God? And he [Amulek] answered No ... Now Zeezrom saith again unto him: Is the Son of God the very Eternal Father? And Amulek said unto him: Yea, he is the very Eternal Father of heaven and of earth ... [and all will] be arraigned before the bar of Christ the Son, and God the Father, and the Holy Spirit, which is one Eternal God ..." (Alma 11:28-29, 38-39, 44).

LDS scholar Boyd Kirkland has commented on these passages:

> [T]he Book of Mormon and early revelations of Joseph Smith do indeed vividly portray a picture of the Father and Son as the same God ... Why is it that the Book of Mormon not only doesn't clear up questions about the Godhead which have raged in Christianity for centuries, but on the contrary just adds to the confusion? This seems particularly ironic, since a major avowed purpose of the book was to restore lost truths and end doctrinal controversies caused by the "great and abominable church's" corruption of the Bible ... In later years he [Joseph] reversed his earlier efforts to completely "mono-theise" the godhead and instead "tritheised" it.[49]

---

49. Boyd Kirkland, "An Evolving God," *Dialogue* 28 (Spring 1995):

That some of our best conservative scholars have produced lengthy articles that try to make these passages and others understandable suggests that these verses are not clear. Moreover, the Community of Christ (RLDS) still interprets Book of Mormon godhead passages as trinitarian.[50]

Other doctrinal "restorations" of the "fullness of the gospel" in the Book of Mormon are closer to evangelical Protestantism than either ancient Jewish or current LDS belief. According to Mark D. Thomas:

> The Book of Mormon must have been written in the nineteenth-century because even a loose translation of an ancient document would reveal an ancient theological context. Such would be expressed by the translator selecting the modern theological concept which best matched the ideas in the text. But on all major theological issues (the doctrines of god, humanity, and salvation), ... the Book of Mormon consistently takes the nineteenth-century position most foreign to the ancient Jewish thought from which the book purports to spring ... Jewish thought is closer to the Unitarian view of God, the New Haven Calvinist view of man as not an enemy to god, and a corporate view of salvation. But ... the Book of Mormon takes a Trinitarian view of deity, a conservative Arminian position on fallen man, and the evangelical position of individual salvation.[51]

Most of the Book of Mormon's theological issues are of little or no interest to Americans today, but in the burned-over district of

---

v-vi. See also Melodie Moench Charles, "Book of Mormon Christology," in *New Approaches to the Book of Mormon: Explorations in Critical Methodology*, ed. Brent Lee Metcalfe (Salt Lake City: Signature Books, 1993), 81-114; and Dan Vogel, "The Earliest Mormon Concept of God," in *Line upon Line: Essays on Mormon Doctrine*, ed. Gary James Bergera (Salt Lake City: Signature Books, 1989), 17-33.

50. Anthony Chvala-Smith, "A Becoming Faith," *Saints Herald* 145 (Apr. 1998): 17.

51. Mark D. Thomas, "Is the Book of Mormon Ancient or Modern History? A Discussion Focusing on the Book of Mosiah," *Sunstone* 13 (Feb. 1989): 55.

western New York in Joseph Smith's era, they were. Its views appear to reflect what Joseph was interested in and personally believed about these issues in 1827-29. By the time the church had moved to Nauvoo, his opinions on the nature of man, eternal punishment, the afterlife, the godhead, ordination, and ministry were different from those in the Book of Mormon.[52] There is nothing in the Book of Mormon about potential exaltation coming through temple ordinances, baptism for the dead, temple marriage for eternity, a graded hereafter, a plurality of gods, a potential to become gods, a positive concept of human nature, or a limitation on punishment. Joseph Smith had not yet embraced these teachings, and the Book of Mormon reflects the limitations of his 1820s understanding. As his successor, Brigham Young, stated in 1862: "If the Book of Mormon were now to be re-written, in many instances it would materially differ from the present translation." Young may have had in mind the book's uncomplimentary view of man. Less than a month before making this statement, he announced that human beings "naturally love and admire righteousness, justice and truth more than they do evil. ... The natural man is of God."[53]

Of the hundreds of religious movements that originated in the nineteenth-century, the LDS church is among only a handful that are still viable in the twenty-first century. From the beginning, the miracle of the Restoration has been the ability of its leaders—Joseph Smith and subsequent prophets—to see things in a new light. Transitional, progressive revelation was and is essential to the successful continuity and expansion of Mormon theology. It is also true for the Book of

---

52. Ostler, "The Book of Mormon as a Modern Expansion," states "Many Book of Mormon doctrines are best explained by the nineteenth-century theological milieu." See also Thomas G. Alexander, "The Reconstruction of Mormon Doctrine," 53-57; G. St. John Stott, "Ordination and Ministry in the Book of Mormon," in *Restoration Studies III* (Independence, MO: Herald Publishing House, 1986), 244-53.

53. Brigham Young, 13 July 1862, 15 June 1862, *Journal of Discourses*, 26 vols. (London and Liverpool: LDS Booksellers Depot, 1854-86), 9:311, 9:305.

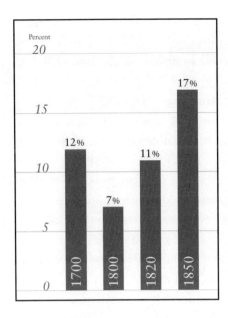

Fig. 25. Percentage of Americans who belonged to a church, 1700-1850. Adapted from Milton V. Backman Jr., *American Religions and the Rise of Mormonism* (Salt Lake City: Deseret Book, 1970).

Mormon which contributes to the modern unfolding revelations rather than revealing an ancient, static one.

Dissenting Anti-Christs

Two concerns of evangelical religion were the "unchurched" (only about 12 percent of the population belonged to a church in Joseph Smith's era; see fig. 25)[54] and the threat of Deism, Unitarianism, Universalism, and liberals. In 1822 Thomas Jefferson and others observed that the country was becoming Unitarian, a claim that alarmed preachers and caused them to label their opponents "anti-Christs."[55] In pamphlets, ministers began denouncing dissenters in mock dialogues between a Christian and the anti-Christ, the unbeliever losing the debate much like the anti-Christs in the Book of Mormon. Sometimes dissenters "attended [evangelical meetings] that they might find subjects for ridicule, or arguments against the utility of revivals of religion: but to their consciences the word has been made quick and

---

54. Backman, *American Religions,* 308.
55. Wood, "Evangelical America," 362-63, 375.

powerful, and conversion to God has been the final result," the pamphlets claimed.[56] One thinks of the anti-Christ Zeezrom in the Book of Mormon. Zeezrom initially came to deride Amulek and ended up accepting Christ (Alma 11:21-12:8; 15:3-12).

In Jacob 7 where Sherem is denounced as an anti-Christ, he has the characteristics of a Deist. Deism emerged out of the Enlightenment in Europe and appeared in America about the time of the Revolutionary War. The general belief was that man, as God's creation, is basically good, self-sufficient, and capable of progress. Deists held that God created the world, including people, like a machine which thereafter runs adequately without further intervention. For a Deist, God could be discovered in history and nature much like a watchmaker can be deduced from the existence of a timepiece. They generally respected Jesus for his religious wisdom, but they denied that he or any other religious leaders were supernaturally gifted. They held the expectation of being rewarded or punished for their works in a future state.[57] Like a Deist, Sherem was also a rationalist. He denied prophecy and believed some things in the Bible but rejected Christ's divinity, miracles, and charismatic religion (Jacob 7:7, 9-11, 13-14).

A more frequent target of evangelicals was Universalism. John Murray established the first Universalist church in America in 1793 (fig. 26). By the 1830s Universalists claimed 500 ministers and published a weekly newspaper. By 1826 there were twenty Universalist preaching stations in Ontario County, New York, where the Smith family lived. Their central tenet was that God "will finally restore the whole family of mankind to holiness and happiness."[58] As Nehor, the dissenter, describes in Alma 1:4: "All mankind should be saved at the

---

56. James H. Hotchkin, *A History of the Purchase and Settlement of Western New York, And the Rise, Progress, and Present State of the Presbyterian Church in that Section* (New York: M. W. Dodd, 1848), 167, 123.

57. Backman, *American Religions*, 197-207.

58. Russell E. Miller, *The Larger Hope: The First Century of the Universalist Church in America, 1770-1870* (Boston: Unitarian Universalist Association, 1979), 45-46; Backman, *American Religions*, 216-23.

Fig. 26. John Murray (1741-1815) founded the first Universalist Church in America in 1793. The Book of Mormon describes and rebuts Universalist theology.

last day ... for the Lord had created all men, and had also redeemed all men; and in the end, all men should have eternal life." Nineteenth-century Universalists embraced this view. They interpreted Matthew 1:21 ("Jesus ... shall save his people from their sins") to mean that everyone will obtain heaven. To combat this interpretation, evangelicals countered, "Christ is a Savior to Save his people from their Sins, and not in them."[59] Amulek rephrases this idea at Ammonihah in Alma 11. The people of Ammonihah, as portrayed in Alma 15, were followers of "the profession of Nehor." Amulek responds to them: "The Lord surely should come to redeem his people, but that he should not come to redeem them in their sins, but to redeem them from their sins" (Hel. 5:10; cf. Alma 11:34-37).

Further evidence that nineteenth-century Universalist ideas and phraseology appear in the Book of Mormon is the debate between the

---

59. Thomas, "Revival Language," 21. Minister Charles Marford, who used this phrase in 1819, lived in Victor, New York, about ten miles from Joseph Smith's home (ibid., 21).

Christian Alma and the Universalist Corianton (Alma 39-42). For some background on the theological context of Joseph Smith's environment, LDS scholar Grant Underwood writes:

> By the early nineteenth century, the Universalist church itself was riven by what came to be known as the "Restorationist Controversy." Essentially, the discord centered around the issue of postmortem punishment. Universalists, or Ultra-Universalists, as their opponents labeled them, denied the proposition that there would be any punishment after death, arguing that all such suffering, by the wicked, would occur *during* mortality and that at death all would be immediately restored to God. The Restorationists, however, felt that there was too much scriptural evidence to deny the future punishment of the wicked and contended that it would occur, if only for a limited duration, before their ultimate "restoration to holiness and happiness" in God's presence.[60]

There appears to be a specific denouncement of Ultra-Universalists and Universal-Restorationists in 2 Nephi 28: "Yea, and there shall be many which shall say: Eat, drink, and be merry, for tomorrow we die; and it shall be well with us. And there shall also be many which shall say: Eat, drink, and be merry: nevertheless, fear God—he will justify in committing a little sin: yea lie a little ... God will beat us with a few stripes, and at last we shall be saved in the kingdom of God" (7-8).

It is the latter brand of Universalism, found in verse 8, that is most frequently condemned in the Book of Mormon. Note Alma's instruction against the Restorationist argument, personified in Corianton:

> And now, my son, I have somewhat to say concerning the restoration of which has been spoken ... Do not suppose, because it hath been spoken concerning restoration, that ye shall be restored from sin to happiness ... the meaning of the word restoration is to bring back again evil for evil, or carnal for carnal, or devilish for devilish—good

60. Grant Underwood, "The Earliest Reference Guides to the Book of Mormon: Windows into the Past," *Journal of Mormon History* 12 (1985): 77-79.

for that which is good; righteous for that which is righteous; just for that which is just; merciful for that which is merciful ... For that which ye do send out shall return unto you again, and be restored; therefore the word restoration more fully condemneth the sinner, and justifieth him not at all. (Alma 41:1-15)

Alma continues by arguing for endless post-mortal punishment. Corianton has said that there is "injustice" in the view that "the sinner should be consigned to a state of misery" forever (Alma 42:1). Alma responds that it is not unjust of God to send a sinner to hell forever because Christ's "infinite atonement" is eternal as well (15-16). Both the concept and the term "infinite atonement," as explained by Alma, were introduced and made famous by Anselm of Canterbury in the twelfth century A.D.[61] In the nineteenth century, Christians used both the idea and phrase, "infinite atonement," to argue against Universalist belief in a limited punishment at death.[62] In brief, Alma argues that because Christ's atonement is "infinite," so are its consequences; therefore, he states that man's "punishment [is as] ... eternal as the life of the soul ... [and] the plan of happiness [is] ... as eternal also as the life of the soul" (42:16). By March 1830 Joseph Smith was using the argument of a Restoration Universalist by saying that "endless punishment" and "eternal damnation" are not endless but refer to limits set by God (D&C 19:6-12).[63]

A prominent dissenter in the Book of Mormon is the agnostic anti-theist Korihor (Alma 30). B. H. Roberts notes the similarity between the Sherem and Korihor narratives, despite being separated by over 400 years of history and reportedly written by two different authors, Nephi and Mormon. Roberts summarizes:

---

61. Alma 34:9-16; 42:9-17; Ostler, "The Book of Mormon as a Modern Expansion," 82; Thomas, "Revival Language," 22-23.

62. Thomas, "Revival Language," 22.

63. Elhanan Winchester, *The Universal Restoration, Exhibited in Four Dialogues between a Minister and His Friend* (Bellow Falls, VT: Bill Blake & Co., 1819), 53. Winchester's work argues that "eternal" and "everlasting" punishment should not be interpreted as literally endless. This was a well-known Universalist argument by the 1820s.

The two Anti-Christs—Sherem and Korihor—the stories of their unbelief and the treatment of them, how alike they are! In both the denial of the Christ; the charge against the ministry, that they mislead the people; that they could not know of things yet future; the denial of the Christ, and of the scriptures; the same method of attack by the prophets—"[B]elievest thou the scriptures?" "[D]eniest thou the Christ," "[B]elievest thou there is a God?" The same hesitancy on the part of the Anti-Christ in answering directly; the same demand for a sign. The same hesitancy on the part of the prophet to invoke the power of God in a sign. In both cases the sign given upon the person of the blasphemer; in one case stricken that he fell of a mortal sickness; in the other stricken with dumbness, shortly afterwards to be run over and trodden to death. In both cases a confession of being deceived by the devil and in both cases a vain repentance.[64]

After examining the narratives of Sherem, Nehor, Nehor's disciples the Amalekites (Alma 21), and Korihor,[65] Roberts concluded: "They are all of one breed and brand; so nearly alike that one mind is the author of them, and that a young and undeveloped, but piously inclined mind. The evidence I sorrowfully submit, points to Joseph Smith as their creator."[66]

Whereas the likely primary source for 1, 2, and 3 Nephi is the Bible (things old), the dominating source for Jacob through Alma 42 is evangelical Protestantism (things new). Book of Mormon prophecy, theology, and history best fit a nineteenth-century setting. When faced with this evidence, our first impulse is often to resort to personal inspiration as our defense of the Book of Mormon. This is a higher means of substantiating the book's antiquity, we assume. As an approach to matters of history and antiquity, this merits our consideration.

Religious Feeling and Truth

In contrast to the rationalism of the Enlightenment, evangelical

---

64. Roberts, *Studies,* 270-71.
65. Ibid., 264-71.
66. Ibid., 271.

Protestantism called for religious emotion. When listeners reacted with strong feelings, including tears, many preachers interpreted this to mean that their audience felt the Holy Spirit. In turn, this was considered to be confirmation of the truth of what had been preached. Jason Whitman described these gatherings in 1834:

> Go to the camp-meeting ground, or into a protracted meeting, and you will hear the preachers declaring that the spirit of God is specially and powerfully present. And what is the proof? The speakers felt great freedom in laying open the truths of the gospel, with great earnestness in exhorting sinners. The people were much affected, and many were in tears ... These revivals, these special manifestations of the Spirit, are represented as proofs that the doctrines advanced at such times are the truths of the gospel.[67]

It is the evangelical affinity of the Book of Mormon that similarly identifies emotion as evidence of the truth. Moroni 10:4-5 predicts that when one reads the book with "real intent," he or she will know the "truth of it ... by the power of the Holy Ghost. And by the power of the Holy Ghost ye may know the truth of all things." The Doctrine and Covenants confirms that when preacher and hearer "are edified," or feel "the Spirit of truth," that which they speak and hear is the truth (D&C 50:21-22).

Most of us have felt this spiritual feeling when reading the Book of Mormon or hearing about Joseph Smith's epiphanies. What we interpret this to mean is that we have therefore encountered the truth, and we then base subsequent religious commitments on these feelings. The question I will pose is whether this is an unfailing guide to truth. Is something true because I and others find it edifying? Hundreds of thousands of people believe in the truthfulness of their own religion because of similar confirming experiences. As one example, many people, including myself, felt this confirming spirit when we heard the World War II stories of Utah Congressman Douglas R.

---

67. Whitman, "The Book of Mormon," 49-50.

Stringfellow. Stringfellow's experiences were later revealed to be a complete hoax.[68] I was about fourteen years old when I heard him speak, and it was a truly inspiring experience. After Stringfellow concluded, I remember that the leader conducting the meeting said, "If you have never felt the Spirit before, it was here today in abundance." He was right. I felt it strongly, as did many others. More recently, I felt the same spirit, along with many others, when hearing Paul H. Dunn, a member of the First Quorum of the Seventy, relate his religious experiences during World War II and as a professional baseball player. Today his stories are known to be contrived.[69]

American psychologist William James in his classic work, *The Varieties of Religious Experience,* studied hundreds of people, including religious founders, who claimed to receive inspiration from the Spirit, from revelation, visions of angels, and from face-to-face appearances of God. He included Joseph Smith with Augustine, Bernard de Clairvaux, the Buddha, Fox, Huss, Loyola, Luther, Mohammed, and Wesley. He concluded that while their experiences and feelings were real to them, they could not be a valid source for determining truth because their claims were doctrinally incompatible.[70] The many Christian denominations that claim God's spirit have not succeeded in winning universal consent for even one theological insight about God beyond his existence and his love for humanity. Doctrinal contradictions appear not only between and within Christian denominations but also within the LDS church itself. Despite the church's claim to exclusive receipt of the Holy Ghost as a gift, a 1985 Gallop Poll reveals that over 40 percent of adults in America claim the same variety of spiritual feelings and experiences enjoyed by Lat-

68. Frank H. Jonas, "The Story of a Political Hoax," in *Institute of Government,* vol. 8 (Salt Lake City: University of Utah, 1966): 1-97.

69. See "Arizona Paper Alleges Many Stories Were Exaggerated," *Deseret News,* 16 Feb. 1991, 5; and "Elder Dunn Offers Apology for Errors, Admits Censure," ibid., 27 Oct. 1991, 1.

70. William James, *The Varieties of Religious Experience* (New York: New American Library, 1958), 362-66, 387-88.

ter-day Saints. Their most common denominator is not religious affiliation but the conviction that "religion is very important in their lives."[71]

The evangelical position of identifying and verifying truth by emotional feelings, which the Book of Mormon advocates, is therefore not always dependable. Such a conclusion may lead some people to believe that these feelings are self-manufactured and that there is no objective existence of something called the Holy Ghost. I assert that the Holy Ghost does exist, that it does speak to human beings. This Spirit of love gives peace, comfort, prompts, and enhances belief in God, but abundant evidence also demonstrates that it is an unreliable means of proving truth. Those who advocate the witness of the Holy Spirit as the foundation for determining the truthfulness of a given religious text need to honestly deal with these epistemological contradictions.

A possible solution may be found in Moroni 7:13: "Wherefore, every thing which inviteth and enticeth to do good, and to love God, and to serve him, is inspired of God." To me, this suggests that the Holy Spirit will witness to that which brings a person to Christ (John 14:6). This does not presume that these promptings will describe objective reality. When a person experiences the Spirit at a Protestant revival meeting or when reading the Book of Mormon, it is not my belief that this feeling proves the truthfulness of the doctrines heard, taught, or read. Nor does the Spirit, which testifies of the Book of Mormon, confirm the historical reality of the book. This sustaining and uplifting religious feeling, in my view, is a God-felt urging to repent and come unto Christ. It does not prove the truthfulness of a doctrine, book, or belief, nor does it need to, to be a valid religious experience to any person.

---

71. George Gallop Jr., "Forty-Three Percent of Americans Admit to Spiritual Experiences," *Salt Lake Tribune,* 15 May 1985, 1-2.

5.
Moroni and "The Golden Pot"

We have observed how Joseph Smith synthesized material from various sources in a way that was relevant to people of his day. Some of the sources he drew from include the King James Bible, evangelical Protestantism, Masonry, and American antiquities. In this chapter and the next, I will discuss how another element that was prevalent in his environment—popular beliefs about the supernatural—informed his experiences and his interpretation of the world and how these became part of the early narratives about his life.

Many of the American assumptions about supernatural beings and phenomena derived from Old World stories about ancient mines and lost civilizations and their forgotten wisdom. People believed that forest and dale held spirits and hidden treasures that the spirits guarded. A pick and shovel would be insufficient to find and exhume such wonders.[1] An example is found in a popular short story pub-

---

1. E. F. Bleiler, ed., *The Best Tales of Hoffmann by E. T. A. Hoffmann* (New York: Dover Publications, 1967), xxviii-xxix. Bleiler cites Mircea Eliade's *Forge and the Crucible* for the "ancient magic associated with metals and minerals" and Novalis's *Heinrich von Osterdingen* relating the "much-envied happiness in learning nature's hidden mysteries ... the hiding places of the metallic powers ... [which] cuts [one] off from the usual life of man, and prevents his sinking into dull indifference as to the deep supernatural tie

lished in Germany in 1814, introduced to America in 1827. Its author, E. T. A. Hoffmann, was born in 1776, worked in Bamberg, Dresden, Leipzig, and Warsaw, and died in Berlin in 1822. He wrote about fifty short stories and novellas and is best known today for "The Nutcracker and the Mouse King" and "The Sandman."[2] In his day, one of his most influential stories was "The Golden Pot," notable for the fact that although it involved gold and money, the principle attraction was esoteric knowledge. For our purposes, its parallels to Joseph Smith's experiences are of interest[3] (figs. 27-28).

To briefly summarize the tale, it is divided into twelve chronological episodes which Hoffmann calls vigils. The main character, Anselmus, is a young theology student who hopes his professor, Conrector Paulmann, has some work for him. Anselmus's life is humdrum and evokes neither sorrow nor joy. He feels that he possesses little influence in the world.

---

which binds man to heaven"; also E. T. A. Hoffmann's story, "The Mines of Falun," about a "quasisupernatural being who knew the intimate secrets of nature, of creation, and of the fructifying force that was believed to create the minerals." See also D. Michael Quinn, *Early Mormonism and the Magic World View,* rev. and enl. (Salt Lake City: Signature Books, 1998), 16-17, 25, 38, 263; and such terms as dwarf, leprechaun, liderc, spriggan, Kvasir, and Siegfried at www.pantheon.org/mythica.html.

2. Hoffmann's influence cannot be overstated, especially on such American authors as Washington Irving, Nathaniel Hawthorne, and Edgar Allan Poe, and in Europe, Dostoevsky and Mayakovsky, as well as on social scientists Sigmund Freud and Carl Jung. He inspired Tchaikovsky's *The Nutcracker,* Delibe's *Coppélia,* Offenbach's *The Tales of Hoffmann,* Wagner's *Die Meistersinger von Nürnberg,* and Paul Hindemith's *Cardillac.* He himself composed nine operas (*The Water Sprite, Undine*), two masses, and chamber pieces. Bleiler, *The Best Tales,* v-xxxiii; Petri Liukkonen, "Books and Writers," www.kirjasto.sci.fi/hoffman.

3. "Der Goldne Topf" first appeared in vol. 3 of *Fantasiestücke in Callots Manier* ("Fantasy Pieces in Callot's Style"), 4 vols. (Bamberg: C. F. Kunz, 1814-15); see also *Selected Writings of E. T. A. Hoffmann,* ed. and trans. Leonard J. Kent and Elizabeth C. Knight (Chicago: University of Chicago Press, 1969), 2:348-49. *Fantasiestücke* was followed two years later by a companion series, *Nachtstücke* ("Night Pieces"), in two volumes and a four-volume series, *Die Erzählungen der Serapionsbrüder* ("Stories of the Serapion Brethren") in 1819-21.

Fig. 27. E. T. A. Hoffmann (1776-1822), self-portrait from *Hoffmanns Werke* (Leipzig und Vienna, 1896), vol. 1.

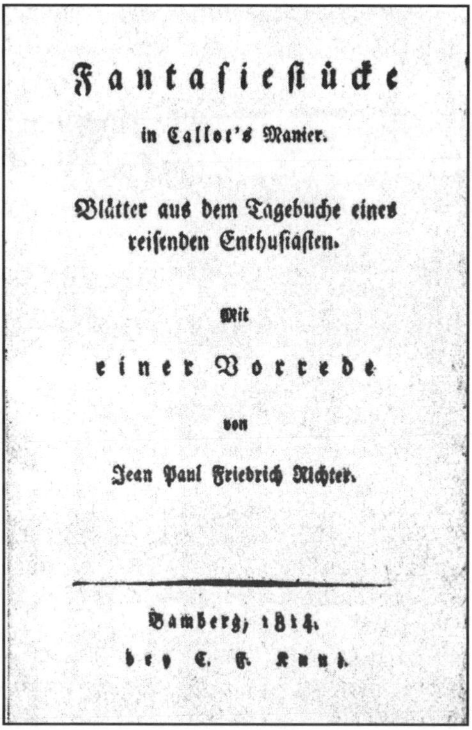

Fig. 28. E. T. A. Hoffmann's "Der Goldne Topf" appeared in volume three of *Fantasiestücke in Callots Manier* in 1814. Photograph from *E. T. A. Hoffmanns Leben und Werk in Daten und Bildern* (Frankfurt am Main: Insel Verlag, 1968).

Fantasiestücke

in Callot's Manier.

Blätter aus dem Tagebuche eines reisenden Enthusiasten.

Mit

einer Vorrede

von

Jean Paul Friedrich Richter.

Bamberg, 1814.

bey C. F. Kunz.

Anselmus begins to have daydreams in which Professor Paulmann becomes a mystical, ancient archivist named Archivarius Lindhorst from the lost civilization of Atlantis. The professor's house and library are transformed into the repository of valuable old records, manuscripts, and treasures from this ancient civilization. When the transformed archivist gives Anselmus work, it is to copy and translate the records of Lindhorst's ancestors. However, Anselmus must first meet certain qualifications to prove his worthiness. After passing these tests, Anselmus receives the Atlantean records on the fall equinox (22 September) and begins to translate them. Throughout the story, the student indulges in daydreams until he can no longer distinguish between his imaginary world and real life. By the story's end, he has permanently withdrawn to the imaginary world.

The ideas and characters for Hoffmann's tales, according to his biographers, came from popular beliefs of the time, readings in the paranormal, and from observing patients at Europe's first psychiatric hospital founded by Hoffmann's friend, Dr. Adalbert Marcus.[4] After its publication in German, "The Golden Pot" was translated into French and English. The English translation was the work of Thomas Carlisle, who had it published in Edinburgh and London in early 1827 (fig. 29).[5] Within weeks, it was already on bookstore shelves in the United States. Of course, the story was already known in some circles in America through its foreign-language editions, as were others of Hoffmann's tales. An advertisement in the Palmyra

---

4. Bleiler, *The Best Tales of Hoffmann*, xxxii; Ronald Taylor, *Hoffmann* (London: Bowes and Bowes, 1963), 70-71; see also Harvey W. Hewett-Thayer, *Hoffmann: Author of the Tales* (New York: Octagon Books, 1971), 167-72, 184-85, 193; *Selected Writings*, 1:28-30; Kenneth Negus, "E. T. A. Hoffmann's Der Goldne Topf: Its Romantic Myth," *German Review* (Columbia University) 34 (1959): 262-75.

5. Thomas Carlyle, *German Romance: Specimens of Its Chief Authors*, 4 vols. (Edinburgh: William and Charles Tait, 1827). "The Golden Pot" appeared in 2:200-317. All 4 vols. were published together sometime between January and March 1827 (*Edinburgh Review* 45 [Dec. 1826-Mar. 1827]: 540, 544).

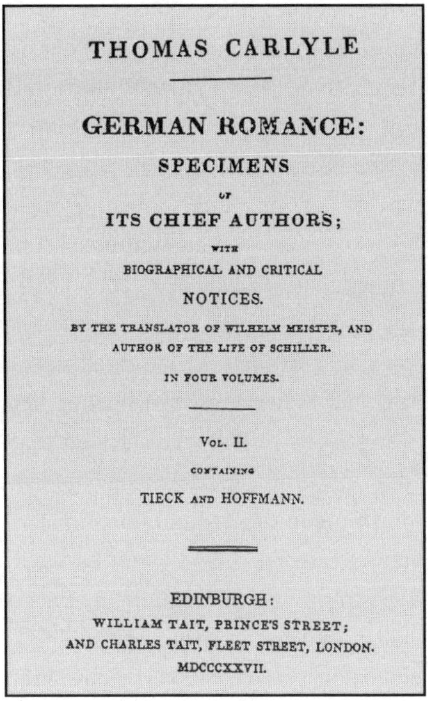

THOMAS CARLYLE

GERMAN ROMANCE:

SPECIMENS

of

ITS CHIEF AUTHORS;

with

BIOGRAPHICAL AND CRITICAL

NOTICES.

BY THE TRANSLATOR OF WILHELM MEISTER, AND
AUTHOR OF THE LIFE OF SCHILLER.

IN FOUR VOLUMES.

VOL. II.

CONTAINING

TIECK AND HOFFMANN.

EDINBURGH:

WILLIAM TAIT, PRINCE'S STREET;
AND CHARLES TAIT, FLEET STREET, LONDON.
MDCCCXXVII.

Fig. 29. "The Golden Pot" first appeared in English in early 1827 in Thomas Carlyle's *German Romance: Specimens of Its Chief Authors*, volume two.

newspaper in 1827 promoted a literary magazine's critique of Hoffmann's works.[6]

Among Joseph Smith's acquaintances, one in particular would have appreciated the German and French editions of Hoffmann's writings. His name was Luman Walters, of Sodus, Wayne County, New York. That the Smith family had contact with Walters in 1822-23 shortly after his move to Sodus is confirmed by Brigham Young,

---

6. The ad promoted *The Museum of Foreign Literature and Science*, published monthly from Philadelphia and available locally through E. B. Grandin. The current issue, according to the ad, carried the article, "On the Supernatural in Fictitious Composition—Works of Hoffmann," a reprint from a London quarterly (*Wayne Sentinel*, 30 November 1827). The review itself includes the following: "The belief [in the supernatural] ... has its origin not only in the facts upon which our holy religion is founded, but upon the principles of our nature, which teach us that while we are probationers in this sublunary state, we are neighbours to, and encompassed by the shadowy

Lorenzo Saunders, Abner Cole, and others.[7] Sodus was twenty–five miles from Palmyra and thirty miles from Mendon where Brigham Young lived. Young met Walters and described him as "a man of profound learning [who] had put himself in possession of all the learning in the States, had been to France, Germany, Italy, and through the world."[8] Young later told a group in 1873, according to Elizabeth Kane: "A man named Walters[,] son of a rich man ... received a scientific education, was even sent to Paris. After he came home he lived like a misanthrope, he had come back an infidel ..."[9]

Clark Braden, a Campbellite college president in Kirtland, Ohio, said that Walters lived in Europe before he met Joseph Smith. His investigations in Palmyra showed that "[w]hile acting in his primitive, super-natural capacity as water-witch and money-digger, [Joseph] Smith made the acquaintance of a ... Walters, who had been a physician in Europe. This person had learned in Europe the secret of Mesmerism or animal magnetism. This was entirely unknown in America except to a few in large cities ..."[10] This European education in medicine suggests that Walters knew French or German or both.

---

world, of which our mental faculties are too obscure to comprehend the laws, our corporeal organs too coarse and gross to perceive the inhabitants" ("On the Supernatural in Fictitious Composition; and particularly on the Works of Ernest Theodore William Hoffmann," *Foreign Quarterly Review,* July 1827).

7. Quinn, *Early Mormonism,* 131.

8. Brigham Young, 19 July 1857, 18 Feb. 1855, *Journal of Discourses,* 26 vols. (London and Liverpool: LDS Booksellers Depot, 1854-86) 5:55, 2:180-81.

9. Qtd. in Elizabeth Kane, *A Gentile Account of Life in Utah's Dixie, 1872-73: Elizabeth Kane's St. George Journal,* ed. Norman R. Bowen (Salt Lake City: Tanner Trust Fund, University of Utah Library, 1995), 72; qtd. in Dan Vogel, ed., *Early Mormon Documents* 3+ vols. (Salt Lake City: Signature Books, 1986-), 3:405.

10. Edmund L. Kelley and Clark Braden, *Public Discussion of the Issues between the RLDS Church and the Church of Christ (Disciples) Held in Kirtland, Ohio, Beginning February 12, and Closing March 8, 1884* (Lamoni, IA: Herald Publishing House, 1913), 367. Braden also called Walters a "drunken vagabond."

Walters is not the only individual in the community who would have encountered "Der Goldne Topf" from Hoffmann's 1814 or 1819 editions or from the 1822 French publication that was widely distributed in Europe.[11] But Walters is the most likely conduit to Joseph Smith. Drawing on extensive observation and treatment of mental patients for some of his character development, Hoffmann would have attracted the attention of someone like Walters who was interested in mesmerism, which was thought at the time to be a cure for mental and physical disorders.[12] Closely associated with mesmerism were the related fields of hypnotism, telepathy, and clairvoyance. Ronald Taylor noted that "no other German writer [than Hoffmann] has absorbed so fully, and re-lived so intensely, the psychological facts of schizophrenia, of hypnotism, of telepathy, and of other irregular and irrational conditions of the mind."[13] Harvey W. Hewett-Thayer writes:

> Once the existence of a magnetic fluid is recognized ... the range of activity that ... may [be] assign[ed] to it is limitless. A mesmerist may project the magnetic fluid over an indeterminate space and control a subject in the faraway ... Persons at a distance may be mysteriously attracted to one another as by a magnet ... Such extensions of the magnetic theory account for a multitude of puzzling phenomena, such as clairvoyance, thought transference, and presentiments ... Hoffmann makes frequent use of these occult phenomena in his tales. The cult of magnetism had by 1813 sufficiently engaged Hoffmann's attention to become the theme of one of his earliest stories.[14]

Although Walters practiced medicine, he earlier dabbled in the

---

11. Bleiler, *The Best Tales of Hoffmann*, xvii, xv.

12. Taylor, *Hoffmann*, 72. Taylor wrote that "the healing powers of 'animal magnetism' ... [were] applied to the body as a cure both for external injuries and for internal disorders"; see also Carl Sagan, *The Demon-Haunted World: Science as a Candle in the Dark* (New York: Random House, 1995), 68.

13. Taylor, *Hoffmann*, 70-71.

14. Hewett-Thayer, *Hoffmann: Author of the Tales*, 171-72.

occult and was a "clairvoyant," according to family tradition.[15] Abner
Cole reported that he was skilled in the magical arts and conducted
treasure digging with Joseph Smith and others at Miner's Hill in Manchester. Cole was interested in these activities because he owned the
property at Miner's Hill from 1820 through 1823.[16] He wrote in the
Palmyra *Reflector* on 12 June 1830 that "Walters the Magician, who
has strange books, and deals with familiar spirits ... produced an old
book in an unknown tongue, ... from whence he read in the presence
of the Idle and Slothful [the money diggers] strange stories of hidden
treasures and of the spirit who had the custody thereof." Cole added
in a subsequent article that when Walters read, he would "interpret,
and explain [the book], as a record of the former inhabitants of America." He believed that Walters must have suggested the idea of a book
to Joseph Smith, as did ten Palmyra residents who, although they may
have been influenced by Cole, added the weight of their opinion in a
letter to the *Painesville Telegraph*. They said that the "idea of a 'book'
was doubtless suggested to the Smiths by one Walters."[17]

One of Joseph Smiths' neighbors, Lorenzo Saunders, who also
lived close to Miner's Hill (fig. 30), remembered that Walters and the
Smiths dug there before Alvin Smith died in late 1823. In Lorenzo's
interview with a counselor in the RLDS presiding bishopric, Edmund
L. Kelley, Lorenzo said, "I am one of them that saw digging there

---

15. Quinn, *Early Mormonism*, 118.

16. Dan Vogel, "The Locations of Joseph Smith's Early Treasure Quests,"
Dialogue: A Journal of Mormon Thought 27 (Fall 1994): 204-207n31.

17. "The Book of Pukei, Chap. 1," *The Reflector*, 12 June 1830, 37; qtd.
in Vogel, *Early Mormon Documents*, 2: 231, 233; "Gold Bible, No. 5," *Reflector*, 28 Feb. 1831, 109; qtd. In Vogel, 2:247; "Letter from Palmyra, NY,"
Painesville [OH] Telegraph, 22 Mar. 1831, [2]; qtd. in Vogel, 3:8. Diedrich
Willers Jr. (1820-1908), of Fayette, New York, wrote: "Fortune tellers are
consulted as to the future, many in this neighborhood where ever they wish
to find out something anything which is lost, or pry in the hidden mysteries
of hidden things will consult Dr Walters." "Ambition and Superstition," Mis-
cellaneous Undated Items, Diedrich Willers Papers, Box 1, Cornell University, Ithaca, New York; in Vogel, "The Locations," 207n33.

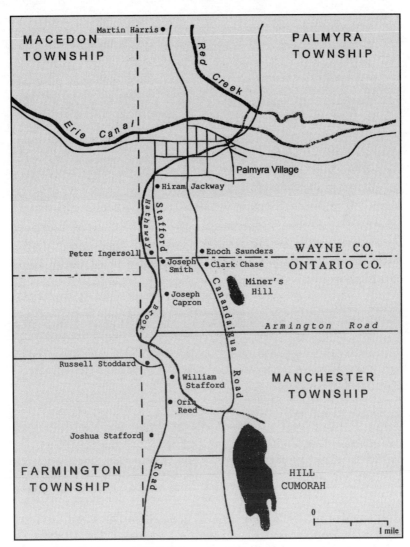

Fig. 30. Map of Palmyra and Manchester townships.

[Miner's Hill] ... Well I will tell you they did dig; Willard Chase & Alvin, the one that died; they dug before Alvin died."[18] Saunders continues:

> At the time the big hole was dug in the hill they was duped by one Walters who pretended to be a conjurer, I heard Willard Chase say that he was duped. They could not be deceived in it after he had gone through with a certain movements & charged them $7. I seen the old man [Joseph Sr.] dig there day in and day out; He was close by. I used to go there & see them work.[19]

Walters is colorful if nothing else; that he is a probable link between Hoffmann's tale and the Palmyra area is also evident.

Before comparing Hoffmann's story to Joseph Smith's life, it is necessary to review the New York sources for Joseph's experiences. There are nine primary sources from 1827 to 1830—five friendly and four unsympathetic.[20] The friendly sources are Lucy Smith,[21] Oliver Cowdery, Joseph Knight Sr., Martin Harris, and Benjamin Saunders, all of whom heard the details of Joseph Jr.'s story directly from Jo-

---

18. Lorenzo Saunders, interview by Edmund L. Kelley, 12 Nov. 1884, 8-9, Edmund L. Kelley Papers, Library-Archives, Community of Christ (RLDS), Independence, Missouri (hereafter RLDS Library-Archives); in Vogel, *Early Mormon Documents*, 2:152-53; and Vogel, "The Locations," 206-7. Lorenzo also mentions that his father, Enoch Saunders, told him to cover up the hole that was dug. His father died in 1825, so the excavation, if Lorenzo's recollection is correct, had to have been completed by then.

19. Lorenzo Saunders, interview by Edmund L. Kelley, 12 Nov. 1884, 12; in Vogel, *Early Mormon Documents*, 2:156-57; see also 2:233n23.

20. In 1833 fifty-one of Palmyra's leading citizens said the Smiths were "famous for visionary projects" (Statement, 4 Dec. 1833, in E. D. Howe, *Mormonism Unvailed* (Painesville, OH: by the Author, 1834), 261-62; qtd. in Vogel, *Early Mormon Documents*, 2:48-55). These included attorneys, a bank president, the fire warden, a justice of the peace, merchants, a minister, a physician, the postmaster, a state legislator, tradesmen and manufacturers (a jeweler, a miller, and several tanners), the village trustee and treasurer, and a U.S. congressman (see W. H. McIntosh, *History of Wayne County, New York* [Philadelphia: Everts, Ensign and Everts, 1877]; Thomas L. Cook, *Palmyra and Vicinity* (Palmyra, NY: Press of the Palmyra Courier-Journal, 1930).

21. Lucy says that the Smith family began discussing Joseph's call to

seph himself.[22] The Knight and Saunders families were good friends of the Smith family. The remaining four sources are Willard Chase, Fayette Lapham, Abner Cole, and the Reverend John A. Clark. Chase and Lapham heard about Joseph's experiences from his father. Chase was a neighbor and fellow treasure hunter and Lapham simply visited the Smiths at their Manchester home. Cole was an attorney in Palmyra who had been a justice of the peace, constable, and overseer of highways before becoming editor of the *Reflector* newspaper. He heard the remarkable stories from Joseph Sr., Joseph Jr., and various neighbors. Reverend Clark, a Palmyra Episcopal minister, heard from

---

translate the record of a lost civilization in September 1823 (Lucy Mack Smith, *History of Joseph Smith by His Mother, Lucy Mack Smith* (Salt Lake City: Bookcraft, 1958), 74-89.); Preliminary Manuscript (1845), 289-98, 302). How detailed their family discussions were is unknown. Lucy refers to "when we [family] get the plates" (L. Smith, 82-85; L. Smith, 1845, 294-96). She said that Martin Harris knew of these things "two or three years previous" to 1827 (ibid., 104-05). Harris clearly disputes this in his own statement. He said he first heard about the angel gold-plates narrative "about the first of October, 1827," Martin Harris, interview by Joel Tiffany, Jan. 1859, in "Mormonism," *Tiffany's Monthly* (New York City) 5 (Aug. 1859): 167; qtd. in Vogel, *Early Mormon Documents,* 2:308. Joseph Knight Jr. recalled in 1862 that "I think" he and his father heard a general statement of Joseph's angelic call in November 1826 (William G. Hartley, *"They Are My Friends": A History of the Joseph Knight Family, 1825-1850* [Provo, UT: Grandin Book Co., 1986], 214). In June 1827 Willard Chase was apparently the first to hear a full recital of the story outside of the Smith family (Affidavit of Willard Chase, 11 Dec. 1833, in Howe, *Mormonism Unvailed,* 242; qtd. in Vogel, *Early Mormon Documents,* 2:66).

22. Lucy Smith, *History of Joseph Smith,* 74-123; and her Preliminary Manuscript "History of Lucy Smith," 1844-45 (hereafter, Lucy Smith, 1845), LDS archives; in Vogel, *Early Mormon Documents,* 1:289-99, 324-29. Oliver Cowdery, "Letters III-VIII," *Latter Day Saints' Messenger and Advocate* (Kirtland, OH), Dec. 1834, 41-43; Feb. 1835, 77-80; Mar. 1835, 95-96; Apr. 1835, 108-12; July 1835, 155-59; Oct. 1835, 195-202; qtd. in Vogel, *Early Mormon Documents,* 2:422-50, 455-66; Dean C. Jessee, ed., "Joseph Knight's Recollection of Early Mormon History," *BYU Studies* 17 (Autumn 1976): 29-39; Martin Harris, in *Tiffany's Monthly* 5 (Aug. 1859):163-170; qtd. in Vogel, *Early Mormon Documents,* 2:300-310; Benjamin Saunders, Interviewed by William H. Kelley, "Miscellany 1795-1948," W. H. Kelly Collection (P19/2:44, 1883-85), RLDS Library-Archives; qtd. in Vogel, *Early*

Martin Harris.[23] I cite all nine individuals in the following comparative presentation by surname.

Between 1832-42, Joseph Smith Jr. himself related four personal accounts of how the golden plates came forth. The first is included in his 1832 letterbook. The second, a conversation with a visitor at Kirtland, Ohio, appears in his diary for November 1835. In 1838, during a time when leading members of the church were apostacizing and persecution was high, he dictated the third account, now canonized as scripture as the "Joseph Smith—History" in the Pearl of Great Price. Finally, in 1842 he dictated another account to John Wentworth, editor of the *Chicago Democrat*.[24] These four accounts are cited below as 1832, 1835, 1838, and 1842.

Now I will compare all of these recitals by Joseph Smith, his family, and their acquaintances with E. T. A. Hoffmann's "The Golden Pot." These are arranged according to the chronology of Hoffmann's story. The general plot narration is mine as a convenience to link significant excerpts, which are quoted. The vigil numbers are Hoffmann's but the titles are mine. Under each title, I will relate the E. T. A. Hoffmann story first, followed by the comparable portions of the New York narratives.

Mormon Documents, 2:136-40; see also Benjamin Saunders, interview by Orson Saunders, 1892, in "Mormon Leaders at Their Mecca," *New York Herald*, 25 June 1893, 12; qtd. in Vogel, *Early Mormon Documents*, 3:201-202.

23. Affidavit of Willard Chase, 11 Dec. 1833, in Howe, *Mormonism Unvailed*, 240-48; qtd. in Vogel, *Early Mormon Documents*, 2:64-74; Joseph Smith Sr., interview by Fayette Lapham about 1830, in "The Mormons," *Historical Magazine* 7 (May 1870): 305-9; in Vogel, *Early Mormon Documents*, 1:456-66; Abner Cole, *The Reflector* (Palmyra, NY), 12 June, 7 July 1830; 14, 28 Feb., 19 Mar. 1831; qtd. in Vogel, *Early Mormon Documents*, 2:231-36, 244-50; Martin Harris, interview by John A. Clark, 1828, *The Visitor, or Monthly Instructor, for 1841* (London: Religious Tract Society, 1841), 61-64; qtd. in Vogel, *Early Mormon Documents*, 2:260-68.

24. Dean C. Jessee, ed., *The Papers of Joseph Smith: Autobiographical and Historical Writings* (Salt Lake City: Deseret Book Co., 1989), 1:1-10, 427-33; and Jessee (ibid., 1992), 2:68-71; "Joseph Smith—History," The Pearl of Great Price, 1:1-65.

Vigil 1: The First Vision of the Evening

He meditates upon his foibles.

E. T. A. Hoffmann

The scene begins with Anselmus, a theology student (pp. 1-2),[25] meditating on his past life. He is discouraged because, as God's servant, he is clumsy and commits many errors. He thinks:

"Now that I've become a student, in spite of Satan, isn't it a frightful fate that I'm still as bumbling as ever? Can I put on a new coat without getting grease on it the first day, or without tearing a cursed hole in it on some nail or other? ... Have I ever got to my college, or any other place that I had an appointment to, at the right time? ... I run into some fellow coming out, and get myself engaged in endless quarrels until the time is clean gone" (p. 3).

Joseph Smith

Meditating on his past life, Joseph is discouraged because he commits many errors and follies. He says: "I frequently fell into many foolish errors, and displayed the weakness of youth, and the foibles of human nature ... not consistent with ... one who was called of God" (1838, v. 28).

He receives a shock, a vision of angels, and a message.

E. T. A. Hoffmann

While Anselmus is meditating upon his foibles in the early evening, several beings from the ancient civilization of Atlantis appear to him. Atlanteans can appear in various forms as humans, serpents, and so forth. On this occasion they are illuminated like "a thousand glittering emeralds ... Through all his limbs there went a shock like elec-

---

25. Page numbers are from Bleiler, *The Best Tales of Hoffmann*, with a reprint of "The Golden Pot" from the 1827 Carlyle English edition, slightly modernized. For a more recent translation, see *Tales of E. T. A. Hoffmann*, ed. and trans. Leonard J. Kent and Elizabeth C. Knight (Chicago: University of Chicago Press, 1972), 14-92.

tricity; he quivered in his inmost heart: he kept gazing up, and a pair of glorious dark-blue eyes were looking at him." This being spoke to Anselmus, but he did not fully comprehend the message (pp. 4-5).

Joseph Smith

After meditating upon his follies, Joseph receives a "vision of angels in the night season after I had retired to bed[.] I had not been a sleep, but was meditating upon my past life and experience ... all at once the room was illuminated above the brightness of the sun [and] an angel appeared before me ... he said unto me I am a messenger sent from God ... " (1835).

Joseph said this bright light "produced a shock that affected the whole body; in a moment a personage stood before me" (1842). Oliver Cowdery said the light "occasioned a shock or sensation, visible to the extremities of the body" (Cowdery, Letter 4).

Vigil 2: The Second Vision of the Evening

He is called to translate ancient records.

E. T. A. Hoffmann

Later in the evening, Anselmus receives a second vision. This time he learns that Archivarius Lindhorst, whom he encountered earlier (pp. 5, 19, 35), is the archivist of a vast library containing Atlantean books and treasures. He also possesses "a number of manuscripts, partly Arabic, Coptic, and some of them in strange characters, which do not belong to any known tongue. These he [Lindhorst] wishes to have copied [and translated] properly, and for this purpose he requires a man who can draw with the pen, and to transfer these marks to parchment, in Indian ink, with the highest exactness and fidelity. This work is to be carried out in a separate chamber of his house, under his own supervision ... he will pay his copyist a *speziesthaler*, or specie-dollar daily, and promises a handsome present" (pp. 10-11).

Joseph Smith

Later in the evening, Joseph receives a second vision in which the custodian of ancient records (later identified as Moroni) commissions him to translate some arcane writings. The being "said unto me that he was a messenger sent from the presence of God to me, and that his name was Moroni; that God had a work for me to do ... He said there was a book deposited, written upon gold plates ... Also that there were two stones ... deposited with the plates; and the possession and use of these stones were ... for the purpose of translating the book" (1838, vv. 33-35).

The next morning he walks to the appointed place.

E. T. A. Hoffmann

Lindhorst instructs Anselmus to come to his "ancient residence" in the morning and meet with him. The next morning Anselmus, in vision, begins walking to Lindhorst's house to initiate the work (p. 11).

Joseph Smith

Moroni instructs Joseph to come in the morning to meet with him on the hill where the records are buried. The vision ends. The next morning Joseph[26] begins walking to the hill to carry out the "commandments which I had received" (1838, vv. 48-50; L. Smith, 80).

He thinks about riches.

E. T. A. Hoffmann

As Anselmus walks to Lindhorst's house, he "saw nothing but clear speziesthalers [dollars], and heard nothing but their lovely clink. Who could blame the poor youth, cheated of so many hopes by capricious destiny, obligated to take counsel about every farthing ... [F]or here, thought he, slapping his pocket, which was still empty, for here [dollars] will soon be clinking" (p. 11).

---

26. Joseph Smith experienced parallels 2-5 after his fourth vision, which occurred in a field (see Vigil 4). I have placed them here for comparison purposes. Surely parallel 5, fighting a serpent-like being, could happen only in a dream-vision.

Joseph Smith

As Joseph walks to Moroni's hill, he "saught the Plates to obtain riches" (1832). Oliver Cowdery added this about Joseph: "[A] thought would start across the mind on the prospects of obtaining so desirable a treasure ... [Thus] a fixed determination to obtain and aggrandize himself, occupied his mind when he arrived at the place where the record was found" (Cowdery, Letter 7; also 1838, v. 46; L. Smith, 83-84).

He encounters an evil force.

E. T. A. Hoffmann

Arriving at Lindhorst's "ancient residence," Anselmus "stood there, and was looking at the large fine bronze knocker; ... [As] he lifted his hand to grasp this same knocker, the metal visage twisted itself ... into a grinning smile" of an ugly old witch. Her menacing thoughts seized his mind: "You fool, fool, fool! ... [You will] fall" (p. 12, also 1, 56-58). This witch becomes the principle adversary throughout the story. Anselmus is unnerved both by the "cursed visage of that witch ... [which] grinned on me from the door knocker" and by her evil thoughts (pp. 15, 16, 21-22, 27, 30-31, 38-40, 64).

Joseph Smith

Lucy Smith said the messenger warned Joseph about a power that would try to control his thoughts: "Now Joseph beware or when you go to get the plates your mind will be filled with darkness and all manner of evil will rush into your mind [t]o prevent you from keeping the commandments of God[,] that you may not succe[e]d in doing his work[,] ... [A]n evil spirit will try to crowd your mind with every evil and wicked thing to keep every good thought and feeling out of your mind but you must keep your mind always staid upon God that no evil may come into your heart" (L. Smith, 1845, 290, 292).

Cowdery said that Joseph "beheld the prince of darkness" (Cowdery, Letter 8), and Joseph confirmed that "the powers of darkness strove hard against me" (1835; 1832).

The messenger harms him.

E. T. A. Hoffmann

Disturbed by the evil one's visage but determined to be rich, Anselmus pulls hard on the bell-rope at the front porch: "The bell-rope lengthened downwards, and became a gigantic, transparent, white serpent, which encircled and crushed him, ... the blood spouted from his veins, penetrating into the transparent body of the serpent and dyeing it red ... On returning to his senses, he was lying on his own poor truckle-bed" (p. 12).

Anselmus has made the mistake of thinking of his special appointment in monetary terms only. Displeased, Lindhorst has appeared to him in a frightful form and inflicted violence upon him. Anselmus awakes from this nightmare.[27]

Joseph Smith

Joseph's pecuniary motives trigger the ire of the guardian of the plates. Joseph Smith Sr. said that, upon arriving at the hill, Joseph "saw in the box something like a toad, which soon assumed the appearance of a man, and struck him on the side of his head ... [T]he spirit struck him again, and knocked him three or four rods, and hurt him prodigiously. After recovering from his fright, he enquired why he could not obtain the plates; to which the spirit made reply, because you have not obeyed your orders" (Chase).

Benjamin Saunders, a good friend of the Smiths, said: "I heard Joe tell my Mother and Sister how he procured the plates. He said he was directed by an angel where it was ... When he took the plates there was something down near the box that looked some like a toad that rose up into a man which forbid him to take the plates" (Saunders).[28]

---

27. It is later disclosed that Lindhorst is an elemental spirit, a salamander. The elemental spirits are sylphs representing air, undines for water, gnomes for earth, and salamanders for fire. Lindhorst's daughters can also appear as snakes, including one named Serpentina with whom Anselmus falls in love. A primeval spirit prince from Atlantis, as Anselmus learns, is named Phosphorus. Bleiler, *The Best Tales of Hoffmann*, xxxii, 4-5, 44-52, 64, 69.
28. In the Hoffmann novel and the New York story, both archivists are

Lucy said her son was "hurled back upon the ground with great violence" (L. Smith, 84). Joseph wrote that he was "excedingly frightened" (1832), though he himself mentions nothing of such magical elements. He does confirm that the guardian angel intervened because Joseph lacked purity of purpose and was therefore "forbidden by the messenger" from obtaining the record (1838, v. 53).

Vigil 3: The Third Vision of the Evening

He receives a brief sketch of the ancients.

E. T. A. Hoffmann

Later in the evening, Anselmus receives a third vision. In this epiphany he hears a "brief" recital of Lindhorst's remarkable life and

---

spirits capable of appearing in a kingly or majestic form, a frightful form, and as a pleasant old man. Normally Lindhorst appears as a pleasant old man (pp. 14-16, 20-21, 31, 35, 48); but when he is displeased, he appears as a frightening old man or as a serpent or salamander (pp. 12, 19, 40, 55, 59-60). When he is pleased with Anselmus, he appears as a king (pp. 35, 43, 52, 61). The majestic form in both narratives is mainly biblical (Ex. 3:2; John 20:12; Acts 10:30; Rev. 1:13-15; 2:18). It is their other forms and their abusive and unpredictable personalities, a characteristic evident in both stories, that is unlike the biblical and Christian tradition. For condemnation of "familiar spirits," see Lev. 19:31; 20:6, 27; Deut. 18:11; 1 Sam. 28:3; 1 Kgs. 21:6; 2 Chr. 10:13; Isa. 8:19; 19:3. The archivist of Cumorah has a kingly form in the 1838 version (vs. 30-33, 44, 47, 49, 53-54, 59). But in the earlier accounts, he appears in the same three forms as Lindhorst: majestic, frightful, or pleasant. For the frightening forms, see Quinn, *Early Mormonism,* 147-54; Joseph and Hiel Lewis, "Mormon History, A New Chapter about to be Published," *Amboy [IL] Journal,* 30 Apr. 1879, 1; "Review of Mormonism—Rejoiner to Elder Cadwell," *Amboy Journal,* 4 June 1879, 1; Sallie McKune, interview by Frederic G. Mather in "The Early Days of Mormonism," *Lippincott's Magazine of Popular Literature and Science* (Philadelphia) 26 (Aug. 1880): 200. For examples of the messenger also appearing as a pleasant old man, see Preston Nibley, *Witnesses of the Book of Mormon* (Salt Lake City: Deseret Book Co., 1968), 70-71; Abner Cole, "Book of Pukei, Chap. 2," *The Reflector,* 7 July 1830, 61, and "Gold Bible No. 4," 14 Feb. 1831, 101, qtd. in Vogel, *Early Mormon Documents* 2:236, 245; Leman Copley, qtd. in E. D. Howe, *Mormonism Unvailed,* 276-77.

family ancestry, including the source from whence this civilization "had sprung" (p. 14). This is told in more detail in Vigil 8 when Anselmus actually translates the history.

Joseph Smith

The same evening that Joseph saw two visions, he received yet another. He says that in this thrice-occurring epiphany, "I was also informed concerning the original inhabitants of this country, and ... [given] a brief sketch of their origin" (1842). It was at this time that he learned "there was a book deposited, written upon gold plates, giving an account of the former inhabitants of this continent, and the source from whence they sprang" (1838, v. 34).

The messenger is a descendant of his people's founders.

E. T. A. Hoffmann

Anselmus learns that Lindhorst is a direct descendant of the founders of Atlantis (p. 14).

Joseph Smith

Joseph learns that Moroni is a direct or "pure descendant" of the founders of the Nephite civilization (3 Ne. 5:20; Morm. 8:13).

The messenger is his people's last archivist.

E. T. A. Hoffmann

Lindhorst is not only an archivist (p. 10) but the last archivist of his race (pp. 14-15, 47, 67).

Joseph Smith

Joseph learns that Moroni is the last archivist of his race (Morm. 8:13-14; Moro. 1:1-4).

The messenger is a spirit prince.

E. T. A. Hoffmann

Being a direct descendant, Lindhorst announces, "I am a prince myself" (p. 14). He is also a "Spirit-prince" and "the Prince of the Spirits" (pp. 43, 45-48, 61).

Joseph Smith

According to Abner Cole, "the elder Smith declared that his son Jo had seen the spirit," also called "the prince of spirits," and "that in due time he (the spirit) would furnish him (Jo) with a book, which would give an account of the Ancient inhabitants (antideluvians), of this country" (Cole, 12 June 1830; 14 Feb. 1831).[29]

Vigil 4: The Morning Vision

He sits under a tree by a green sward.

E. T. A. Hoffmann

Several days later, Anselmus receives a fourth vision while lying under an "elder-tree" by a "green kindly sward" (p. 18). When in vision, Anselmus is in "deep thought" and looks "ill" (pp. 6-7).

Joseph Smith

Lucy says of her son's fourth vision: "The next day he and his father and Alvin were reaping in the field togather [. S]uddenly Joseph stopped and seemed to be in a deep study ... [His father] urged him to go to the house and tell his mother that he was sick[. H]e went a short distance till he came to a green sward under an apple tree[. H]ere he lay down ... The personage whom he saw the night before came to him again ..." (L. Smith, 1845, 291).

Joseph says that the messenger "appeared unto me three times in one night and once the next day" (1832). Of the fourth vision he states that "while in the field at work with my Father he asked me if I

---

29. Some people in Joseph Smith's era believed Atlantis to have been "the continent of America." See entry for "Atlantis" in *Noah Webster's First Edition of an American Dictionary of the English Language* (facsimile of the 1828 ed., San Francisco: Foundation for American Christian Education, 1980).

was sick ... I started and went part way [to the house] and was finally deprived of my strength and fell, but how long I remained I do not know; the Angel came to me again" (1835) and "related unto me all that he had related to me the previous night" (1838, v. 49).[30]

The message is repeated and expanded.

E. T. A. Hoffmann

After his fourth vision, Anselmus says "it was clearer to him now than ever" (p. 18). He adds, "[F]or I now see and feel clearly ... remarkable dreams" (p. 22). These progressive experiences deepen his understanding of the spiritual world as they unfold.

Joseph Smith

Joseph says, "The angel appeared to me again and related the same things and much more" (1835). In his 1838 recital he said that the messenger "related the very same things which he had done at his first visit, without the least variation," and then provided evidence the envoy did in fact give additional information each time (1838, vv. 45-46, 49). Cowdery explained, "[T]he vision was renewed twice before morning, unfolding farther and still farther the mysteries" (Cowdery, Letter 7).

He is chastised for disobedience.

E. T. A. Hoffmann

Several days later Lindhorst appears again in vision and chastises Anselmus, calling him by name (cf. 1838, v. 33): "[T]here suddenly stood before him a tall lean man, wrapped up in a wide light-gray surtout [frock], who, looking at him with large fiery eyes, exclaimed: ... 'Hey, hey, this is Herr Anselmus that was to copy my manuscripts.'

---

30. In this vision, the messenger instructed Joseph to leave the field and come to the hill for the records (JS—History (1838), vv. 48-50; Lucy Smith, *History of Joseph Smith*, 80). He said that parallels 2-5 (Vigil 2) occurred on the way and upon arriving at the hill.

The Student Anselmus felt not a little terrified at hearing this voice ...
For fright and astonishment, he could not utter a word. 'What ails
you, Herr Anselmus,' continued Archivarius Lindhorst, for the stran-
ger was no one else ... '[W]hy did you not come to me and set about
your work?'" (p. 19). Anselmus explains his fear of the evil witch and
white serpent (p. 19).

Joseph Smith

Before obtaining the record, Joseph tells his parents: "I have
taken the severest chastisement that I have ever had in my life ... As I
passed by the hill of Cumorah, where the plates are, the angel met me
and said that I had not been engaged enough in the work of the Lord"
(L. Smith, 100).

According to Martin Harris, as Joseph returned home from hunting for treasure at Cumorah, "the angel of the Lord met him clad in
terror and wrath. He spoke in a voice of thunder ... The terror of the
Divine Messenger's appearance instantly struck Smith to the earth ...
In language most terrific did the angel upbraid him for his disobedi-
ence, and then disappeared" (Clark).

Vigil 5: Waiting for the Fall Equinox

He has to wait one year.

E. T. A. Hoffmann

Because of Anselmus's sloth, Lindhorst determined: "[W]e will
talk of it this time a year from now" (p. 23).

Joseph Smith

Moroni tells Joseph that he is "under transgression, but to come
again in one year from that time" (1835; 1838, v. 53).

He will be accompanied by a woman.

E. T. A. Hoffmann

The evil witch encounters Veronica, Anselmus's sweetheart-fian-

cee. Disguised as a pleasant old woman, the witch induces Veronica
to come with her on an equinox adventure. The witch will conjure
Anselmus and assure a happy future for them, but only if Veronica is
present. Veronica should come on "the next [fall] equinox" (pp.
26-30).

Joseph Smith

Joseph informs Joseph Knight Sr. that to obtain the plates he
must bring "Emma Hale" on the next fall equinox (Knight Sr.). Joseph's father says that "to insure success," his son "courted and married" Emma (Lapham).

Vigil 6: Another Visit to the Appointed Place

The door opens automatically.

E. T. A. Hoffmann

Remembering Lindhorst's chastisement, Anselmus makes a second visionary trip to Lindhorst's residence. The door simply swings
open and Anselmus "mount[s] the fine broad stair. ... Archivarius
Lindhorst, in a white damask nightgown, emerged and said ... Come
this way, if you please" (pp. 30-31).

Joseph Smith

According to Brigham Young, Joseph entered the Hill Cumorah
several times to see the archivist and his library of plates.[31] Apostle

---

31. Brigham Young, 17 June 1877, *Journal of Discourses* 19:37-39;
Wilford Woodruff, 11 Dec. 1869, *Wilford Woodruff's Journal, 1833-98*,
typescript, ed. Scott G. Kenny, 9 vols. (Midvale, UT: Signature Books, 1983-
85), 6:508-9; Hyrum Smith, qtd. by William W. Phelps, in William H. Dame,
"Journal of Southern Exploring Company, 1854-1858," 14 Jan. 1855, Della
Dame Edmunds Collection, Ms 515, Manuscripts Division, Marriott Library,
University of Utah, Salt Lake City, Utah; William Blood, 17-18 June 1877,
The Life Sketch of William Blood (np, nd), 47; John Whitaker, Journal,
6:104, Manuscripts Division, Marriott Library. Cowdery and others reported these events, according to Young's memory. It should be noted that
dream-visions can be misremembered as having been real events.

Heber C. Kimball said this occurred while Joseph was in "vision."[32] Joseph's brother Hyrum said that Cowdery and others visited the hill in 1829: "As they were walking up the hill, a door opened." Young said "the hill opened, and they walked into a cave."[33] Hyrum said they were met by "an angel" whom Young calls "a Messenger who was the keeper of the room."[34]

He tours the vast chambers.

E. T. A. Hoffmann

Anselmus follows Lindhorst through an indoor "house garden" with "great trees" and "high groves" (pp. 31, 42). Next they "stepped through many a strangely decorated chamber." They enter "a large apartment," the "azure chamber," then the outer library described as "a high room" (pp. 31-33).

Joseph Smith

Young and Kimball said that Joseph and his companions "walked from cell to cell." Orson Pratt was informed by the Smiths that the hill contained various "chambers."[35] Hyrum said "they walked into a room about 16 ft square." Young described it as "a large and spacious room."[36] According to Cole, the Smiths said the hill contained "large and spacious chambers" (Cole, 14 Feb. 1831).

He sees illuminated treasures.

E. T. A. Hoffmann

As Anselmus walks through the azure chamber, he notices that

---

32. Heber C. Kimball, 28 Sept. 1856, *Journal of Discourses* 4:105.

33. Hyrum Smith in Dame Journal; Brigham Young, 17 June 1877, *Journal of Discourses* 19:37-39.

34. Hyrum Smith in Dame Journal; Woodruff quoting Brigham Young, 11 Dec. 1869, *Wilford Woodruff's Journal*, 6:508-9.

35. Heber C. Kimball, qtd. in "Brigham Young Manuscript History," 5 May 1867, LDS archives; Orson Pratt, "The Hill Cumorah," *Latter-day Saints' Millennial Star*, 7 July 1866, 419.

36. Hyrum Smith in Dame Journal; Brigham Young, *Journal of Discourses* 19:38.

"[a] magic dazzling light shone over the whole, though you could not discover where it came from, for no window whatever was to be seen" (p. 31). Anselmus "could scarcely give a glance at all the glittering wondrous furniture and other unknown things with which all the rooms were filled" (p. 32).

Joseph Smith

Cowdery "did not think, at the time, whether they had the light of the sun or artificial light; but that it was just as light as day," according to Young's retelling. Church member William Blood heard Young say in his 1877 discourse that "they entered a large room that was brilliantly lighted, but [they] did not notice the source of the light."[37] Joseph Sr. said the rooms contained "substance, consisting of costly furniture, etc" (Cole, 14 Feb. 1831). Young also said that Joseph and the others saw "tons of choice treasures and records" and that "there were a great many treasures hid up by the Nephites."[38]

He views Egyptian artifacts.

E. T. A. Hoffmann

Anselmus enters the azure chamber which houses the records of Lindhorst's ancestors (pp. 32, 43). "[I]n the middle of the chamber, and resting on three Egyptian lions, cast out of dark bronze, lay a porphyry plate; and on this stood a simple flower pot made of gold" (p. 32). Porphyry is a hard Egyptian rock with embedded crystals[39] similar to the design of Aaron's breastplate in the Bible (Ex. 28:15-20).

---

37. Brigham Young, *Journal of Discourses* 19:38; Blood, *Life Sketch*, 47.

38. Brigham Young, *Journal of Discourses* 19:37-39; *Wilford Woodruff's Journal*, 11 Dec. 1869, 6:508-9; see also Dame, Journal, 14 Jan. 1855; John Whitaker, Journal, 6:104. Heber C. Kimball, 28 Sept. 1856, *Journal of Discourses* 4:105; and "Brigham Young Manuscript History," 5 May 1867, LDS archives; Statement of Abigail Harris, 28 Nov. 1833, in Howe, *Mormonism Unvailed*, 253; and the Affidavit of William Stafford, 8 Dec. 1833, ibid., 237-39; both qtd. in Vogel, *Early Mormon Documents*, 2:32, 60.

39. *Noah Webster's First Edition*, "Porphyry."

Joseph Smith

Cowdery reported that "[f]rom the bottom of the box, or from the breastplate, arose three small pillars ... and upon these three pillars was placed the record" that was inscribed in "Egyptian characters" (Cowdery, Letter 8; 1838, v. 52; L. Smith 1845, 291; J. Smith, 1842). Hyrum Smith said that "Aaron's breastplate" was among the artifacts housed in the chamber.[40]

He encounters the seeric device.

E. T. A. Hoffmann

Anselmus is drawn to the golden pot, a seeric device. Anselmus "could not turn away his eyes. It was as if, in a thousand gleaming reflections, all sorts of shapes were sporting on the bright polished gold ... Anselmus was beside himself with frantic rapture" (p. 32). Later the pot is described as being of "the fairest metal ... [its radiant] beams borrowed from the diamond" (p. 47).

Lindhorst has previously shown Anselmus "the stone of the ring"; Anselmus "looked in, and O wonder! The stone emitted a cluster of rays; and the rays wove themselves into a clear gleaming crystal mirror ... " In the mirror, a face appears and begins to speak (p. 20).

Joseph Smith

On 22 September, Joseph tells Knight that the spectacles are "ten times Better th[a]n I expected." In elaborating, Knight says that Joseph "seemed to think more of the glasses or the Urim and Thummem then [than] he Did of the Plates, for says he, I can see any thing; they are Marvelous" (Knight). Joseph Sr. also said that Joseph "could see everything" in the glasses (Lapham). Joseph describes the device as "two stones in silver" (1838, v. 35). Lucy said they were "two large bright diamonds set in" metal and two "diamonds ... set in silver" (L. Smith, 1845, 221, 329).

---

40. Dame, Journal, 14 Jan. 1855.

The special treasures are kept separate from the library.

E. T. A. Hoffmann

Most of the books and manuscripts are in the general library. However, the special records of Lindhorst's ancestry, the golden pot, and the breastplate are kept in the inner, azure chamber (pp. 32-33, 43-44, 48).

Joseph Smith

When Moroni deposited the artifacts in the Hill Cumorah—the gold plates, the urim and thummim, and the breastplate (1838, vv. 35, 59)—he was "inspired to select a department of the hill separate from the great sacred depository of the numerous [other] volumes hid up ... [and stored] in another department of the hill," according to Orson Pratt, quoting Joseph Jr.[41]

He describes the general library.

E. T. A. Hoffmann

Lindhorst leads Anselmus to the library, "a high room lined on all sides with bookshelves, and no wise differing from a common library and study. In the middle stood a large writing table" (p. 33). By contrast, the table in the azure chamber was "encircled ... [with] large books with gilt leaves" (p. 41).

Joseph Smith

John Whitaker heard Young's 1877 sermon and reported that he said there were "great volumes of ancient records ... [at the time Joseph] entered this underground ancient library."[42] Blood said, "The room had shelves around it ... There was also a table."[43] Young said "[i]t was a large table that stood in the room."[44] He reported that "in that room were deposited a large amount of gold plates, containing

---

41. Orson Pratt, "The Hill Cumorah," 417.
42. John Whitaker, Journal, 6:104.
43. Blood, *Life Sketch*, 17-18 June 1877, 47.
44. Young, *Journal of Discourses* 19:38.

sacred records."[45] Kimball said, "There were books piled up on tables, book upon book."[46]

He enters a period of instruction.

E. T. A. Hoffmann

In the library "Lindhorst now brought out ... an Arabic manuscript" which Anselmus eagerly begins transcribing. "While laboring here," Lindhorst says, "you are undergoing a season of instruction." At the close of the first day's work, Lindhorst is obviously pleased and appears in kingly form to praise Anselmus (pp. 34-35). During the season of instruction, "at the moment when Anselmus had finished the last letter of some manuscript; then the Archivarius would hand him another" (p. 42).

Joseph Smith

When Joseph went to the hill for the plates, "he fully expected to carry them home with him" (L. Smith, 83). However, he "made an attempt to get them out but was forbidden." Instead, he received a period of "instruction and intelligence" (1838, vv. 53-54). He told Saunders that it was "in a cave, where I began the first translation of the inspired pages" (Saunders). Thomas Cook, a local Palmyra historian, says the angel met Joseph and instructed him in "a cave. There he would meet him and reveal to him the hieroglyphics on the golden plates."[47] Lucy reportedly said, "The angel brought each plate as Jo[seph] began to translate it and took it away as he finished it."[48]

---

45. *Wilford Woodruff's Journal*, 11 Dec. 1869, 6:508-9.

46. Kimball, *Journal of Discourses*, 28 Sept. 1856, 4:105.

47. Cook, *Palmyra and Vicinity*, 309, 238; see also Pomeroy Tucker, *Origin, Rise, and Progress of Mormonism* (New York: D. Appleton & Co., 1867), 48-49; qtd. in Vogel, *Early Mormon Documents*, 3:112.

48. Lucy Mack Smith, qtd. in Kelley and Braden, *Public Discussion of the Issues*, 180-81.

He understands the higher purpose of his work.

E. T. A. Hoffmann

Lindhorst says in parting at the end of the first day's work: "'The fee for this day is lying in your right waistcoat pocket'; the Student Anselmus actually found the [dollar] in the pocket indicated; but he derived no pleasure from it" (p. 36). After working "several days with Archivarius Lindhorst ... every little care of his needy existence had vanished from his thoughts" (pp. 41-42).

Joseph Smith

Joseph understood that he would receive the plates in "due time ... [if I had] an eye single to the glory of God ... [I] obtained them not untill I was twenty one years of age" (1832). He could not "get the plates for the purpose of getting rich ... I must have no other object in view in getting the plates ... otherwise I could not get them" (1838, v. 46). After "due time," or "four years," he saw the higher purpose in the work (1832; 1838, v. 53).

Vigil 7: The Final Test

The fall equinox has significance.

E. T. A. Hoffmann

In this vision, the witch reappears and seeks the golden pot for herself. Her plan is to eliminate her competition by killing Anselmus on "the Equinox" (p. 36). She chooses this day because one "can prosper ... [It] favours the work" (pp. 36, 37, 48).

Joseph Smith

Joseph regards the autumnal equinox as a special day. He says, "At length the time arrived for obtaining the plates ... [o]n the twenty-second day of September" (1838, vv. 29, 48-54, 59). The equinox is also when Joseph received the plates back after losing them in June 1828 because of Harris's transgression (L. Smith, 133-34).

His companion prays against the howling spirits.

E. T. A. Hoffmann

"On this twenty-second of September," Veronica and the old witch "went at midnight on the Equinox to the crossing of the roads: she [the witch] conjured certain hellish spirits ..." by drawing a magic circle and performing other rituals. "[K]neeling" in the circle, Veronica summoned "with prayers her guardian angel to deliver her from the monsters of the Pit, which, in obedience to this potent spell are to appear at any moment" (pp. 37-38, 41, 64).

"She heard, indeed, the howling and the raging around her; all sorts of hateful voices bellowed and bleated, and yelled and hummed; but she did not open her eyes, for she felt that the sight of the abomination and horrors with which she was encircled might drive her into incurable destroying madness" (p. 39).

Joseph Smith

Emma Smith accompanied Joseph to the hill on the 1827 fall equinox and "kneeled down and prayed" (Harris). Joseph Sr. added that his son "proceeded, punctually, with his wife, to find the hidden treasure ... [and while they were on the hill] a host of devils began to screech and to scream, and made all sorts of hideous yells, for the purpose of terrifying him and preventing the attainment of his object" (Lapham).

He is wounded in a fight with the spirits.

E. T. A. Hoffmann

The witch commands her "hellish spirits" to destroy Anselmus and obtain the golden treasure, screaming "Bite him to death!" This is interrupted by a rushing wind as Lindhorst arrives as an eagle, swooping in, pouncing, and "striking round him [Anselmus] with his pinions" to fight off the spirits. He then sends the crone home (pp. 40, 48, 64).

Joseph Smith

"With Lucifer at their head, ... those spirits knew when Joseph

Smith got the plates," the Smiths told Young. "They were there at the time, and millions and millions of them opposed Joseph in getting the plates; and not only they opposed him, but also men in the flesh."[49]

After moving to Pennsylvania in late 1827, Joseph told Mrs. Harriet Marsh "he saw legions of devils, ... that he had had a personal encounter with the chief devil, and that he (the Prophet) was severely wounded by a blow."[50] According to Harris and others in the Palmyra area, the Smiths said that Joseph encountered infernal spirits and "[o]ne of the devils struck him a blow," seeking to kill him (Harris; Lapham; Cole, 14 Feb. 1831).

Joseph told Saunders that: "a thousand devils sprang into light. They were all around the hill; the mountain seemed alive with them; they were in the air[,] they perched on my shoulders ... I was protected by the angel of God. But I had to fight for it" (Saunders). Joseph's own later account reports that after receiving the plates, "multitudes" sought them and that only through his diligence were they "protected" (1838, vv. 59-60).

Midnight to dawn on the equinox.

E. T. A. Hoffmann

Veronica and the witch were out all night from "midnight on the Equinox" until "broad daylight" (pp. 40, 64).

Joseph Smith

Joseph asserted that "[o]n the twenty-second day of September," in making a second attempt for the plates (1838, vv. 53-54, 59), he and Emma left for the hill at "[a]bout twelve o'clock" midnight and did not return home until after breakfast time (L. Smith, 102-03; also L. Smith, 1845, 326-27).[51]

---

49. Brigham Young, 19 July 1857, *Journal of Discourses* 5:55.

50. Harriet Marsh, interview by Frederic G. Mather, in "The Early Mormons," *Binghamton Daily Republican*, 29 July 1880.

51. On 15 June 1828, almost exactly nine months after 22 September 1827, Emma Smith delivered a stillborn son (Lucy Smith, *History of Joseph*

He receives the ancestral records on the equinox.

E. T. A. Hoffmann

Veronica looks into a "bright polished metallic mirror" and sees Anselmus "sitting in a stately chamber (not the usual library), with the strangest furniture, and diligently writing" at a desk encircled by "large books with gilt leaves" (p. 41). Thus on the fall equinox, having passed his test, Anselmus has been allowed to enter the stately azure chamber with the golden pot, porphyry, and Lindhorst's special records.

Joseph Smith

On the fall equinox, having passed the test of his probation, Joseph receives "the plates, the Urim and Thummim, and the breastplate" from Moroni (1838, v. 59).

Vigil 8: Translating the History

He describes the records.

E. T. A. Hoffmann

In vision, Lindhorst appears before Anselmus in kingly form, standing in the stately azure chamber, and says: "You have gained my confidence; but the hardest is still ahead; and that is the transcribing or rather painting of certain works, written in a peculiar character; I keep them in this room, and they can only be copied on the spot. You will, therefore, in the future work here" (pp. 42-43).

Smith, 125). Joseph had previously said to six people that the child would play an important role in translating the golden plates. See Willard Chase, 11 Dec. 1833, in Howe, *Mormonism Unvailed*, 247; qtd. in Vogel, *Early Mormon Documents*, 2:72; Martin Harris, interview by John A. Clark, in *The Visitor, or Monthly Instructor, for 1841*, 63; qtd. in Vogel, *Early Mormon Documents*, 2:264; Affidavit of Isaac Hale and statements by Joshua McKune and Sophia Lewis, *The Susquehanna Register and Northern Pennsylvanian* (Montrose, PA), 1 May 1834, 1; Sallie McKune, in the *Binghamton Daily Republican*, 29 July 1880.

In the chamber are "books with gilt leaves ... [of] parchment." After several days, Lindhorst gives Anselmus some "parchment leaves from the books" and Anselmus begins to translate these "little leaves" (pp. 41, 43, 60).

Joseph Smith

"These records," wrote Joseph, "were engraven on plates which had the appearance of gold, each plate was six inches wide and eight inches long and not quite so thick as common tin. They were filled with engravings, in Egyptian characters and bound together in a volume, as the leaves of a book" (1842).

Emma, when handling the record through a cloth, said the leaves were "pliable like thick paper and would rustle with a metallic sound when the edges were moved by the thumb, as one does sometimes thumb the edges of a book."[52]

The characters are in an unknown language.

E. T. A. Hoffmann

Looking at the special parchments, "Anselmus wondered not a little at these strangely intertwisted characters; and as he looked over the many points, strokes, dashes, and twirls in the manuscript, he almost lost hope of ever copying it" (p. 43). Elsewhere these markings are described as "Arabic" or "partly Arabic, Coptic, and some of them in strange characters, which do not belong to any known tongue," (p. 10) "the twisted strokes of ... foreign characters" (p. 34).

Joseph Smith

Joseph Sr. said the marks on the plates were "written over in characters of some unknown tongue" and explained that Harris took "the strange characters" to New York City "where the most learned man then in the city told him that with few exceptions, the characters were Arabic" (Lapham). A missionary in 1831 said the "thin plates resem-

---

52. Nibley, *Witnesses of the Book of Mormon*, 27.

Fig. 31. Charles Anthon (1787-1867), engraved from a photograph by Matthew Brady, *Harper's Weekly,* 1861. His 1828 library included works on hieroglyphic and demotic Egyptian.

bling gold" had "Arabic characters inscribed on them."[53] Harris said that classical scholar Charles Anthon in New York pronounced the characters "Egyptian, Chaldaic, Assyriac, and Arabic" (1838, v. 64).

Anthon later wrote (figs. 31-32): "This paper was in fact a singular scrawl. It consisted of all kinds of crooked characters ... Greek and Hebrew letters, crosses and flourishes, Roman letters inverted or placed sideways, ... decked with various strange marks" ...[54]

Joseph said of the characters: "[N]o one can interpret them; ... [They are written] in a language that ... cannot be read, ... [for the language is] confounded" (Eth. 3:22, 24; Morm. 9:32, 34).

---

53. "Mormonism," *New-Hampshire [Portsmouth] Gazette,* 25 Oct. 1831, 1.

54. Charles Anthon to E. D. Howe, 17 Feb. 1834, in Howe, *Mormonism Unvailed,* 271-72; Anthon to T. W. Colt, 3 Apr. 1841, *Church Record* 1 (1841): 231.

Fig 32. Facsimile of the characters on the gold plates. Holograph, Community of Christ (RLDS) Library-Archives.

He translates by inspiration.

E. T. A. Hoffmann

When sitting in the azure chamber where things are "seen," Anselmus receives "help" in translating. At first he "look[s]" (pp. 43, 67-69) as Lindhorst unfolds a piece of oblong parchment and places it on the table before him. He studies "the foreign characters" (p. 43), then "directed his eyes and thoughts more and more intensely on the superscription of the parchment roll ... till it sounded in his inmost heart ... like a burning ray" (pp. 44-45). He "felt" and thus knew that it was the story of Lindhorst and "his history" (pp. 44-49).

"It was as if, in his inmost soul, a voice were whispering in audible words ... [and as] he caught these sounds, the unknown characters grew clearer and clearer to him; he scarcely needed to look at the original at all; nay, it was as if the letters were already standing in pale ink on the parchment and he had nothing more to do but mark them black" (pp. 34-35).

Joseph Smith

Joseph said he could "look" in a seer stone "and translate all records" (cf. Mosiah 8:13). He did so by "sight and power," which he defined as the Holy Ghost "tell[ing] you in your mind and in your heart" what the foreign letters said (D&C 3:12, 8:1-2, 11:11). David Whitmer said Joseph told "me and others" that he concentrated his thoughts on his seer stone, then he "would see, not the stone, but what appeared like an oblong piece of parchment, on which the hieroglyphics would appear, and also the translation in the English language."[55]

Joseph told Orson Pratt that he only used "the Urim and Thummim when he was inexperienced in the Spirit of inspiration"[56] and that it was "by the gift, and power of God," rather than by the stone itself, that he translated (1842).

He produces a most correct book.

E. T. A. Hoffmann

Lindhorst specified that his special records needed to be interpreted and copied "with the highest exactness and fidelity" and "the greatest clearness and correctness" (pp. 10, 21). When Anselmus translated, his work stood "perfect on the parchment" (p. 34). As he became experienced, he "scarcely needed to cast his eye upon the manuscript," and yet it was interpreted "rapidly and correctly" (pp. 42-43).[57]

Joseph Smith

Joseph said that "the Book of Mormon was the most correct of any book on earth."[58]

In conclusion, what do these parallels mean? Clearly, there are

---

55. David Whitmer, interview by James H. Hart, 10 Mar. 1884, in the *Deseret News*, 25 Mar. 1884; see also David Whitmer, interview by Zenas H. Gurley Jr., 14 Jan. 1885, Ms d 4681, LDS archives; David Whitmer, *An Address to All Believers in Christ* (Richmond, MO: by the Author, 1887), 12.

56. Orson Pratt, "Two Day's Meeting at Brigham City, June 27 and 28, 1874," *Latter-Day Saints' Millennial Star,* 11 Aug. 1874, 499.

57. In vigils nine through twelve, Anselmus's visions increase until, in Vigil 12, he withdraws completely "to the mysterious land of wonders" (pp. 49, 61, 65).

58. Joseph Smith Jr. et al., *History of the Church of Jesus Christ of Latter-day Saints*, ed. B. H. Roberts (Salt Lake City: Deseret Book Co., 1978 printing), 4:461.

similar motifs, descriptions, and occasionally the same terminology in both the New York and "Golden Pot" narratives. Moreover, how could Joseph control the many detailed events and descriptions that are clearly beyond his power to duplicate and which are common to both narratives? It would stretch credulity to believe that this could be a coincidence, and I therefore think that a debt is owed to E. T. A. Hoffmann and the European traditions for at least some of the details that passed from the Smith family to neighbors and from there to outsiders. Interestingly, it is only after the appearance of Carlyle's translation in January-February 1827 that the first full narrative of the angel and gold plates was reported outside the Smith family (see note 21). Joseph Sr. related it in some detail to Willard Chase in June 1827 (Chase). The community began to hear the full report after 22 September 1827.[59]

Hoffmann's tale is not a very religious story; Joseph's is. There are spirits and apparitions in both. In both stories, the archivist has the characteristics of a wizard or elemental spirit, one that has the ability to appear as a king, a pleasant old man, and as a frightening old man and serpent. These qualities are more than a resurrected being would demonstrate, according to current LDS theology. When Anselmus and Joseph make mistakes, the messenger exhibits the passions of a Greek god rather than the personality of the God of Mount Sinai or of New Testament angels. A personage appearing in frightful form and administering physical abuse is not an inspiring figure in the Christian tradition.

---

59. There are other similarities between Hoffmann's story and the New York narratives that could be cited. For instance, Anselmus wears clothing that is "at variance with all fashion. His pike-gray frock was shaped as if the tailor had known the modern style only by hearsay." His clothing consists of an old fashioned "neckcloth ... black silk stockings ... pike-gray frock and black satin lower habiliments" (pp. 11, 1-2). By comparison, Joseph Sr. said that his son wore "an old-fashioned suit of clothes, of the same color" (Lapham). He also told Willard Chase that his son "must repair to the place where was deposited this manuscript, dressed in black clothes ... They accordingly fitted out Joseph with a suit of black clothes" (Chase).

In the variants of the story that were told, then standardized after 1830, the sometimes abusive spirit is presented as a resurrected human being, the mild-mannered Moroni who appears in stately form and quotes scripture (1838, vv. 36-41). He is a physical being rather than a spirit, an earthly visitant who descends and ascends through Joseph's bedroom ceiling. This corporeal resurrected visitor quoting the Bible at length and conducting "interviews" at Cumorah and by Joseph's bedside is impressive in a way that the angel of the dream visions originally spoken of is not (1832; 1838, vv. 30, 43, 46-47, 54). In other words, Joseph's later narratives provide a more biblical-type angel and a setting that sounds religiously authoritative.

While almost all of the motifs in Joseph's 1827-30 narratives are found in the German novel, there are exceptions, the most notable being that Joseph is told to bring another person with him each year that he visits the hill from 1824-27. Joseph said he failed to obtain the plates from 1823 through 1826 but claimed success in 1827 (Knight; Chase; Lapham).[60] On the other hand, his mother, Lucy, said there were only two attempts to obtain the records (L. Smith, 1845, 326-27). In his 1830 accounts, Joseph concurs. He said that after his first failure in 1823, he had no chance to obtain the plates until a four-year probation had passed (1838, vv. 53-54), which is more in line with Hoffmann's tale.

In the preface to his 1827 translation, Thomas Carlyle explained that he had selected six representative novellas of different genres and by different authors. He observed that often, within a genre, the same basic story is retold with different details. "If the reader will impress himself with a clear view of these six kinds" of genre, he wrote, "and then conceive some hundreds of persons incessantly occupied in imitating, compounding, separating, distorting, exaggerating, diluting them, he may have formed as correct an idea of the actual state of German novel writing, as it seemed easy with such means to afford him."[61]

---

60. See also Quinn, *Early Mormonism*, 159-65.
61. Carlyle, *German Romance: Specimens of Its Chief Authors*, 1:xi-xii;

The same could be said of frontier storytelling in Joseph Smith's day, as well as of the nuances that may have colored personal experiences.

Regardless of where the motifs in the New York narratives came from, most of them, including the basic storyline, were already present in some form in the environment. Similarly, many of the magical elements of the story began disappearing around 1830. At least, no one reported hearing such details from Joseph after 1828 or from Joseph Sr. after 1830.[62] By making the story less magical, it and the messenger became more traditionally religious. On 19 March 1831, just prior to the Smith family's move from New York to Ohio (L. Smith, 195, 199), Abner Cole wrote in the Palmyra *Reflector* that, from his perspective, the Smith family was telling "a new edition" of the story.[63] When Joseph was asked on 25 October 1831 to relate "all the particulars of the coming forth of the book of Mormon" to a mixed group of New York and Ohio church members, he replied "that it was not expedient for him to relate these things."[64] He may have understood that the Ohio converts, from their largely institutional Protestant backgrounds, would not relate to some aspects of the story as it had been told and enthusiastically received by Joseph's followers in New York. By November 1832, he had written the narrative which is now part of the Pearl of Great Price.

What I believe from this is that the European beliefs about spirit guardians of wealth and wisdom influenced the early accounts of how the Book of Mormon came to be. The influence must have been from

rptd. in Thomas Carlyle, *German Romance: Translations from the German,* 2 vols. (London: Chapman and Hall, 1898), 1:4.

62. Joseph Smith Jr., interview by Hiel and Joseph Lewis (1828), in the *Amboy Journal,* 30 Apr. 1879, 1; ibid., 4 June 1879, 1; Joseph Smith Sr., interview by Fayette Lapham (1830), in *Historical Magazine* 7 (May 1870): 305; qtd. in Vogel, *Early Mormon Documents,* 1:456.

63. "Gold Bible, No. 6," *The Reflector,* 19 Mar. 1831, 126; qtd. in Vogel, *Early Mormon Documents,* 2:250.

64. Donald Q. Cannon and Lyndon W. Cook, eds., *Far West Record: Minutes of The Church of Jesus Christ of Latter-day Saints, 1830-1844* (Salt Lake City: Deseret Book Co., 1983), 19, 23.

several different directions at once. It must have been that when Joseph's family and acquaintances—some of whom knew Luman Walters, and especially those who had been involved in treasure-seeking ventures—heard that Joseph was translating an ancient record, they heard and interpreted this news with ears tuned to familiar themes. Some of the similarities probably came from their retellings as they unintentionally blended motifs that they heard from Walters and elsewhere. Nor was Joseph immune to a tendency toward the same, perhaps first visualizing himself in the role of an Anselmus, then interpreting his experiences in that light. In his recounting of these experiences, he appears to have borrowed many elements of the storyline, terms, and concepts that were familiar to his audience. Over time, the story was altered; one could say that it was gentrified and Christianized much as Joseph himself was.

6.

Witnesses to the Golden Plates

The 1820s view of how the Book of Mormon was dictated is different than what we currently assume, as we have already seen. A corollary to this is that the perspective of the eleven men who testified to viewing and handling the gold plates differs from what we now assume. Their published statements tell only part of the story, and even then, we tend to read into their testimonies a rationalist perspective rather than a nineteenth-century magical mindset.[1] We are told that the witnesses never disavowed their testimonies, but we have not come to know these men or investigated what else they said about their experiences. They are eleven individuals—Martin Harris, Oliver Cowdery, Hiram Page, David Whitmer, John Whitmer, Christian Whitmer, Jacob Whitmer, Peter Whitmer Jr., Hyrum Smith, Samuel Smith, and Joseph Smith Sr.—whose lives and personalities varied. They shared a common world view, and this is what drew them together in 1829.

More specifically, they believed in what has been called second sight. Traditionally, this included the ability to see spirits and their

---

1. Richard L. Anderson, *Investigating the Book of Mormon Witnesses* (Salt Lake City: Deseret Book Co., 1981), is in my opinion the best example of the tendency.

dwelling places within the local hills and elsewhere. Josiah Stowell of Bainbridge, New York, hired Joseph Smith to hunt for buried treasure because Joseph "could discern things invisible to the natural eye."[2] Ezra Booth, an early Mormon convert, reported of Joseph: "He does not pretend that he sees them [spirits and angels] with his natural, but with his spiritual eyes; and he says he can see them as well with his eyes shut, as with them open."[3] Joseph reported that the antediluvian prophet Enoch beheld "things which were not visible to the natural eye" and explained that he, like Enoch, could "see" with the spiritual "mind" (Moses 6:36; D&C 67:10). Joseph Smith and Oliver Cowdery would later perceive Jesus, Moses, Elias, and Elijah in a worship service in Ohio while the congregants discerned "convoy after convoy of angels," all with "the eyes of our understanding."[4] The eleven witnesses to the Book of Mormon claimed second-sight abilities, as well. This chapter seeks to understand the mindset, the shared magical perspective of these men as a key to understanding their affirmations of seeing and handling the golden plates.

Martin Harris (fig. 33) moved to the Palmyra area with his parents in 1794 when he was ten years old. He married his cousin Lucy in 1808 and established a farm on his father's estate. Before becoming a Mormon, he had been a Quaker, Universalist, Restorationist, Baptist, Presbyterian, and perhaps Methodist.[5] He shared with neighbors discoveries he said he had made through his gift of seeing. BYU professor Ronald W. Walker has written:

---

2. Lucy Mack Smith, *History of Joseph Smith by His Mother, Lucy Mack Smith* (Salt Lake City: Bookcraft, 1958), 92, 104.

3. Ezra Booth to Presiding Elder, 8 Nov. 1831, in E. D. Howe, *Mormonism Unvailed* (Painesville, OH: by the Author, 1834), 186.

4. D&C 110:1 (see also 76:12, 19; the depiction of Jesus in 110:2-4 follows precisely John's description in Revelation 1:14-18). Sylvester Smith, qtd. by Jedediah M. Grant, 28 June 1854, *Journal of Discourses,* 26 vols. (London and Liverpool: Latter-day Saints Book Depot, 1854-86), 6:254.

5. Ronald W. Walker, "Martin Harris: Mormonism's Early Convert," *Dialogue: A Journal of Mormon Thought* 19 (Winter 1986): 30-33.

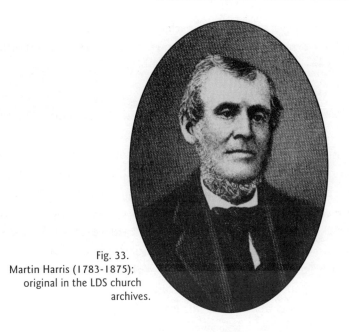

Fig. 33.
Martin Harris (1783-1875);
original in the LDS church
archives.

The Reverend Jesse Townsend, who had been installed at Palmyra's Western Presbyterian Church in 1817, found Harris ... a "visionary fanatic" ... Many accounts suggest that Harris was a visionary. "Marvelousness" was his "predominating phrenological development," remembered Pomeroy Tucker, who seemed to like and respect the man. He was given to a "belief in dreams, ghosts, hobgoblins" ... John Gilbert, the Palmyra printer, likewise found him to be "superstitious," someone who "pretended to see things" ... Lorenzo Saunders, who claimed to know the Harris family well, was more colloquial. "There can't anybody say a word against Martin Harris," he asserted. "Martin was a good citizen ... a man that would do just as he agreed with you. But, he was a great man for seeing spooks."

Walker continued the examples of Harris's world view:

His imagination was excitable and fecund. Once while reading scripture, he reportedly mistook a candle's sputtering as a sign that the devil desired to stop him. Another time he excitedly awoke from his sleep believing that a creature as large as a dog had been upon his chest, though a nearby associate could find nothing to confirm his

fears. Several hostile and perhaps unreliable accounts told of visionary experiences with Satan and Christ, Harris once reporting that
Christ had been poised on a roof beam.[6]

After meeting Joseph Smith, Harris participated in his own treasure adventures and said that he could "see things" in the Hill
Cumorah. On one occasion he described how he, Porter Rockwell,
and another man were digging for Cumorah's treasures in 1827. He
reported: "We found a stone box ... [and] we were ready to take it up:
but behold by some unseen power it slipped back into the hill." As it
was sinking, according to Harris, one of them "took his pick and
struck into the lid of it ... The blow took off a piece of the lid, which a
certain lady kept in her possession until she died."[7] On another occasion Brigham Young mentioned that this souvenir, a rock chip, was
actually kept in the "possession of mother Smith" until her death.[8] It
is interesting that Harris informed Joseph Smith about the gold
plates: "The Lord has showed to me ten times more about it than you
know."[9] This was before the collective experience with the other witnesses. He also said, "I saw them [the gold plates] just as distinctly as I
see any thing around me, though at the time they were covered over
with a cloth."[10] Did Harris encounter a treasure chest and watch it

6. Ibid., 34-35.
7. Ole A. Jensen, "Testimony Given to Ole A. Jensen by Martin Harris," July 1875, 3, archives, Historical Department, Church of Jesus Christ of
Latter-day Saints, Salt Lake City (hereafter LDS archives); qtd. in Dan Vogel,
ed., *Early Mormon Documents*, 3+ vols. (Salt Lake City: Signature Books,
1996-), 2:376; Brigham Young, 17 June 1877, *Journal of Discourses* 19:37.
Brigham Young clearly believed the incident.
8. Brigham Young, Office Journal, 21 Nov. 1861, LDS archives.
9. Martin Harris, interview by Joel Tiffany, Jan. 1859, in "Mormonism," *Tiffany's Monthly* (New York City) 5 (Aug. 1859): 166; qtd. in Vogel,
Early Mormon Documents, 2:306.
10. Martin Harris, interview by John A. Clark, 1828, in "Modern Superstition—The Mormonites," *The Visitor, or Monthly Instructor, for 1841*
(London: Religious Tract Society, 1841), 239; qtd. in Vogel, *Early Mormon
Documents*, 2:270.

sink into the hill? Did he see the gold plates through a cloth—by means of a spiritual gift or mental visualization?

Oliver Cowdery, Hiram Page, and the five Whitmers were related by marriage. They all believed in second sight. The Whitmers were especially close-knit and all believed that seers could discern things with seeing stones and dowsing sticks. Oliver Cowdery came from a similar background. He was a treasure hunter and "rodsman" before he met Joseph Smith in 1829. William Cowdery, his father, was associated with a treasure-seeking group in Vermont, and it is from them, one assumes, that Oliver learned the art of working with a divining rod.[11] Joseph told Oliver that he knew the "rod of nature" Oliver used "has told you many things"[12] (figs. 34-35). Oliver saw "the plates in vision" before the two men met.[13] This means that two of three special witnesses (Harris and Cowdery) had seen these plates in vision before Joseph prophesied that they would view them together.[14] David Whitmer, the third of this group, reported in early June 1829 before their group declaration that he, Cowdery, and Joseph Smith observed "one of the Nephites" carrying the records in a knapsack on his way to Cumorah. Several days later this trio perceived "that the Same Person was under the shed" at the Whitmer farm.[15]

Ezra Booth named Hiram Page as "one of the 'Money Diggers'"

---

11. Barnes Frisbie, *The History of Middletown, Vermont* (Rutland, VT: Tuttle and Co., 1867), 43-64; rptd. in Abby Maria Hemenway, ed., *Vermont Historical Gazetteer* (Claremont, NH: Claremont Manufacturing Co., 1877), 3:810-19; qtd. in Vogel, *Early Mormon Documents*, 1:599-621.

12. Book of Commandments 7:3 (1833), in Wilford C. Wood, ed., *Joseph Smith Begins His Work: The Book of Commandments,* 2 vols. (Salt Lake City: by the Author, 1962), vol. 2; cf. D&C 8:6-8.

13. Dean C. Jessee, ed., *The Papers of Joseph Smith: Autobiographical and Historical Writings* (Salt Lake City: Deseret Book Co., 1989), 1:10.

14. See D&C 5:11 (Mar. 1829); 17:1-5 (mid-late June 1829); Ether 5:2-4; 2 Ne. 27:12-13 (Apr.-June 1829).

15. David Whitmer, interview by Edward Stevenson, 22 Dec. 1877, Edward Stevenson Journal, 4806/2, LDS archives.

Fig. 34.
Oliver Cowdery (1806-50).
Photograph ca. 1848,
C. R. Savage.

who had searched for treasure.[16] We know that Page used a seer stone and said he received revelations.[17] Diedrich Willers, the German Reformed Church minister for Page and the Whitmer family since 1822, described Page as a good man who was nevertheless "full of superstition." Willers characterized the Whitmers as good citizens but "gullible to the highest degree and even believe in witches."[18] Their neighbors stated that they were "noted" for being prone "to the Marvelous, and a firm believer in witches."[19]

Along with Hiram Page, two or three of the Whitmers—Jacob,

---

16. Ezra Booth to Presiding Elder, 8 Dec. 1831, in Howe, *Mormonism Unvailed*, 215.

17. Jessee, *Papers of Joseph Smith*, 1:322-23.

18. Diedrich Willers to Reverends L. Mayer and D. Young, 18 June 1830, trans. and ed. by D. Michael Quinn in "The First Months of Mormonism," *New York History* 54 (July 1973): 333. For the Whitmers' reputation and religious involvement, see Anderson, *Investigating the Book of Mormon Witnesses*, 125.

19. Howe, *Mormonism Unvailed*, 16, 97. See also, "Letter from Palmyra, NY," 12 Mar. 1831, *Painesville [OH] Telegraph*, 22 Mar. 1831, [2].

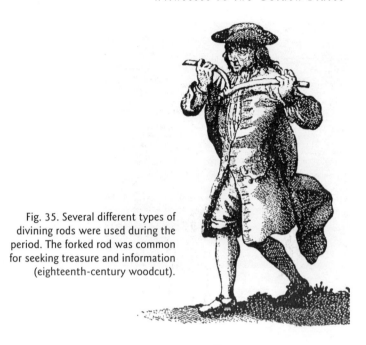

Fig. 35. Several different types of divining rods were used during the period. The forked rod was common for seeking treasure and information (eighteenth-century woodcut).

David, and perhaps John—owned seer stones[20] (figs. 36-38). This seeing gift continued among the Whitmer children and grandchildren. In September 1847 Page and the Whitmers joined the schismatic Church of Christ; David was sustained as their "Prophet, Seer, Revelator, and Translator" to receive revelations for them.[21] When David reorganized this movement in 1875, he ordained and authorized his grandson George Schweich and nephew John C. Whitmer (Jacob's son) to translate some records that were said to be hidden in caves. John L. Traughber knew of this later movement and wrote: "David Whitmer has a peep-stone ... [and] John C. Whitmer has a stone, the one which his son [John Whitmer Jr.] uses, and states that it belonged to his

---

20. D. Michael Quinn, *Early Mormonism and the Magic World View,* rev. and enl. (Salt Lake City: Signature Books, 1998), 239-40, 247-48.

21. William E. McLellin, "The Successor of Joseph, the Seer," *The Ensign of Liberty of the Church of Christ,* ed. William E. McLellin (Kirtland, OH) 1 (Mar. 1848): 78, and McLellin, "Our Tour West in 1847," 1 (Aug. 1849): 104, copy in LDS archives.

Fig. 36. Jacob Whitmer (1800-56), from a painting owned by Mayme Koontz, a granddaughter.

Fig. 37. This seer stone belonged to one of the Whitmers, probably Jacob or John. Hiram Page's stone was reportedly destroyed at Joseph Smith's orders. Courtesy Rick Grunder Books.

Fig. 38.
John Whitmer (1802-78),
about age sixty; original in
Community of Christ (RLDS)
Library-Archives.

father, Jacob Whitmer"[22] (figs. 39-40). David also reported that his grandson George Schweich was a "seer" who, "through his peepstone, sees caves in which are vast stores of records; cave in succession to cave, all filled with treasures of golden plates and sacred records. He sees in the north pole a gigantic race of people; in the south a liliputian race."[23]

The remaining witnesses to the Book of Mormon were members of the Smith family. They also held a magical view of the world. Residents of the Palmyra area reported on the family's enthusiasm for treasure hunting between 1820 and 1827.[24] Martin Harris remembered:

---

22. John L. Traughber, "David Whitmer, 'The Last Witness' of the Book of Mormon," J. L. Traughber Collection, 1446/2:39, Manuscripts Division, Marriott Library, University of Utah, Salt Lake City, Utah. Traughber said Whitmer obtained his stone in Kirtland, Ohio; see also Lucy Smith, *History of Joseph Smith*, 241-42.

23. Joseph Fielding Smith, *Life of Joseph F. Smith* (Salt Lake City: Deseret News Press, 1938), 239. Jacob Whitmer's grandson, John Whitmer Jr., may have been the one with the reported seeric gift quoted here (J. L. Traughber Collection, 1446/2:39).

24. Pomeroy Tucker, *Origin, Rise, and Progress of Mormonism* (New

Fig. 39.
David Whitmer (1805-88)
in old age; original in Community of
Christ (RLDS) Library-Archives.

There was a company there in that neighborhood, who were digging for money supposed to have been hidden by the ancients. Of this company were old Mr. Stowel[l]—I think his name was Josiah—also old Mr. Beman, also Samuel Lawrence, George Proper, Joseph Smith, Jr., and his father, and his brother Hiram Smith. They dug for money in Palmyra, Manchester, also in Pennsylvania, and other places.[25]

These nocturnal excursions took the treasure hunters to a nearby drumlin, later called Cumorah. Orsamus Turner, who had known the Smiths since their arrival, noted that "[l]egends of hidden treasure had long designated Mormon Hill as the depository." He continued:

Old Joseph had dug there, and young Joseph had not only heard his

---

York: D. Appleton & Co., 1867), 21-26; qtd. in Vogel, *Early Mormon Documents*, 3:96-99; Affidavit of Willard Chase, 11 Dec. 1833, in Howe, *Mormonism Unvailed*, 240; qtd. in Vogel, *Early Mormon Documents*, 2:65.

25. Martin Harris, in *Tiffany's Monthly* 5 (Aug. 1859): 164-65; qtd. in Vogel, *Early Mormon Documents*, 2:303-4.

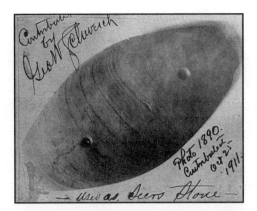

Fig. 40. Two views of David Whitmer's seer stone. They were used in his church during the 1870s and 1880s by his grandson George Schweich.

father and mother relate the marvelous tales of buried wealth, but had accompanied his father in the midnight delvings, and incantations of the spirits that guarded it. ... Long before the Gold Bible demonstration, the Smith family had ... pretended that in digging for money, at Mormon Hill, they came across "a chest, three by two feet in size, covered with a dark colored stone, ... [the large stone] then exploded with a terrible noise. The chest vanished and all was utter darkness."[26]

---

26. O[rsamus]. Turner, *History of the Pioneer Settlement of Phelps and Gorham's Purchase* (Rochester, NY: William Alling, 1851), 214-16; qtd. in Vogel, *Early Mormon Documents*, 3:50-53. Pomeroy Tucker also stated that the Smiths were digging at Cumorah before the gold plates were found. See Tucker, *Origin, Rise, and Progress*, 34; qtd. in Vogel, *Early Mormon Documents*, 3:104.

Figs. 41-43. Joseph Smith Jr. (left), Hyrum Smith (center, 1800-44), and Joseph Smith Sr. (right, 1771-1840), all searched for hidden treasure from 1820 to 1827.

The Smiths (figs. 41-43) shared freely with neighbors and relatives about their ability to see subterranean chambers in the local hills. They told of seeing the guardian spirits, or angels, and their caves that contained books, tables, swords, and treasures. Brigham Young heard from the Smiths and believed all his life that "these treasures that are in the earth are carefully watched; they can be removed from place to place" by the angels.[27] The Smiths told their neighbor Joseph Capron, who lived just south of the Smith home, that Joseph "discovered ghosts, infernal spirits, mountains of gold and silver, and many other invaluable treasures deposited in the earth. He would often tell his neighbors of his wonderful discoveries." Another neighbor, William Stafford, recounted the Smiths' profession of what they had seen in one hill:

> keys, barrels and hogsheads of coined silver and gold—bars of gold, golden images, brass kettles filled with gold and silver—gold candlesticks, swords, &c, &c. They would say, also, that nearly all the hills in this part of New York, were thrown up by human hands, and in them were large caves, which Joseph, Jr., could see ... [and that]

---

27. Brigham Young, 17 June 1877, *Journal of Discourses* 19:36-37.

within the above mentioned caves [were] large gold bars and silver plates; that he could also discover the spirits in whose charge these treasures were, clothed in ancient dress.

Joshua Stafford said that the family "told marvelous stories about ghosts, hob-goblins, caverns and various other mysterious matters."[28] Joseph's uncle Jesse Smith wrote of his nephew: "[H]e says he has eyes to see things that are not, and then has the audacity to say they are; and [that] the angel of the Lord ... has put [him] in possession of great wealth, gold & silver and precious stones."[29] Joseph informed Bainbridge, New York, resident Jonathan Thompson, when they were hunting treasure, that he "discovered distinctly the two Indians who had buried the trunk ... and that one of said Indians was ... guard[ing] it, as he supposed."[30] Sylvia Walker, who lived in sight of the Smith home and attended school with the Smith children, stated that Joseph had described to her a nearby "cave that contained gold furniture, chairs and table."[31]

Lorenzo Saunders said that while digging in a hill, Joseph asserted he could "see a man sitting in a gold chair. Old Joe said he was [a] king."[32] Roswell Nichols, another neighbor, mentioned that Joseph

28. Affidavit of William Stafford, 8 Dec. 1833, and statements of Joseph Capron, 8 Nov. 1833, and Joshua Stafford, 15 Nov. 1833, in Howe, *Mormonism Unvailed*, 237-38, 258-59; qtd. in Vogel, *Early Mormon Documents*, 2:24, 27, 60. Joshua Stafford is thought to be William's nephew.

29. Jesse Smith to Hyrum Smith, 17 June 1829, Joseph Smith Letterbook, 2:59-61, LDS archives; qtd. in Vogel, *Early Mormon Documents*, 1:552.

30. Jonathan Thompson's statement was made under oath for the defendant at Joseph Smith's 20 March 1826 pre-trial examination, *The State of New York v. Joseph Smith*, recorded in the Docket Book of Albert Neely, first printed in *Fraser's Magazine* (London) 7 (Feb. 1873): 229-30.

31. Statement of Sylvia Walker in Arthur B. Deming, ed., *Naked Truths About Mormonism* 1 (Oakland, CA, Apr. 1888): 1; publication available at the Beinecke Library, Yale University; qtd. in Vogel, *Early Mormon Documents*, 2:192.

32. Statement of Lorenzo Saunders, 17 Sept. 1884, in E. L. Kelley Papers, P16:7, Library-Archives, Community of Christ (hereafter RLDS Library-Archives); qtd. in Vogel, *Early Mormon Documents*, 2:130.

Sr. "pointed to a small hill on my farm, and said, 'in that hill there is a stone which is full of gold and silver. I know it to be so, for I have been to the hole, and God said unto me, go not in now, but at a future day you shall go in [the hill] and find the book open, and then you shall have the treasures.'"

Joseph Sr. indicated to Peter Ingersoll a nearby place that held "one chest of gold and another of silver ... '[I]f you knew what I had seen, you would believe.'"[33] W. R. Hine of Windsor heard from Joseph Jr. that:

> he [Joseph] saw Captain Kidd [the pirate] sailing on the Susquehanna River during a freshet, and that he buried two pots of gold and silver. He claimed he saw writing cut on the rocks in an unknown language telling where Kidd buried it, and he translated it through his peepstone ... [and] dug for Kidd's money, on the west bank of the Susquehanna, half a mile from the river ... Jo became known all over New York and Pennsylvania. Sometimes his brothers were with him ... Jo and his father were all the time telling of hidden things, lead, silver, and gold mines which he could see.[34]

Emily Coburn became acquainted with Joseph Jr. at the Joseph Knight Sr. farm in Colesville, New York, where the two men were digging for money. She often went to visit her sister Sally who married Newell Knight. She wrote of Joseph:

> He also told his friends that he could see money in pots, under the ground ... and [he would] dig for the treasures, which were hidden in the earth; a great share of which, he said, was on Joseph Knights farm ... While I was visiting my sister, we have walked out to see the places where they [Smith, Knight, and company] dug for money, and

---

33. Affidavit of Peter Ingersoll, 2 Dec. 1833, and statement of Roswell Nichols, 1 Dec. 1833, in Howe, *Mormonism Unvailed*, 233, 257; qtd. in Vogel, *Early Mormon Documents*, 2:38, 41.

34. Statement of W. R. Hine in Deming, *Naked Truths* 1 (Jan. 1888): 2.

laughed to think of the absurdity of any people having common intellect to indulge in such a thought or action.[35]

This is a sampling of many New York and Pennsylvania stories that could be cited. They are too numerous, too similar in content, and too diverse in origin to be dismissed as non-Mormon contrivances. The fact that the Smiths organized and participated in treasure digging expeditions indicates their belief in the physical reality of what they saw by second sight. Significantly, none of the Smiths' seeric ventures yielded any real, physical treasure. This is why, when the family began telling of gold plates in mid-1827, people were skeptical about "their pretended revelations."[36] The unsuccessful treasure episodes had created credibility problems, especially among those who were more rational in orientation. It was especially difficult for neighbors because Joseph's religious experiences bore the trappings of his previous endeavors.[37]

For instance, Henry Harris said Joseph told him "he looked in his stone" to find the gold plates in their "place of deposit."[38] Martin Harris confirmed that "[i]t was by means of this stone he first discovered these plates."[39] Joseph said a "vision was opened to my mind

---

35. Emily M. Coburn, *Mormonism: Or Life among the Mormons* (Madison, WI: M. J. Cantwell, 1882), 32-33.

36. Statement of fifty-one Palmyra area citizens, 4 Dec. 1833, in Howe, *Mormonism Unvailed*, 261-62; qtd. in Vogel, *Early Mormon Documents*, 2:48-49.

37. Affidavit of Isaac Hale, 20 Mar. 1834, in *Susquehanna Register and Northern Pennsylvanian*, 1 May 1834, 1. Hale insisted that "[t]he manner in which he [Joseph] pretended to read and interpret [the gold plates] was the same as when he looked for the money-diggers, with the stone in his hat, and his hat over his face, while the Book of Plates were at the same time hid in the woods." See also Turner, *History of the Pioneer Settlement*, 216; Martin Harris in *Tiffany's Monthly* 5 (Aug. 1859): 169; qtd. in Vogel, *Early Mormon Documents*, 2:309; affidavit of Willard Chase in Howe, *Mormonism Unvailed*, 240-41, 247; qtd. in Vogel, *Early Mormon Documents*, 2:65-66, 73.

38. Affidavit of Henry Harris in Howe, *Mormonism Unvailed*, 252; qtd. in Vogel, *Early Mormon Documents*, 2:76.

39. Martin Harris in *Tiffany's Monthly*, 163; qtd. in Vogel, *Early Mormon Documents*, 2:302.

Fig. 44. Sketch of Lucy Mack Smith (1776-1856), from *Piercy's Route from Liverpool to Great Salt Lake Valley.*

that I could see where the plates were deposited" (JS—History 1:42). His mother (fig. 44) recalled of her son in 1842: "The angel of the Lord appeared to him fifteen years since, and shewed him the cave where the original golden plates of the book of Mormon were deposited. He shewed him also the Urim and Thummim ... [and the] golden breastplate."[40] Abigail Harris, an in-law of Martin Harris, heard from Lucy Smith that there were so many records hidden in Cumorah, "it would take four stout men to load them into a cart, [and] that Joseph had also discovered by looking through his stone, the vessel in which the gold was melted from which the plates were made, and also the machine with which they were rolled; he also discovered in the bottom of the vessel three balls of gold, each as large as his fist."[41] Joseph told convert and apostle Orson Pratt that within Cumorah "numer-

---

40. Lucy Smith, interview by Henry Caswall, 18 Apr. 1842, in "The Mormons," *The Visitor, or Monthly Instructor, for 1842,* 407, LDS archives; qtd. in Vogel, *Early Mormon Documents,* 1:220-21.

41. Statement of Abigail Harris, 28 Nov. 1832, in Howe, *Mormonism Unvailed,* 253; qtd. in Vogel, *Early Mormon Documents,* 2:32.

ous records of the ancient nations of the western continent was located ... [and] under the charge of holy angels."[42] What should a fair-minded researcher make of this? Did the witnesses perceive secular and spiritual personages and their treasures within the local hills by a spiritual gift or by their creative imaginations?[43]

The ability to see into hidden crevices within the local hills was not limited to Joseph Jr. and his father. Heber C. Kimball spoke of "the vision that Joseph and others had [Joseph Sr. and Oliver Cowdery are identified] when they went into a cave in the Hill Cumorah, and saw more records than ten men could carry ... books piled upon tables, book upon book."[44] Young named more witnesses in connection with these visits to Cumorah's cave. Although parts of his statement have already been quoted, the complete excerpt is useful:

> Oliver [Cowdery] says that when Joseph and Oliver went there, the hill opened, and they walked into a cave, in which there was a large and spacious room. He says he did not think, at the time, whether they had the light of the sun or artificial light; but that it was just as light as day. They laid the plates on a table; it was a large table that stood in the room. Under this table there was a pile of plates as much as two feet high, and there were altogether in this room more plates than probably many wagon loads; they were piled up in the corners and along the walls. The first time they went there the sword of Laban hung upon the wall; but when they went again it had been taken down and laid upon the table across the gold plates ... I tell you this as coming not only from Oliver Cowdery, but others who were familiar with it ... Carlos Smith ... was a witness to these things. Sam-

---

42. Orson Pratt, "The Hill Cumorah," *Latter-day Saints' Millennial Star,* 7 July 1866, 417.

43. Joseph Smith apparently believed that what he discerned in his mind was real, especially if one believes the reports of four people who said he told them he could not literally see images in his stone (See chapter 1, nn. 23-26).

44. Heber C. Kimball, 28 Sept. 1856, *Journal of Discourses* 4:105; "Brigham Young Manuscript History," 5 May 1867, LDS archives.

uel Smith saw some things, Hyrum saw a good many things, but Joseph was the leader.[45]

In fact, Hyrum Smith related more about this to William W. Phelps, identifying still others who made the excursion to the hill's interior. Phelps recounted: "Joseph, Hyrum, Cowdery & Whitmere[s?] went to the hill Cormoroh. As they were walking up the hill, a door opened and they walked into a room about 16 ft square. In that room was an angel and a trunk. On the trunk lay a book of Mormon & gold plates, Laban's sword, Aaron's brestplate."[46] In another statement Young mentioned that they viewed "a Messenger" who was the "keeper of the room" and that they conversed with him.[47]

In Young's accounts, he specifies at least three visits to the hill's chambers. It is interesting that Lucy refers to three occasions when witnesses saw the gold plates, each time within a "grove."[48] Describing the circumstances in each instance, she said the first event involved the

---

45. Brigham Young, 17 June 1877, *Journal of Discourses* 19:38. Young refers to this same incident when they "went into a cave in the Hill Cumorah" and returned the plates, in *Wilford Woodruff's Journal, 1833-98*, typescript, ed. Scott G. Kenny, 9 vols. (Midvale, UT: Signature Books, 1984], 11 Dec. 1869, 6:508-9. As early as 1849, Young discussed "finding the Plates ... & returning them again to Cumorah, who did it &c," Quorum of the Twelve Minutes, 6 May 1849, LDS archives, qtd. in *New Mormon Studies CD-ROM: A Comprehensive Resource Library* (Salt Lake City: Smith Research Associates, 1998). He recounted statements by Cowdery and others and may have misremembered that they were real events rather than visionary. These may have proceeded like the vision received in 1832 when Joseph would say, "I see" such and such, followed by Sidney Rigdon declaring, "I see the same." All was perceived by "the eyes of our understandings" according to Philo Dibble, "Recollections of the Prophet Joseph Smith," *Juvenile Instructor*, 15 May 1892, 303-4; D&C 76:19.

46. Hyrum Smith, qtd. by William W. Phelps in William H. Dame, "Journal of Southern Exploring Company, 1854-1858," 14 Jan. 1855, Della Dame Edmunds collection, Ms 515, Manuscripts Division, Marriott Library.

47. As qtd. in *Wilford Woodruff's Journal*, 11 Dec. 1869, 6:508-9.

48. Brigham Young, qtd. by Elizabeth Kane in *A Gentile Account of Life in Utah's Dixie, 1872-73: Elizabeth Kane's St. George Journal*, ed. Norman R. Bowen (Salt Lake City: Tanner Trust Fund, University of Utah Library, 1995), 76; qtd. in Vogel, *Early Mormon Documents*, 3:408; Lucy Smith, Pre-

three witnesses and took place in a grove near the Whitmer cabin in Fayette. Immediately afterward, Lucy and Joseph Sr. returned to their Manchester home. "In a few days," she wrote, "we were follow[ed] by Joseph, Oliver and the whitmers[,] ... [S]oon after they came[, T]hey all[,] that is the male part of the company[,] repaired to a little grove" near the Smiths' farm. This is where the experience of the eight witnesses transpired. Of the third event, Lucy stated that directly after the eight returned to the Smith house, Joseph returned the plates to the angel. Cowdery told Young that he was with Joseph at the time and that they "laid the plates on a table" inside Cumorah's interior. Later that evening "all the witnesses" conversed about their experiences, including fourteen-year-old Carlos Smith who testified to the divinity of the work.[49] Carlos later informed Young that he "was a witness" to some of these events within Cumorah, although no specific information is available about his experiences.[50]

If the reports are correct, then there were more than eleven witnesses to the Book of Mormon. The Smith brothers Hyrum, Carlos, and Samuel, Joseph Sr., Oliver Cowdery, at least one of the Whitmers, and unnamed "others" participated in the remote viewings of Cumorah's cave. If Lucy Smith is correct, at least one of these experiences—returning the plates to the angel—occurred nearly at the same time as the eight witnesses' experience. Perhaps the three and eight also saw the contents of the cave. In these metaphysical excursions within Cumorah, the participants saw a bright light, a table, the sword of Laban, many other plates and treasures, and an angel.

David Whitmer's and Martin Harris's descriptions of the three witnesses' experience at Fayette are strikingly similar. Whitmer stated in 1878 at his Richmond, Missouri, home: "It was just as though Jo-

---

liminary Manuscript (MS), 1844-45, LDS archives; qtd. in Vogel, *Early Mormon Documents*, 1:392-96.

49. Lucy Smith, *History of Joseph Smith*, 155; Joseph also reported returning the plates to the angel, although he provides no details (see JS—History" 1:60).

50. Brigham Young, 17 June 1877, *Journal of Discourses* 19:38.

seph, Oliver and I were sitting just here on a log. ... When we see things in the spirit and by the power of God they seem to be right here." Continuing, Whitmer said that they saw a bright light, a table, the sword of Laban, many plates and treasures and an angel: "We not only saw the plates of the Book of Mormon but also the brass plates ... and many other plates ... [W]e were overshadowed by a light ... [I]n the midst of this light ... there appeared as it were, a table with many records or plates upon it, besides the plates of the Book of Mormon, also the Sword of Laban, the Directors ... [and the angel which] stood before us."[51]

Harris said that Hyrum, Joseph Jr., Joseph Sr., and others viewed marvelous things while they were digging for treasure and that these things "were real to them." On one occasion a log school house suddenly lit up. On another adventure a spirit nine feet tall communicated with them. On still another occasion a spectral group of charging horsemen appeared.[52] Alan Taylor, director of the Institute of Early American History and Culture, has observed that treasure-seeking groups of that era often encountered spectral apparitions and sinking treasure chests. With expectations high, a suggestion from one participant would trigger a group vision, according to his research. Taylor found that years later some of these groups, still believing their experiences were real, would not deny them and never had.[53]

Far removed from our own modern empiricism, the world view of the witnesses is difficult for us to grasp. The gold plates they saw

---

51. Preston Nibley, *The Witnesses of the Book of Mormon* (Salt Lake City: Deseret Book Co., 1968), 68-69, 71; for Harris, see p. 135.

52. Martin Harris, *Tiffany's Monthly* 5 (Aug. 1859): 165; qtd. in Vogel, *Early Mormon Documents*, 2:305.

53. Alan Taylor, "The Early Republic's Supernatural Economy: Treasure Seeking in the American Northeast, 1780-1830," *American Quarterly* 38 (Spring 1986): 13-14. For a detailed description of a company of seven men who never denied that they viewed a guardian and his "glittering" metal treasure, see Daniel P. [Judge] Thompson, *May Martin: Or the Money Diggers. A Green Mountain Tale* (London: J. Clements Lytle, 1841), 19-22.

and handled disappeared when placed on Cumorah's ground.[54] The witnesses believed that a toad hiding in the stone box became an apparition that struck Joseph on the head.[55] Harris and Rockwell saw a treasure chest sink into Cumorah's interior.[56] Cowdery helped lay the gold plates on a table inside the hill. These examples and others underscore the witnesses' mindset. Thus it may not be as significant as we have assumed that three signatories to the Book of Mormon saw and heard an angel.

In discussing the witnesses, we should not overlook the primary accounts of the events they testified to. The official statements published in the Book of Mormon are not dated, nor is a specific location given for where the events occurred. There are not eleven affidavits but rather one statement signed by three men and one signed by eight. The three witnesses' testimony was written in June 1829, as was Doctrine and Covenants 17. The Doctrine and Covenants reveals what was expected of these men, while the formal testimony recounts what they saw. I believe they show the marks of common authorship:

54. Dean C. Jessee, ed., "Joseph Knight's Recollection of Early Mormon History," *BYU Studies* 17 (Autumn 1976): 30-31; Lucy Smith, *History of Joseph Smith*, 83-88; Affidavit of Willard Chase, in Howe, *Mormonism Unvailed*, 242; qtd. in Vogel, *Early Mormon Documents*, 2:67.

55. Benjamin Saunders, interview by William H. Kelley (an RLDS apostle), 1884, in William H. Kelley Collection, "Miscellany 1795-1948," P19/2:44, RLDS Library-Archives; qtd. in Vogel, *Early Mormon Documents*, 2:137; Affidavit of Willard Chase, 11 Dec. 1833, in Howe, *Mormonism Unvailed*, 242; qtd. in Vogel, *Early Mormon Documents*, 2:67; Joseph Smith Jr., interview by Joseph and Hiel Lewis, 1828, "Mormon History, A New Chapter about to be Published," *Amboy [IL] Journal*, 30 Apr. 1879, 1; Joseph Smith Sr., interview by Fayette Lapham, ca. 1830, in "The Mormons," *Historical Magazine* 7 (May 1870): 305-6; qtd. in Vogel, *Early Mormon Documents*, 1:458-59.

56. For another example of a chest "rumbling" away, see Martin Harris, qtd. in "Modern Superstition—The Mormonites," 63; qtd. in Vogel, *Early Mormon Documents*, 2:265; Orlando Saunders, qtd. in Frederic G. Mather, "The Early Days of Mormonism," *Lippincott's Magazine of Popular Literature and Science* (Philadelphia) 26 (Aug. 1880): 200.

Doctrine and Covenants 17

And it is by your faith that you shall obtain a view of them [the plates] (v. 2) ... And after that you have ... seen them with your eyes, you shall testify of them, by the power of God (v. 3) ... And ye shall testify that you have seen them, even as my servant Joseph Smith, Jun., has seen them (v. 5) ... [And] you shall be lifted up at the last day (v. 8).

THE TESTIMONY OF THREE WITNESSES

Be it known unto all nations, kindreds, tongues, and people, unto whom this work shall come, that we, through the grace of God the Father, and our Lord Jesus Christ, have seen the plates [see v. 2] which contain this record, which is a record of the people of Nephi, and also of the Lamanites, his brethren, and also of the people of Jared, which came from the tower of which hath been spoken; and we also know that they have been translated by the gift and power of God, for his voice has declared it unto us; wherefore we know of a surety, that the work is true. And we also testify that we have seen the engravings which are upon the plates; and they have been shewn unto us by the power of God [see v. 3] , and not of man. And we declare with words of soberness, that an Angel of God came down from heaven, and he brought and laid before our eyes, that we beheld and saw the plates, and the engravings thereon [see v. 5]; and we know that it is by the grace of God the Father, and our Lord Jesus Christ, that we beheld and bear record that these things are true; and it is marvellous in our eyes: Nevertheless, the voice of the Lord commanded us that we should bear record of it; wherefore, to be obedient unto the commandments of God, we bear testimony of these things.—And we know that if we are faithful in Christ, we shall rid our garments of the blood of all men, and be found spotless before the judgement seat of Christ, and shall dwell with him eternally in the heavens [see v. 8]. And the honor be to the Father, and to the Son, and to the Holy Ghost, which is one God. Amen.

OLIVER COWDERY,
DAVID WHITMER,
MARTIN HARRIS.

This document gives the impression that there was an actual visitation of an angel who displayed physical plates. Church members today generally interpret the statement in this way. But the individual affirmations by Joseph Smith and the witnesses themselves indicate that their experience occurred as a vision.[57]

James H. Moyle, a young LDS attorney, interviewed David Whitmer for two and one-half hours in 1885 and wrote that Whitmer "was somewhat spiritual in his explanations. He was not as materialistic in his descriptions as I wished."[58] Zenas H. Gurley, an RLDS apostle, also interviewed Whitmer and asked, "Do you know the plates seen with the angel on the table were real metal, [and] did you touch them? [Whitmer:] We did not touch nor handle the plates. [Gurley:] Was the table literal wood? or was the whole a vision such as often occurs in dreams &c? [Whitmer:] The table had the appearance of literal wood as shown in the vision, in the glory of God ... I [also] saw the 'interpreters' in the holy vision."[59]

In another account, Whitmer remembered:

In June 1829, I saw the angel by the power of God ... The angel appeared in the light ... Between us and the angel there appeared a table, and there lay upon it the sword of Laban, the Ball of Directors, the Record, and interpreters. The angel took the Record, and turned the leaves, and showed it to us by the power of God. They were taken away by the angel to a cave, which we saw by the power of God while we were yet in the Spirit.[60]

57. Jessee, *Papers of Joseph Smith,* 1:296.

58. James Henry Moyle, Journal, 28 June 1885, James Henry Moyle Papers, F508:1, LDS archives; also Nibley, *Witnesses of the Book of Mormon,* 92-95.

59. David Whitmer, interview by Zenas H. Gurley Jr., 14 Jan. 1885, typescript, D4681, LDS archives. Gurley published portions of this interview in *Autumn Leaves* (Lamoni, IA) 5 (1892): 453, RLDS Library-Archives.

60. David Whitmer, interview by Edmund C. Briggs, in "Letter from Edmund C. Briggs to Joseph Smith III," 4 June 1884, *Saints' Herald,* 21 June 1884, 396; David Whitmer, interview by Edward Stevenson, Journal, 22 Dec. 1877, 4806:2, LDS archives.

In his own pamphlet, *An Address to All Believers in Christ,* and elsewhere, Whitmer referred to this experience as a "vision."[61]

Harris testified to Anthony Metcalf of Elk Horn, Idaho, that "I never saw the golden plates, only in a visionary or entranced state ... While praying I passed into a state of entrancement, and in that state I saw the angel and the plates."[62] Another person asked Harris, "Did you see the plates and the engraving on them with your bodily eyes? ... [Harris:] I did not see them as I do that pencil case, yet I saw them with the eye of faith."[63] John H. Gilbert, Jesse Townsend, and Reuben T. Harmon all independently recalled that Harris said he saw the records with his "spiritual eyes" only. Harmon announced: "I am well acquainted with Martin Harris, who was often at my house ... He never claimed to have seen them [the plates] with his natural eyes, only [in a] spiritual vision."[64]

According to the authorized testimony, the witnesses saw the plates but did not handle them. The angel turned the leaves for them to see the engravings. However, according to some of the witnesses' individual affirmations, they handled the plates. Lucy Smith was at the Peter Whitmer home when Harris arrived immediately after the witnesses' experience. He reported to her: "I have now seen an angel from Heaven ... I have also looked upon the plates and handled them with my hands and can testify of the same to the whole world."[65] To a

---

61. David Whitmer, *An Address to All Believers in Christ* (Richmond, MO: by the Author, 1887), 32; Francis Kirkham, *A New Witness for Christ in America* (Salt Lake City: Utah Printing Co., 1959), 2:349-50.

62. Martin Harris, interview by Anthony Metcalf, ca. 1873, in *Ten Years before the Mast* (Malad, ID: Author, 1888), 70; qtd. in Vogel, *Early Mormon Documents,* 2:346-47.

63. Martin Harris, qtd. in *The Visitor, or Monthly Instructor, for 1841,* 239; qtd. in Vogel, *Early Mormon Documents,* 2:270.

64. Marvin S. Hill, "Secular or Sectarian History? A Critique of 'No Man Knows My History,'" *Church History* 43 (Mar. 1974): 92-93; qtd. in Vogel, *Early Mormon Documents,* 2:385, 526.

65. Lucy Smith, Preliminary Manuscript, in Vogel, *Early Mormon Documents,* 1:395.

group in Painesville, Ohio, in 1831, Harris declared that he knew "all about the gold plates, Angels, Spirits, and Jo Smith.—He had seen and handled them all, *by the power of God!*"[66] Edward Stevenson, a member of the First Quorum of the Seventy, reported after interviewing Harris in August 1870: "He says he saw the plates, handled them and saw the angel that visited Joseph Smith, more than 40 years ago."[67] Harris testified in the Salt Lake Tabernacle in September 1870, "I would rather have my right hand cut off than deny the knowledge of seeing and handling the plates, and hearing the words of the Angle [angel] regarding the truth of the Records."[68] LDS bishop Simon Smith wrote that on his deathbed, Harris "did truly testify to me that he both saw and handled the plates that the Book of Mormon was translated from and that an angel of God did lay them before him."[69]

When asked about his vision, David Whitmer told RLDS member J. W. Chatburn in 1882: "These hands handled the plates, these eyes saw the angel, and these ears heard his voice." In 1886 a newspaper correspondent interviewed Whitmer and wrote: "Mr. Whitmer describes every detail of the 'vision' with great precision and much fervency and insists that he handled and scrutinized the plates, and that the form and appearance of the strangely engraved characters were so impressed upon his memory that he would never forget them."[70] Re-

---

66. *Painesville Telegraph,* 15 Mar. 1831, [3], emphasis in original.

67. Edward Stevenson to editor, 10 Aug. 1870, *Deseret Evening News,* 19 Aug. 1870, [3]; qtd. in Vogel, *Early Mormon Documents,* 2:388.

68. Statement of Charlotte H. B. Adams (1938), Special Collections, Harold B. Lee Library, Brigham Young University, Provo, Utah, qtd. in Vogel, *Early Mormon Documents,* 2:389. Harris's testimony was less adamant in 1844 when he affiliated with the Shakers. Young said, "[H]is testimony is greater [in Shakerism] than it was of the Book of Mormon." Phineas H. Young to Brigham Young et al., 31 Dec. 1844, Journal History of the Church, LDS archives.

69. Simon Smith to Joseph Smith III, 29 Dec. 1880, in "Correspondence," *Saints' Herald,* 1 Feb. 1881, 43; qtd. in Vogel, *Early Mormon Documents,* 2:380.

70. David Whitmer, interview by J. W. Chatburn, in "Answer to a Question," *Saints' Herald,* 15 June 1882, 189; David Whitmer, interview by W. W.

call that when asked by Gurley if the three witnesses actually did "touch" the "real metal," Whitmer responded, "We did not."[71] In other words, if they handled them, it was in vision rather than in plain sight. Moyle said that Whitmer "repeated to me that he did see and handle the plates; that he did see and hear the angel"[72] in a vision, but that he "did not handle the plates" physically.[73]

According to Reuben Miller, Oliver Cowdery said, "I beheld with my eyes and handled with my hands the gold plates from which it was translated." In 1873 Brigham Young informed Elizabeth Kane and others that the plates that Cowdery saw "were in a cave; that Oliver Cowdery ... would not deny that he had seen [and handled] them. He had been to the cave." It appears that this cave was not a physical reality but rather something that was visited in a dream-vision.[74]

The event, as the three witnesses describe it, was similar to the many second-sight experiences of Apostle John E. Page, John Landers, John Young (Brigham's brother), Harrison Burgess, and Apostles Luke S. and Lyman E. Johnson (brothers), and other early Mormons. Elder Page related to John Landers his "vision" of 1833 when "three ancient-looking men" stood together in a room. According to Landers's report: "They had the plates from which the Book of Mormon was translated between them. He [Page] stood directly in front of them and saw them turn over the leaves, leaf by leaf, until they came to a thick mass of leaves that had a seal on them. While looking upon them, he heard the voice of the Lord say to him, 'This is shown you, and you are to bear witness of it ...'"[75]

Blair, in "David Whitmer Reviewed," *Saints' Herald,* 13 Nov. 1886, 706.

71. David Whitmer, interview by Zenas H. Gurley Jr., 14 Jan. 1885, LDS archives.

72. Moyle, Journal, 28 June 1885.

73. Nibley, *Witnesses of the Book of Mormon,* 94-95.

74. Reuben Miller, Journal, 21 Oct. 1848, 1: [12], LDS archives; qtd. in "Testimonies of Oliver Cowdery and Martin Harris," *Latter-day Saints' Millennial Star* 21 (Aug. 1859): 544; Kane, *A Gentile Account,* 75; qtd. in Vogel, *Early Mormon Documents,* 3:407-408; also see Brigham Young, 17 June 1877, *Journal of Discourses* 19:38.

75. John Landers to Mary Page Eaton, in *Autumn Leaves,* 3 Feb. 1890, 198.

John Young was "in vision" in 1832 and was escorted by a guide:

We arrived at a cave in the side of a hill, into which we entered ... [M]y guide went to a corner in the room, where lay a large chest, and opened it[;] there, said he, is the Plates ... My guide handled the Plates of fine Gold ... [A]fter We examined them, he said We could depart. As we were leaving the cave, he gave me the Box containing the Plates, and told me to preserve them.[76]

Harrison Burgess was baptized in 1832. He said of an 1833 experience: "The vision of my mind was opened and a glorius personage clothe[d] in white stood before me and exhibited to my view the plates."[77] Ohio member John Landers chronicled a day vision in 1836 that is similar to the others:

I was carried away in vision and stood on the hill of Cumorah. I looked and saw the box containing the plates ... The bottom of the box was covered by the breastplate; in the center of the box and resting on the breastplate, were three pillars ... Upon the pillars rested the plates which shone like bright gold. I saw also lying in the box a round body, wrapped in a white substance, and this I knew to be the ball of directors ...[78]

Lyman Johnson preached to a Vermont congregation in 1834, resulting in Ethan Barrows joining the church. Barrows wrote that Johnson said a "holy angel had ministered with him and had shown him the plates from which the Book of Mormon was translated, and commanded him to testify to all the world that it was true."[79] Luke Johnson told John D. Lee in 1846 "about seeing the angel and the

---

76. John Young, "A Vision of John Young," Archives and Manuscripts, Lee Library.

77. Harrison Burgess, Autobiography, D893, LDS archives.

78. "Autobiography of John Landers," *Autumn Leaves* 3 (1890): 68.

79. "The Journal of Ethan Barrows," *Journal of History* 15 (Jan. 1922): 36-7. This journal is an autobiography of Barrows, not daily entries.

plates" in vision.[80] Thirteen years later Brigham Young announced in the Salt Lake Tabernacle:

> Some of the witnesses of the Book of Mormon, who handled the plates and conversed with the angels of God, were afterwards left to doubt ... One of the Quorum of the Twelve, a young man full of faith and good works [one of the Johnsons], prayed, and the vision of his mind was opened, and the angel of God came and laid the plates before him, and he saw and handled them, and saw the angel ...[81]

Apparently such visions of the mind erased the boundaries that separate the spiritual and the physical worlds, a perspective consistent with how a number of people of that day perceived reality.

The experiences are similar in tone and often have a connection to Cumorah and its subterranean chambers. The similarity with E. T. A. Hoffmann's German story is also apparent, as discussed in the previous chapter. For Europeans and Americans of that era who perceived an invisible parallel world of spiritual forces, these were usually uplifting, inspiring experiences and were not considered odd.[82] (fig. 45).

The eight witnesses' formal statement, probably dictated by Joseph Smith, appeared in the 1830 Book of Mormon as follows:

AND ALSO THE TESTIMONY OF EIGHT WITNESSES

> Be it known unto all nations, kindreds, tongues, and people, unto whom this work shall come, that Joseph Smith, Jr., the Author and Proprietor of this work, has shewn unto us the plates of which

---

80. Anderson, *Investigating the Book of Mormon Witnesses*, 162-63.

81. Brigham Young, *Journal of Discourses*, 5 June 1859, 7:164.

82. See Ronald W. Walker, "The Persisting Idea of American Treasure Hunting," *BYU Studies* 24 (Fall 1984): 443-46. Since 1947 the descriptions of and experiences with aliens in flying saucers have been similar (see Carl Sagan, *The Demon-Haunted World: Science as a Candle in the Dark* [New York: Random House, 1995], 63-64, 127, 130-31). Psychiatrists say that these people demonstrate no evidence of psychopathology but that their experiences occur within inner space (the mind), rather than in outer space.

Fig. 45. The Hill Cumorah in Manchester, New York. Americans and Europeans who shared a magical mindset, including the witnesses to the Book of Mormon, were seeing many of the same things in the hills and elsewhere during this era. Photograph by George E. Anderson, 1907.

hath been spoken, which have the appearance of gold; and as many of the leaves as the said Smith has translated, we did handle with our hands; and we also saw the engravings thereon, all of which has the appearance of ancient work, and of curious workmanship. And this we bear record, with words of soberness, that the said Smith has shewn unto us, for we have seen and hefted, and know of a surety, that the said Smith has got the plates of which we have spoken. And we give our names unto the world, to witness unto the world that which we have seen: and we lie not, God bearing witness of it.

> CHRISTIAN WHITMER,
>
> JACOB WHITMER,
>
> PETER WHITMER, JR.
>
> JOHN WHITMER,
>
> HIRAM PAGE,
>
> JOSEPH SMITH, SEN.
>
> HYRUM SMITH,
>
> SAMUEL H. SMITH.

Although this collective declaration again seems to describe a literal event, the supporting evidence points to a less physical incident. If the three witnesses and others inspected the plates in a vision, perhaps the eight did also. Their statements indicate that this is likely the case.

On 25 March 1838, Martin Harris testified publicly that none of the signatories to the Book of Mormon saw or handled the physical records. His statement, made at the height of Ohio's banking-related apostasy, became the final straw that caused Apostles Luke S. Johnson, Lyman E. Johnson, and John F. Boynton, and high priest Stephen Burnett and seventy Warren Parrish to exit the church. Stephen Burnett, in a letter dated 15 April 1838, three weeks after this meeting, wrote to Lyman Johnson:

> I have reflected long and deliberately upon the history of this church & weighed the evidence for & against it—loth to give it up—but when I came to hear Martin Harris state in public that he never saw the plates with his natural eyes only in vision or imagination, neither Oliver nor David & also that the eight witnesses never saw them & hesitated to sign that instrument for that reason, but were persuaded to do it, the last pedestal gave way, in my view our foundations was sapped & the entire superstructure fell a heap of ruins, ... I was followed by W. Parish[,] Luke Johnson & John Boynton[,] all of who[m] concurred with me[. A]fter we were done speaking[,] M Harris arose & said he was sorry for any man who rejected the Book of Mormon for he knew it was true, he said he had hefted the plates repeatedly in a box with only a tablecloth or handkerchief over them, but he never saw them only as he saw a city through a mountain. And said that he never should have told that the testimony of the eight was false, if it had not been picked out of [h]im but should have let it passed as it was ...[83]

Warren Parrish, like Stephen Burnett, also heard Harris say at this

---

83. Stephen Burnett to Lyman E. Johnson, 15 Apr. 1838, Joseph Smith Letterbook, 2:64-66, d155/2:2, LDS archives; qtd. in Vogel, *Early Mormon Documents*, 2:288-93.

meeting that none of the eleven men examined physical records. On 11 August Parrish wrote in a letter: "Martin Harris, one of the subscribing witnesses, has come out at last, and says he never saw the plates, from which the book purports to have been translated, except in vision and he further says that any man who says he has seen them in any other way is a liar, Joseph [Smith] not excepted."[84]

Of the eight signatories, only three individually reported that they saw and touched the records. A fourth, Hiram Page, curiously mentioned neither handling nor seeing plates. He said that he could not deny "what I saw. To say ... that [I did not see] those holy Angels who came and showed themselves to me as I was walking through the field ... would be treating the God of heaven with contempt."[85] Hyrum Smith said his "eyes had seen ... [and] my hands had handled" the plates. According to LDS member Daniel Tyler, Samuel Smith said that "he had handled them and seen the engravings thereon."[86] John Whitmer provides the only detailed statement when he said in 1839, according to church member Theodore Turley: "I handled those plates; there were fine engravings on both sides ... they were shown to me by a supernatural power."[87] This added detail of how he saw in-

---

84. Warren Parrish to E. Holmes, 11 Aug. 1838, *The Evangelist* (Carthage, OH), 1 Oct. 1838, 226. George A. Smith to Josiah Flemming, 30 March 1838, Journal History, confirms the meeting of 25 March 1838. Smith wrote: "Last Sabbath a division arose among the Parrish party about the Book of Mormon. John Boyington, W. Parrish, Luke Johnson and others said it was nonsense. Martin Harris then bore testimony of its truth and said all would be damned, if they rejected it."

85. Hiram Page to William E. McLellin, 30 May 1847, *The Ensign of Liberty* 1 (Jan. 1848): 63.

86. Hyrum Smith, "To the Saints Scattered Abroad," Dec. 1839, *Times and Seasons* 1 (Dec. 1839): 23; Daniel Tyler, "Incidents of Experience," *Scraps of Biography: Tenth Book of the Faith-Promoting Series* (Salt Lake City: Juvenile Instructor Office, 1883), 23.

87. Joseph Smith Jr. et al., *History of the Church of Jesus Christ of Latter-day Saints*, ed. B. H. Roberts (Salt Lake City: Deseret Book Co., 1978 printing): 3:307; Theodore Turley, Memorandas, 4 Apr. 1839, LDS archives. In a statement by John Whitmer to P. Wilhelm Poulson three weeks before Whitmer's death (Poulson to editors, *Deseret Evening News*, 6 Aug. 1878),

dicates that the eight probably did not observe or feel the actual artifact, just as Harris testified. If Joseph Smith placed the gold records
uncovered into their hands, as the authorized statement seems to imply, there would be no reason for John Whitmer to say that a
supernatural power was involved or for Harris to say that the eight
witnesses viewed them in vision, like imagining "a city through a
mountain." Having handled the plates in vision, the eight witnesses
therefore "hesitated to sign" their testimony because it seemed to say
that their experience was physical. Both the Harris and Whitmer
statements lead me to believe that the eight, like the three, saw and
scrutinized the plates in a mind vision.

This would mean that the golden record belongs to another world
rather than to this one. They are, therefore, unlike the Dead Sea
Scrolls or other ancient documents that are physically real. Like supernatural treasures, the gold plates were in the custody of, and trans-
ported by, other-worldly beings to various witnesses and New York locations.[88] The plates were able to "sink" and "glide" underground and
could be heard "rumbling" through the hill, according to contemporary accounts. They vanish when laid upon the ground.[89] They can

---

Whitmer reportedly said that the eight witnesses viewed the plates in the
Smith home. He also allegedly said that only four saw them at the time and
that "at another time he showed them to four persons more." This contra-
dicts Lucy Smith's statement of 1844-45. She said that the eight "repaired to
a little grove ... as Joseph had been instructed that the plates would be carried
there by one of the ancient Nephites. Here it was that those 8 witnesses ...
looked upon the plates and handled them" (Lucy Smith, *History of Joseph
Smith*, 154-55; Preliminary Manuscript, in Vogel, *Early Mormon Documents*, 1:395-96). Whitmer also reportedly asserted in this interview that Joseph Smith handed them the plates "uncovered into our hands," thus contra-
dicting his 1839 declaration to Theodore Turley. Whitmer died before
reading this article. Poulson also interviewed David Whitmer (Poulson to Editor, *Deseret Evening News*, 16 Aug. 1878), and David complained about the
inaccuracies in that interview (David Whitmer to S. T. Mouch, 18 Nov. 1882,
RLDS Library-Archives).

88. Lucy Smith, *History of Joseph Smith*, 149-50, 154-55.
89. Martin Harris, qtd. in John A. Clark, "Modern Superstition—The
Mormonites," 63; qtd. in Vogel, *Early Mormon Documents*, 2:265; Orlando

cause physical death if viewed too soon.[90] The witnesses seem to have seen the records with their spiritual eyes and inspected them in the context of a vision, apparently never having actually possessed or touched them. But for them, the spiritual was material; thus, in their official declarations, their experiences sounded more physical than was intended.[91]

Believers and skeptics alike report that they physically hefted the box and handled something through a cloth. The weight, size, dimensions, and rings running through the metal were described by Martin and Lucy Harris, William Smith, Emma Smith, Isaac Hale, and others.[92] According to Dan Vogel, the literary phrases of Joseph's day (1823) described how the ancient mound builders and Jews were thought to have preserved their writings. They were said to have fashioned books of "brass ... connected together by rings at the back," "plates of brass, with characters inscribed resembling letters," placed in "stone boxes."[93] These ideas may have been Joseph's inspiration for making a plate-like object to persuade belief.

Saunders, qtd. in Mather, "The Early Days of Mormonism," 200; Affidavit of Willard Chase, 11 Dec. 1833, in Howe, *Mormonism Unvailed*, 242; qtd. in Vogel, *Early Mormon Documents* 2:67; Jessee, "Joseph Knight's Recollection," 30-31; Lucy Smith, *History of Joseph Smith*, 83-84.

90. JS—History 1:42; Affidavit of Sophia Lewis, 20 Mar. 1834, *Susquehanna Register*, 1 May 1834, 1; Charles Anthon to E. D. Howe, 17 Feb. 1834, in Howe, *Mormonism Unvailed*, 272.

91. Moses 6:36 (Pearl of Great Price); D&C 67:10; 131:7; Lucy Smith, *History of Joseph Smith*, 92.

92. Martin Harris, qtd. in *Tiffany's Monthly* 5 (Aug. 1859): 165-66; Martin Harris, interviewed by Edward Stevenson, 4 Sept. 1870, LDS archives; both in Vogel, *Early Mormon Documents* 2:305-6, 333. Stevenson wrote that "Martins Wife had hefted them & felt them under cover as had Martin" (Joseph Smith III, "Last Testimony of Sister Emma," *Saints' Herald*, 1 Oct. 1879, 290); William Smith, *William Smith on Mormonism* (Lamoni, IA: Herald Steam Book and Job Office, 1883), 11; in Vogel, *Early Mormon Documents*, 1:497; Affidavit of Isaac Hale, 20 Mar. 1834, in *Susquehanna Register*, 1 May 1834, 1.

93. Dan Vogel, *Indian Origins and the Book of Mormon: Religious Solutions from Columbus to Joseph Smith* (Salt Lake City: Signature Books,

Fig. 46. James J. Strang (1813-56)
at age forty-three.

Joseph was not alone in producing witnesses of ancient records. James J. Strang (fig. 46), like Joseph, produced eleven signatories who testified that they too had seen and inspected ancient metal plates. After Joseph's death in June 1844, Strang professed to be his successor.[94] On 1 September 1845, he further reported that he had been visited by an angel regarding "the record which was sealed from my servant Joseph. Unto thee it is reserved," the angel said. Strang said he received the "Urim and Thummim," which revealed the location of a record of "an ancient people." Two weeks later four witnesses—Aaron Smith, Jirah B. Wheelan, James M. Van Nostrand, and Edward Weitcomb—unearthed these plates under Strang's direc-

---

1986), 18, 80nn40, 47. See also Brent Lee Metcalfe, "Apologetic and Critical Assumptions about Book of Mormon Historicity," *Dialogue* 26 (Fall 1993): 156-57.

94. James J. Strang, "Letter from Joseph Smith to James J. Strang," 18 June 1844, in *Voree* [WI] *Herald* 1 (Jan. 1846): [1]; Roger Van Noord, *King of Beaver Island: The Life and Assassination of James Jesse Strang* (Urbana: University of Illinois Press, 1988), 4, 7-10.

tion. In a joint affirmation, the signatories reported how they found the plates and testified that they saw and examined them. The plates were covered with "characters, but in a language of which we have no knowledge."[95] Hundreds of others examined these plates. C. Latham Sholes, editor of the nearby *Southport Telegraph,* wrote shortly after their discovery: "The plates were shown us, and we visited and examined the spot from which they purport to have been taken." Sholes offered no editorial opinion but stated that, in his judgment, Strang was "honest and earnest in all he said" and that his witnesses were "among the most honest and intelligent in the neighborhood."[96]

Sometime after Strang had translated these writings, he announced that it had been revealed to him where the ancient plates of Laban were buried. (This was the same Laban from whom Nephi took the brass plates in Jerusalem during the reign of Zedekiah, king of Judah.) From these records, Strang translated forty-seven chapters of what he called the "Book of the Law of the Lord" (fig. 47). Seven signatories testified in the preface of the first edition:

TESTIMONY

Be it known unto all nations, kindreds, tongues and people, to whom this Book of the Law of the Lord shall come, that James J. Strang has the plates ... and has shown them to us. We examined them with our eyes, and handled them with our hands. The engravings are beautiful antique workmanship, bearing a striking resemblance to the ancient oriental languages ... [The plates] are eighteen in number, about seven inches and three-eights wide, by nine inches long ...

---

95. James J. Strang, "Revelation Given to James J. Strang," 1 Sept. 1845, *Voree Herald* 1 (Jan. 1846): [3-4]; Van Noord, *King of Beaver Island,* 33-35. None of these four witnesses had been Latter-day Saints.

96. C. Latham Sholes, Editorial, 30 Sept. 1845, *Southport* [WI] *Telegraph,* 30 Sept. 1845; Van Noord, *King of Beaver Island,* 35-36. For others, see *Gospel* [Voree, WI] *Herald,* 23 Sept. 1847; 21 Sept., 26 Oct. 1848).

Fig. 47. *The Book of the Law of the Lord,* which Strang said God
commissioned him to translate from eighteen metal plates.
Seven witnesses, in a joint testimony, said: "We examined
them with our eyes, and handled them with our hands. The
engravings are beautiful antique workmanship."

SAMUEL GRAHAM,

SAMUEL P. BACON,

WARREN POST,

PHINEAS WRIGHT,

ALBERT N. HOSMER,

EBENEZER PAGE,

JEHIEL SAVAGE.[97]

Samuel Graham was the scribe in the translation of these plates of
Laban. Later he was excommunicated, but there is no direct evidence
that he or any of the other ten men ever denied their testimonies.[98]

It is interesting that three of the Whitmers—David, John, and
Jacob—and Martin Harris, Hiram Page, William Smith, and Lucy
Smith all followed Strang's leadership from 1846 to 1847, even
though none of them had ever met him. They became Strangites after
reading a pamphlet in early 1846 that reprinted the January 1846 issue of the *Voree Herald*, the official organ of Strang's church. It reported his appointment from Joseph Smith, his angelic visitations, an
account by his witnesses of how the metal plates were unearthed, and
a translation of part of the first set of plates.[99]

On 11 May 1846, Lucy Smith, in a letter to Reuben Hedlock,
wrote: "I am satisfied that Joseph appointed J. J. Strang. It is verily
so." The same day former apostle William Smith informed Hedlock:
"James J. Strang has the appointment and we have evidence of it. The
whole Smith family excepting Hyrum's widow uphold Strang."[100]

---

97. James J. Strang, *Book of the Law of the Lord* (St. James [Beaver Is-
land], MI, 1851 & 1856), 2; Van Noord, *King of Beaver Island*, 97. Page and
Savage were former LDS members.

98. Van Noord, *King of Beaver Island*, 56-57, 163-64.

99. *Voree Herald* 1 (Jan. 1846): [1-4]; William Smith to James J. Strang,
1 Mar. 1846, in *Voree Herald* 1 (July 1846): [3]. Lucy Smith and six members
of her family signed this letter sustaining Strang.

100. Lucy Smith to Reuben Hedlock, 11 May 1846; William Smith to
Reuben Hedlock, 11 May 1846, both in *Voree Herald* 1 (June 1846): [1]; see
also "Brigham Young Manuscript History," 27 Jan. 1847, LDS archives.

William further testified: "As to the claims of Brother James J. Strang, as the President of the Church of Jesus Christ of Latter Day Saints, Prophet, Seer, and Revelator, I entertain no doubt whatever, as his appointment by my brother [Joseph], and his confirmation by angelic administration ... for so Jehovah hath revealed it unto me."[101]

The three Whitmers and Hiram Page read Strang's pamphlet in the spring of 1846 and wrote letters of allegiance.[102] John Whitmer testified, "God knowing all things prepared a man whom he visited by an angel of God and showed him where there were some ancient Record hid ... whose name is James J. Strang."[103] By September 1846, the *Voree Herald* named Harris as a member of Strang's high council in Kirtland and announced his missionary call to England.[104] In this same issue, the editor stated, "There are engaged in the faith with us nearly all the best preachers of the church, all the living witnesses of the book of Mormon save one, and every surviving member of the family of Joseph Smith."[105]

The one living witness who had not yet joined with Strang was Oliver Cowdery. His father, William Cowdery, converted in the summer of 1846.[106] A year later Oliver had moved to Elkhorn, Wisconsin, twelve miles from Strang's Voree headquarters, although it is unknown how close his affiliation was with the church.[107]

In conclusion, all of the living signatories to the Book of Mor-

---

101. William Smith to the "Church of Jesus Christ of Latter Day Saints" [Strang], 28 July 1846, in *Zion's* [Voree, WI] *Reveille* 1 (Dec. 1846): 3.
102. Hiram Page to James J. Strang, Apr. 1846, paraphrased by Strang in the *Gospel Herald*, 20 Jan. 1848, 206.
103. Bruce N. Westergren, ed., *From Historian to Dissident: The Book of John Whitmer* (Salt Lake City: Signature Books, 1995), 194. John Whitmer later lined out these words.
104. "Kirtland," in *Voree Herald* 1 (Sept. 1846): [1-2]; see also Orson Hyde, "Martin Harris," *Latter-day Saints' Millennial Star*, 15 Nov. 1846, 124-28.
105. "Kirtland," *Voree Herald*, [4].
106. Ibid., [2].
107. Stanley R. Gunn, *Oliver Cowdery: Second Elder and Scribe* (Salt Lake City: Bookcraft, 1962), 189.

mon, except possibly Cowdery, accepted Strang's leadership, angelic call, metal plates, and his translation of these plates as authentic. This replication of an earlier pattern of belief confirms that it must have been relatively easy for the witnesses to accept Joseph's golden plates as an ancient record. Appreciating their mindset helps us understand Mormon origins in their terms.

7.

Priesthood Restoration

Like the early narratives about how the Book of Mormon came to be, the early accounts of priesthood restoration are more nuanced and fascinating than the simple, unified story that is told today. The earliest reference to priesthood authority appeared in the 1833 Book of Commandments, the earliest version of, and precursor to, the Doctrine and Covenants (fig. 48). According to a revelation received in June 1829, Oliver Cowdery was "baptized [one month earlier on 15 May] by the hand of my servant [Joseph Smith], according to that which I have commanded him."[1] Lucy Smith, the prophet's mother, explained the circumstances and medium by which she understood that this command from God had come to her son:

> One morning however they sat down to their usual work [Joseph and Oliver were translating in Third Nephi in the Book of Mormon] when the first thing that presented itself to Joseph was a commandment from God that he and Oliver should repair to the water & each of them be baptized[. T]hey immediately went down to the susquehana river and obeyed the mandate given them through the urim and

---

1. BofC 15:6-7 in Wilford C. Wood, *Joseph Smith Begins His Work: The Book of Commandments*, 2 vols. (Salt Lake City: by the Author, 1962), vol. 2; cf. D&C 18:7.

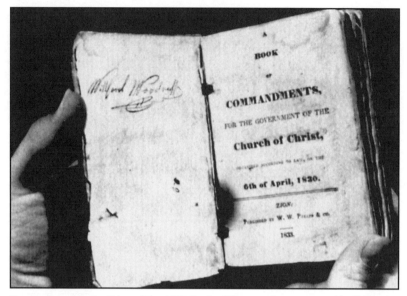

Fig. 48. An original edition of the 1833 Book of Commandments owned by Wilford Woodruff; LDS church archives

Thummim[. A]s they were on their return to the house they over-heard samuel [Smith] in a secluded spot engaged in secret prayer[.] They had now received authority to baptize ... and they [then] spoke to Samual who went withe them straightway to the water and was baptized (fig. 49).[2]

At this early date the view was that the commandment received through the urim and thummim is what gave Joseph and Oliver the authority to baptize.

In 1885 David Whitmer, another New York church member and one of the three special witnesses to the Book of Mormon, told the same version of how Joseph and Oliver received their authority:

---

2. Lucy Smith's Preliminary Manuscript, dictated to Martha Jane Coray, 1844-45, original in the archives of the Historical Department, Church of Jesus Christ of Latter-day Saints, Salt Lake City, Utah (hereafter LDS archives); qtd. in *Early Mormon Documents,* ed. Dan Vogel, 3+ vols. (Salt Lake City: Signature Books, 1996-), 1:381.

Fig. 49. The Susquehanna River in Harmony, Pennsylvania, where Joseph Smith and Oliver Cowdery baptized each other. Photograph by George E. Anderson, 1907.

I moved Joseph Smith and Oliver Cowdery to my fathers house in Fayette[,] Seneca County New York, from Harmony, Penn. in the year [June] 1829 [so they could finish translating the Book of Mormon. O]n our way I conversed freely with them upon this great work they were bringing about, and Oliver stated to me in Josephs presence that they had baptized each other seeking by that to fulfill the command ... I never heard that an Angel had ordained Joseph and Oliver to the Aaronic priesthood until the year 1834[, 183]5[,] or [183]6—in Ohio. My information from Joseph and Oliver upon this matter being as I have stated, and that they were commanded so to do by revealment through Joseph. I do not believe that John the Baptist ever ordained Joseph and Oliver as stated and believed by some. I regard that as an error, a misconception.[3]

---

3. David Whitmer, interview by Zenas H. Gurley Jr., 14 Jan. 1885, typescript, LDS archives. See Edward Stevenson Journal, 9 Feb. 1886, cited

Shortly after arriving at the Peter Whitmer Sr. home, according to statements, Joseph and Oliver received additional authority in the same manner as before. Now they would be able to bestow the gift of the Holy Ghost. Because Joseph had been promised this higher authority when they were baptized, he was "anxious" and "diligent in prayer" to receive it. He explained how God gave them this greater authority in the Whitmer home in June 1829 (fig. 50):

> We had for some time made this matter a subject of humble prayer, and at length we got together in the Chamber [upper story] of Mr Whitmer's house in order more particularly to seek of the Lord what we now so earnestly desired ... [W]e had not long been engaged in solemn and fervent prayer, when the word of the Lord, came unto us in the Chamber, commanding us; that I should ordain Oliver Cowdery to be an Elder in the Church of Jesus Christ, And that he also should ordain me to the same office, and then to ordain others ... [W]e were however commanded to defer this our ordination untill, such times, as it should be practicable to have our brethren, who had been and who should be baptized, assembled together ...[4]

This meeting and the anticipated ordinations took place on 6 April 1830, the day the church was organized.[5] Two months later a revelation published in the Book of Commandments referred to their new, higher priesthood authority by affirming that "commandments were given to Joseph, who was called of God and ordained an apostle

---

in Joseph Grant Stevenson, *Stevenson Family History* (Provo, UT: by the Author, 1955), 1:177-78. Some have argued that the reason no one heard of angelic ministrations early on was because, as Joseph Smith said in 1838: "[W]e were forced to keep secret the circumstances of having received the Priesthood and our having been baptized, owing to a spirit of persecution in the neighborhood ... [Harmony, Pennsylvania]. We had been threatened with being mobbed" (JS—History 1:74-75). In light of the David Whitmer and Lucy Smith statements, Joseph intended to keep his and Oliver's baptisms and receipt of authority to baptize from their enemies, not from devoted believers.

4. Dean C. Jessee, ed., *The Papers of Joseph Smith: Autobiographical and Historical Writings* (Salt Lake City: Deseret Book Co., 1989), 1:299.

5. Ibid., 302-03.

Fig. 50. A reconstructed log house at the Whitmer homesite in Fayette, New York. This is where Joseph and Oliver received the authority to ordain each other and where they finished the Book of Mormon transcript. It is also where many early revelations were received and where the three witnesses signed their testimony.

of Jesus Christ, an elder of this church; And also to Oliver, who was also called of God an apostle of Jesus Christ, an elder of this church, and ordained under his [Joseph's] hand." In other words, they received a calling in the Whitmer home and ordained each other at the first church meeting, and this authorized the two men to function as elders; angelic ordinations were not mentioned. The Book of Commandments goes on to explain that an elder holds the authority to preside, ordain other elders, and bestow the gift of the Holy Ghost.[6]

The term elder was also at this time synonymous with the term apostle and should not be confused with the later office or apostolic keys, both of which would not be introduced until early 1835. At

---

6. BofC 24:3-4, 32-35; cf. D&C 20:2-3, 38-45.

first, anyone who was ordained an elder was considered to be an apostle. The Book of Commandments says, "An apostle is an elder."[7] In an 1830 letter of introduction for Orson Pratt to the Colesville branch, Joseph Smith and John Whitmer called Pratt "another Servant and apostle."[8] Pratt had just been ordained an elder the day before. Sidney Rigdon wrote on 4 January 1831: "I send you this letter by John Whitmer. Receive him, for he is a brother greatly beloved, and an Apostle of this church." Whitmer was an elder. Ezra Booth recorded in 1831 that Ziba Peterson, an early missionary who had committed a wrongdoing, "was deprived of his Elder and Apostleship."[9] Jared Carter noted in his 1831 journal about being ordained an elder, "I received the authority of an apostle."[10]

The Book of Commandments outlines Joseph's authority to found the church. Chapter 24, dated June 1830, states that Joseph: (1) "received a remission of his sins"; (2) received a "call ... to his holy work" from an angel who gave him the means to translate the Book of Mormon; (3) that angels showed the book to others and thus "confirmed" it to them; (4) that the Church of Christ was organized on 6 April 1830; and that (5) on that same day, Joseph and Oliver ordained each other elders, having been "called of God" to do so; concluding, (6) "Wherefore having so great witnesses, by them shall the world be judged."[11] Nothing yet suggested that Joseph and Oliver had received authority by angelic ordination.

Significantly, teachings on ministerial authority in the Book of Commandments mirror what is found in the Bible as well as in the Book of Mormon and the Book of Moses. Aside from the New Testa-

---

7. BofC 24:32; cf. D&C 20:38; 21:1, 10-11.
8. Joseph Smith and John Whitmer to Colesville Saints, 2 Dec. 1830; qtd. in Vogel, *Early Mormon Documents,* 1:19.
9. Ezra Booth to Edward Partridge, 20 Sept. 1831; Sidney Rigdon to Ohio Brethren, ca. 4 Jan. 1831, in E. D. Howe, *Mormonism Unvailed* (Painesville OH: by the Author, 1834), 110, 208.
10. Jared Carter Journal, Sept. 1831, 35, LDS archives.
11. BofC 24: 1-12; also D&C 20:1-13, which dates this as April 1830.

ment influence on the Book of Moses, notice that Adam receives priesthood by the voice of God which directed him to open a gospel dispensation by baptizing, bestowing the Holy Ghost, and ordaining others (5:4-9; 6:51-7:1). Adam then gave these ordinances to his worthy descendants: "And thou art after the order of him who was without beginning of days or end of years, from all eternity to all eternity. Behold, thou art one in me, a son of God; and thus may all become my sons" (6:67-68).

In the Bible God's command to his prophets authorizes them to carry out various assignments and to ordain others. Moses was called by God's voice out of a burning bush, and it was God's spirit that commanded him to ordain Aaron. The voice of God called Samuel to be a prophet and judge and to anoint Saul and David as kings. Isaiah, Jeremiah, Ezekiel, and Zechariah, as well as Lehi in the Book of Mormon, were called by the voice of the Lord in dreams and visions. Following the biblical pattern, Lehi ordained other Nephites.[12]

Four hundred and fifty years later the Nephite civilization divided into two separate geographical centers, one at Zarahemla and the other at Lehi-Nephi under the wicked king Noah. Abinadi, a citizen of Lehi-Nephi, said "the Lord ... commanded me" to preach. In preaching he converted Alma, a young man in Noah's court, who taught Abinadi's words and converted more than two hundred. By God's command alone, Alma baptized and ordained followers and organized a church: "Alma took Helam, he being one of the first, and went and stood forth in the water, and cried, saying: O Lord, pour out thy Spirit upon thy servant, that he may do this work ... and ... the Spirit of the Lord was upon him, and he [Alma] said: Helam, I baptize thee, having authority from the Almighty God ..." Alma and Helam both submerged themselves and "arose and came forth from the water rejoicing, being filled with the Spirit." They baptized each other,

---

12. Ex. 3:1-12; 40:13-16; 1 Sam. 3:1-18; 9:15-17; 10:1; 16:1-13; Isa. 6:1-10; Jer. 1:1-10; Ezek. 1:1, 26-2:3; Zech. 1:1-16; 1 Ne. 1:4-8, 18-2:3; 2 Ne. 5:26; Jac. 1:18.

in other words. Afterwards, Alma baptized the rest of the multitude, who were "filled with the grace of God. And they were called the church of God, or the church of Christ, from that time forward. And it came to pass that whosoever was baptized by the power and authority of God was added to his church. And it came to pass that Alma, having authority from God, ordained priests."[13]

A generation passed and Noah's son King Limhi "and many of his people were desirous to be baptized; but there was none in the land that had authority from God ... Therefore they did not at that time form themselves into a church, waiting upon the Spirit of the Lord. Now they were desirous to become even as Alma and his brethren, who had fled into the wilderness" (Mosiah 21:32-34).

The Nephite model is a consistent one in that "the Spirit of the Lord" authorizes men to baptize and ordain each other and to organize a church. This corresponds exactly to the Book of Commandments pattern for receiving authority. There are periods during which ordinations occur in an orderly succession, but when the chain is broken, another prophet is called by God's voice or by his Spirit to begin the cycle anew.

To continue the Nephite example, another prophet named Nephi is introduced, this one a son of Helaman in about A.D. 1. As a successor to a line of prophets from Alma's time, Nephi has the authority to baptize, to bestow the Holy Ghost, and to ordain. Christ appears in

---

13. Mosiah 11:20-25; 17:1-4; 18:1, 12-18; 21:30. The bestowal of the Holy Ghost follows the Pentecostal pattern of Joseph Smith's day and our own. In Mosiah 18:14, 16, the Holy Ghost fell upon the newly baptized as they emerged from the water. In Alma 31:36, the Holy Ghost is not associated with baptism but falls upon members when Alma "clapped his hands upon them." I have seen a Pentecostal congregation exhibit this phenomenon when the minister poured water onto the ground or touched congregants with one or both hands (cf. Alma 19:12-17, 29-30; 3 Nephi 7:21-22). In 3 Nephi 18:36-37, Jesus "touched with his hand the disciples whom he had chosen ... [and thereby] gave them power to give the Holy Ghost." Moroni 2:3 adds, "On as many as they [the disciples] laid their hands, fell the Holy Ghost."

A.D. 34 and declares that the old law is fulfilled, then introduces a new covenant by orally reaffirming Nephi's authority to baptize. By this oral authority, the Nephite twelve are commissioned to bestow the Holy Ghost and to ordain others. Thereafter, these Nephites ordain other men in an orderly succession. As the twelve die, "there were other disciples ordained in their stead."[14]

These recitals in the Bible and in Joseph's revelations, including those in the Book of Commandments, are consistent. God calls a man by voice or by spirit to open a gospel dispensation or to commence a mission of preaching repentance. This call authorizes the individual to baptize and to ordain others. In none of these scriptural writings do we find other-worldly beings laying hands upon mortals to bestow priesthood authority.

Joseph Smith was commanded to search the Book of Mormon itself for instructions on how to receive and dispense priesthood authority. A revelation (BofC 15:3/D&C 18:3-4) given June 1829 instructed him: "I give unto you a commandment, that you rely upon the things which are written [on the gold plates]; For in them are all things written concerning the foundation of my church, my gospel, and my rock." When Joseph receives a spiritual prompting to begin to baptize and ordain others, he is following the pattern in the Book of Mormon.

Further evidence lies in the fact that early missionaries declared that they were called of God but did not say that their authority originated with heavenly messengers.[15] Accounts of angelic ordinations from John the Baptist and Peter, James, and John are in none of the

---

14. 3 Ne. 7:21-25; 11:18-22, 33-36; 12:1; 13:25; 4 Ne. 14. For other Book of Mormon examples, see G. St. John Stott, "Ordination and Ministry in the Book of Mormon," in *Restoration Studies III* (Independence, MO: Herald Publishing House, 1986), 244-53.

15. BofC 5:2; 10:2, 11; 11:2; 12:2; 15:30; cf. D&C 6:4; 11:4, 27; 12:3-4; 14:4; 18:28. Note that whoever has desire is called to the work, and if he does the work, he is "called of God."

journals, diaries, letters, or printed matter until the mid-1830s.[16] Zenas H. Gurley, an RLDS apostle, asked David Whitmer in 1885:

> Were you present when Joseph Smith received the revelation commanding him and Oliver Cowdery to ordain each other to the Melchizedek Priesthood? ... [Whitmer:] "No I was not, neither did I ever hear of such a thing as an angel ordaining them until I got into Ohio about the year 1834, or later ... [and regarding the Aaronic Priesthood,] I never heard that an angel had ordained Joseph and Oliver to the Aaronic priesthood until the year 1834[, 183]5[,] or [183]6, in Ohio."[17]

An example would be the diaries of early convert and apostle William E. McLellin from 1831 to 1836, wherein he never mentioned that the church claimed angelic priesthood restoration.[18] After leaving the church, McLellin recorded: "I joined the church in 1831. For years I never heard of John the Baptist ordaining Joseph and Oliver. I heard not of James, Peter, and John doing so."[19] He elaborated in 1870: "I heard Joseph tell his experience of his ordination [by Cowdery] and the organization of the church, probably, more than twenty times, to persons who, near the rise of the church, wished to know and hear about it. I never heard of Moroni, John, or Peter, James and John."[20] Two years later he repeated: "But as to the story

---

16. LaMar Petersen, *Problems in Mormon Text* (Salt Lake City: by the Author, 1957), 8. Some scholars view an 18 December 1833 statement as the first evidence that Oliver and Joseph were ordained under the hands by angels (see appendix to this chapter).

17. David Whitmer, interview by Zenas H. Gurley Jr., 14 Jan. 1885. An apostle in the RLDS church, Gurley believed in the ordination by John the Baptist and the verbal command but not in a physical ordination by Peter, James, and John.

18. Jan Shipps and John W. Welch, eds., *The Journals of William E. McLellin, 1831-1836* (Urbana: University of Illinois Press, 1994), 29-225.

19. William E. McLellin to J. L. Traughber, 25 Aug. 1877, J. L. Traughber Collection, 1446/2, Manuscripts Division, Marriott Library, University of Utah, Salt Lake City. See also "Notebook of William E. McLellin," 10, J. L. Traughber Collection, Ms 666, Manuscripts Division, Marriott Library.

20. William E. McLellin to D. H. Bays, 24 May 1870, *True Latter Day Saints' Herald*, 15 Sept. 1870, 556.

of John, the Baptist ordaining Joseph and Oliver on the day they were baptized; I never heard of it in the church for years, altho I carefully noticed things that were said."[21]

There is other corroborating evidence in an episode that occurred in September 1830 when Hiram Page, who held the office of teacher, claimed to receive revelations for the church through a seer stone. Many, "especially the Whitmer family and Oliver Cowdery," accepted Page's revelations as authoritative for "the upbuilding of Zion, the order of the Church [speaking for God] &c &c."[22] If Cowdery's authority came literally from the hands of John the Baptist and Peter, James, and John in an unequivocal bestowal of apostolic keys of priesthood succession, rather than in a more subtle apprehension of divine will, it should have been obvious to Cowdery that Page's claim lacked comparable weight. If this restoration of authority and truth which had been lost for centuries occurred dramatically and decisively in a show of glory in 1829, then it seems unlikely that a year later Cowdery would accept Page's authority over that of Joseph Smith. Why would those claiming to hold the exclusive keys of apostolic succession from Peter, James, and John seek direction and revelation from one holding the office of a teacher in the church? It seems more likely that simple and undramatic commandments were the source of these early authority claims.

The first mention of authority from angels dates to 22 September 1832, a revelation that appears as section 84 of the Doctrine and Covenants. This revelation elaborates on a Bible passage and states that John the Baptist was "ordained by the angel of God at the time he was eight days old ... to overthrow the kingdom of the Jews,"

---

21. William E. McLellin to Joseph Smith III, July 1872, 3, Library-Archives, Community of Christ (RLDS).

22. Jessee, *Papers of Joseph Smith*, 1:322-23; D&C 28; Donald Q. Cannon and Lyndon W. Cook, eds., *Far West Record: Minutes of the Church of Jesus Christ of Latter-day Saints, 1830-1844* (Salt Lake City: Deseret Book Co., 1983), 1. The minutes for 9 June 1830 list Hiram Page as a teacher in the church.

while Moses, Jethro, Caleb, Elihu, Jeremy, Gad, and Esaias all received priesthood authority "under the hand" of men, "and Esaias received it under the hand of God." These examples do not refer to the actual physical laying on of hands by an angel, but one sees the seed of a concept here.[23]

When Joseph Smith began writing his first history in November 1832, he described "thirdly the reception of the holy Priesthood by the ministering of Aangels to administer the letter of the Gospel—(—the Law and commandments as they were given unto him—) and the ordinencs."[24] Here he begins to apprehend the significance of angels who were said to have attended his ordination. Finally, on 12 February 1834, Joseph mentioned in public for the first time that his priesthood "office" had "been conferred upon me by the ministring of the Angel of God, by his own will and by the voice of this Church."[25] This is still not an unequivocal assertion of authority by angelic ordination. That was yet to come in Oliver Cowdery's 7 September 1834 letter in the October issue of the *Messenger and Advocate*. Cowdery tells a highly dramatic, if poetic, version of how he and Joseph received the priesthood from an unnamed angel:

> [T]he angel of God came down clothed with glory, and delivered the anxiously looked for message, and the keys of the Gospel of repentance!—What joy! what wonder! what amazement! ... [W]e were rapt in the vision of the Almighty! Where was room for doubt? No where: uncertainty had fled ... [W]e received under his hand the holy priesthood, as he said, "upon you my fellow servants ..."[26]

---

23. D&C 84:28, 6-12. See Moses 8:19: "And the Lord ordained Noah after his own order." This probably refers to ordination by a mortal being already possessing authority since D&C 36:2 said concerning the gift of the Holy Ghost: "And I [God] will lay my hand upon you [Edward Partridge] by the hand of my servant Sidney Rigdon."

24. Jessee, *Papers of Joseph Smith*, 1:3.

25. Kirtland Council Minutes, (12 Feb. 1834), 27, LDS archives; qtd. in Vogel, *Early Mormon Documents*, 1:32.

26. Oliver Cowdery, "History of the Rise of the Church of the Latter

Notice that this experience occurred while they "were rapt in the vision of the Almighty," according to Cowdery. A year later, in September 1835, Cowdery repeated: "While we were in the heavenly vision the angel came down and bestowed upon us this priesthood."[27] Future apostle Franklin D. Richards recorded a sermon by Joseph Smith in 1844 that "related the vision of his ordination to the priesthood of Aaron."[28] The phrasing is similar to the accounts of how Cowdery and others visited the chambers within the Hill Cumorah (see chapter 6), occurring in a spiritual rather than physical dimension. Given the tendency to blend the spiritual and physical, we can understand how the angel's appearance was transmitted through church history as a literal, physical event.

When Joseph and Oliver began mentioning their angelic ordinations in late 1834 and early 1835, they were facing a credibility crisis that threatened the church's survival. In late 1833 a group in Kirtland, Ohio, denounced Joseph Smith for ministering "under pretense of Divine Authority." They employed D. P. Hurlbut to investigate Joseph's past, hoping to bring him down "from the high station which he pretends to occupy."[29] Hurlbut traveled to Palmyra, New York, and collected affidavits from residents about Joseph's early treasure seeking and other aspects of his youth. Hurlbut began a lecture tour starting in January 1834 to "numerous congregations in Chagrin, Kirtland, Mentor, and Painesville; and ... [he] fired the minds of the people with much indignation against Joseph and the Church."[30]

Day Saints," *Latter Day Saints' Messenger and Advocate* 1 (Oct. 1834): 15-16; qtd. in Vogel, *Early Mormon Documents*, 2:420-21. The statement is also in JS—History after verse 75.

27. The Book of Patriarchal Blessings 1:8-9, LDS archives; qtd. in Vogel, *Early Mormon Documents*, 2:453.

28. Joseph Smith, sermon of 10 Mar. 1844, in Andrew F. Ehat and Lyndon W. Cook, eds., *The Words of Joseph Smith: The Contemporary Accounts of the Nauvoo Discourses of the Prophet Joseph* (Provo, UT: Religious Studies Center, 1980), 334.

29. "To the Public," *Painesville* [OH] *Telegraph*, 31 Jan. 1834, [3].

30. Joseph Smith Jr. et al., *History of the Church of Jesus Christ of*

Finding disillusionment spreading among the Saints, Joseph and Sidney Rigdon began preaching against Hurlbut.[31] It was under these circumstances, exacerbated by problems associated with the failure of Zion's Camp—the paramilitary trek to assist fellow Saints in Missouri—that Joseph mentioned for the first time in public that his priesthood had "been conferred upon me by the ministering of the Angel of God."[32] Ironically, Hurlbut's, Rigdon's, and Joseph Smith's speeches all became advance publicity for E. D. Howe's scathing *Mormonism Unvailed* [sic].

By May 1834, Joseph's Pennsylvania in-laws had issued similar affidavits about Joseph's treasure digging and his supposed motivations for starting Mormonism. Howe published all of these in his book in November 1834. Meanwhile, Oliver Cowdery, with Joseph's assistance and sensitive to the negative impact of the recent disclosures, decided to write "on the subject of those affidavits."[33] Oliver's first refutation, published in the October 1834 *Messenger and Advocate,* included the narrative of being ordained by an unnamed angel. Shortly thereafter, this angel was identified as John the Baptist. Simultaneously, a statement about Peter, James, and John appearing to Joseph and Oliver was added to an earlier revelation.[34] This information appeared in the 1835 Doctrine and Covenants. Thus, by degrees,

---

Latter-day Saints, ed. B. H. Roberts (Salt Lake City: Deseret Book Co., 1978 printing), 1:475.

31. Donna Hill, *Joseph Smith: The First Mormon* (Garden City, NY: Doubleday & Co., 1977), 157.

32. Kirtland Council Minutes, (12 Feb. 1834), 27, LDS archives; qtd. in Vogel, *Early Mormon Documents,* 1:32. Cowdery wrote in December 1834 about "... the angel while in company with President [Joseph] Smith, at the time they received the office of the lesser priesthood" (Jessee, *Papers of Joseph Smith,* 1:21).

33. Oliver Cowdery, "Answer," *The Evening and the Morning Star* (Kirtland, OH) 2 (Sept. 1834): 190.

34. See D&C 27:8, 12-13. "In 1835 the original edition of the Doctrine and Covenants gave the first precise published account of the appearance of Peter, James, and John to Joseph and Oliver," writes Brian Q. Cannon et al., "Priesthood Restoration Documents," *BYU Studies* 35 (1995-96): 167.

the accounts became more detailed and more miraculous. In 1829 Joseph said he was called by the Spirit; in 1832 he mentioned that angels attended these events; in 1834-35 the spiritual manifestations became literal and physical appearances of resurrected beings. Details usually become blurred over time; in this case, they multiplied and sharpened. These new declarations of literal and physical events facilitated belief and bolstered Joseph's and Oliver's authority during a time of crisis.

No contemporary narrative exists for a visitation to Joseph and Oliver by Peter, James, and John. In fact, the date, location, ordination prayer, and any other circumstances surrounding this experience are unknown. B. H. Roberts confirmed: "There is no definite account of the event in the history of the Prophet Joseph or, for matter of fact, in any of our annals."[35] Scholars have produced scenarios about when and where this may have occurred. The most popular views are May 1829, July 1830, and June 1831.[36]

The earliest statement about the higher priesthood being restored in a literal, physical way, including named angels, appears in the September 1835 Doctrine and Covenants:

> Which John I have sent unto you, my servants, Joseph Smith, Jun., and Oliver Cowdery, to ordain you unto the first priesthood which you have received ... And also with Peter, and James, and John, whom I have sent unto you, by whom I have ordained you and confirmed you to be apostles, and especial witnesses of my name, and bear the keys of your ministry and of the same things which I revealed unto them; Unto whom I have committed the keys of my kingdom, and a dispensation of the gospel for the last times (27:8, 12-13, current LDS edition).

---

35. *History of the Church*, 1:40n.

36. For May 1829, see Larry C. Porter, "The Restoration of the Aaronic and Melchizedek Priesthoods," *Ensign* 26 (Dec. 1996): 30-47; for July 1830, see Richard L. Bushman, *Joseph Smith and the Beginnings of Mormonism* (Urbana: University of Illinois Press, 1984), 162-3, 240n55; for June 1831, see Marvin S. Hill, *Quest for Refuge: The Mormon Flight from American Pluralism* (Salt Lake City: Signature Books, 1989), 25-26.

These verses plus two in section 7 pertaining to John the Baptist and Peter, James, and John and literal priesthood restorations do not appear in the 1833 Book of Commandments.[37]

Section 7 tells us that "the keys" were given anciently to Jesus' three apostles to "minister for those who shall be heirs of salvation who dwell on the earth" (6-7). Section 27 has Peter, James, and John bestowing apostolic keys upon Joseph and Oliver, as already quoted.[38] It is difficult to explain why these important names and the bestowal of their keys of authority would not be included in the Book of Commandments. The most plausible explanation is that they were retrofitted to an 1829-30 time period to give the impression that an impressive and unique authority had existed in the church from the beginning.

It may be more than a coincidence that in February 1835 when the Quorum of the Twelve Apostles was organized, the detail regarding Peter, James, and John was added to the revelations. It was sometime between January and May 1835 that Peter, James, and John were first mentioned as the restorers of apostolic keys to Joseph and Oliver.[39] This new link of succession undoubtedly bolstered President

37. Cf. D&C 27 and D&C 7 with Book of Commandments chaps. 28 and 6 in Wood, *Joseph Smith Begins His Work*, vol. 2.

38. Joseph Smith, in speaking to the newly formed high council, said: "The apostle, Peter, was the president of the Council in ancient days and held the keys of the Kingdom of God on the earth" (Kirtland Council Minutes, 17 Feb. 1834, 30, LDS archives). This may be the beginning of the development for D&C 7:7. In later recollections by Philo Dibble and Benjamin Winchester, published in the 1880s, their statements about Peter, James, and John were probably influenced by D&C 27:12-13. See "Philo Dibble's Narrative," *Early Scenes in Church History: Eighth Book of the Faith-Promoting Series* (Salt Lake City: Juvenile Instructor Office, 1882), 80; Benjamin Winchester, "Primitive Mormonism," *The Daily Tribune* (Salt Lake City), 22 Sept. 1889, 2.

39. Joseph revised his earlier revelations between January and May 1835. Section 20 represents the first textual evidence of his revisions in the January 1835 Kirtland reprint of the *Evening and Morning Star*, 1:2-4. By June, the Doctrine and Covenants was being printed (ibid., 80).

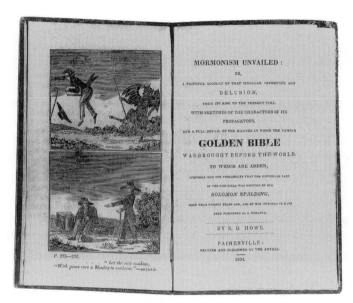

Fig. 51. Eber D. Howe's *Mormonism Unvailed* (1834) was the most influential anti-Mormon book of the nineteenth century.

Smith's and Assistant President Cowdery's authority in the eyes of the new Quorum of the Twelve and the church.

The early claim to be "the only true ... church," with Christ's exclusive authority, may have caused members to ask how the church's authority was in fact unique (D&C 1:30). The attacks against the character and early life of Joseph Smith must have raised questions, as well (fig. 51). Howe's book, published less than twelve miles from Kirtland, posed a threat to the credibility and authority of the Restoration. This provided motivation for Joseph and Oliver to counter with detailed accounts of physical appearances by these impressive biblical figures. For the survival and continued growth of the young church, the changes appear to have been necessary. In a single stroke, the new accounts legitimized the leadership's religious authority, giving them exclusive rights and setting them apart from anyone who claimed a nonliteral or metaphysical reception of authority.[40] Angelic

---

40. After Joseph's death, recent convert James J. Strang claimed that an

ordinations and apostolic keys of succession provided an incontestable and singular credential for being the only true spokesmen for Christ on earth.

As in his accounts of an angel and the gold plates, Joseph was willing to expand on another foundational narrative. The events surrounding priesthood restoration were reinterpreted, one detail emphasized over another. A spiritually charged moment when participants felt that the veil between heaven and earth was thin became, in the retelling, an event with no veil at all. The first stories about how Joseph received his authority show that, like other prophets and religious founders throughout history, he and Oliver first received their callings in a metaphysical way. Within a few years, their accounts became more impressive, unique, and physical.

Appendix

A statement that Joseph Smith reportedly made on 18 December 1833 exists only in Oliver Cowdery's entry in the 1835 Book of Patriarchal Blessings. It reads:

> These blessings shall come upon him [Cowdery] according to the blessings of the prophecy of Joseph [of Egypt], in ancient days, ... [and Cowdery] should be ordained with him [Smith], by the hand of the angel in the bush, unto the lesser priesthood, and after receive the holy priesthood under the hands of those who had been held in reserve for a long season; even those who received it under the hand of the Messiah ...[41]

---

angel appointed him to be the successor. Strang first said that this angel metaphysically granted him authority, then later said it ordained him by the laying on of hands. This embellishment led Reuben Miller, a stake president in Strang's church, to disillusionment. Miller converted to Mormonism in 1843 and was apparently unaware of Joseph's similar priesthood development. Richard L. Anderson, "Reuben Miller: Recorder of Oliver Cowdery's Reaffirmations," *BYU Studies* 8 (Spring 1968): 280-85.

41. The Book of Patriarchal Blessings 1:8-9, LDS archives; qtd. in Vogel, *Early Mormon Documents*, 2:454.

There are researchers who consider this to be the earliest statement of literal priesthood bestowal.[42] I find it unconvincing. On 18 December 1833 Joseph gave blessings to Oliver Cowdery and four members of the Smith family—Hyrum, Samuel, William, and Joseph Sr.—all of which were recorded on that date in Joseph's personal diary.[43] Twenty-one months later Oliver began copying these blessings into the first volume of the Book of Patriarchal Blessings.[44] A comparison indicates that Oliver liberally added to and deleted from the original blessings.[45]

For example, some sentences from Joseph's 1833 record are found scattered throughout the rewritten secondary version. In addition, some of the expansions contain motifs that derive from 1834-35 rather than from an earlier setting. The words "the church of the Latter Day Saints" are added; this was the name of the church between May 1834 and April 1838. The 1835 version of Joseph Sr.'s blessing says, "[H]e shall be called a prince over his posterity; holding the keys of the patriarchal priesthood over the kingdom of God on earth, even the church of the Latter Day Saints." This sentence is not in the diary. Furthermore, this and other references to "patriarchal priesthood" do not appear in the diary. The concept of a patriarchal priesthood

---

42. Gregory A. Prince, *Power from on High: The Development of Mormon Priesthood* (Salt Lake City: Signature Books, 1995), 8-9n24. Prince believes that this document has "integrity," meaning that it is a valid copy of the original blessing. See also Bruce R. McConkie, comp., *Doctrines of Salvation: Sermons and Writings of Joseph Fielding Smith* (Salt Lake City: Bookcraft, 1956), 3:101.

43. Jessee, *The Papers of Joseph Smith*, 2:15-17.

44. The Book of Patriarchal Blessings 1, LDS archives.

45. Scott H. Faulring, ed., *An American Prophet's Record: The Diaries and Journals of Joseph Smith* (Salt Lake City: Signature Books in association with Smith Research Associates, 1987), 19n8. Faulring writes: "In September 1835, Oliver Cowdery recorded Joseph Smith's blessings to members of his immediate family into what would become the first volume, 8-20, of the Patriarchal Blessing Books, located in the archives of the Historical Department, Church of Jesus Christ of Latter-day Saints. In so doing, however, Cowdery greatly expanded the blessings beyond their contents as initially recorded."

comes from Joseph's attention to the Egyptian papyri scrolls and the resulting stories of Old Testament patriarchs Joseph and Abraham in July 1835.[46] These ideas would have occupied Cowdery's mind in 1835 as well.

The diary version of William's blessing says: "[N]otwithstanding his rebellious heart ..." This phrase was deleted from the 1835 transcript probably because William had been ordained to be one of the twelve apostles in February. In Oliver's own blessing, the following words appear: "[N]evertheless there are two evils in him that he must needs forsake or he cannot altogeth[er] escape the buffitings of the adver[sar]y ..." Again, this is deleted.

Cowdery also added a preface to the blessings for his 1835 transcript, including the following:

> [W]e diligently sought for the right of the fathers, and the authority of the holy priesthood, and the power to administer in the same; for we desired to be, followers of righteousness, and the possessors of greater knowledge, even the knowledge of the mysteries of the kingdom of God. [These phrases became part of Abraham 1:2 in 1835.] Therefore we repaired to the woods, even as our father Joseph [of Egypt] said we should, that is, to the bush ... [T]he angel came down and bestowed upon us this priesthood.[47]

The similarities between this and the alleged 1833 statement are striking. I conclude that the 1833 statement, recorded by Cowdery in 1835 and cited as an early reference to the bestowal of priesthood by angels, has too many anachronisms to support this idea. The view of a literal, physical laying on of hands by angels is just one more of the many anachronisms in this document.

---

46. *History of the Church,* 2:235-36.

47. The Book of Patriarchal Blessings, 1:9-10, LDS archives; qtd. in Vogel, *Early Mormon Documents,* 2:452-53.

8.

The First Vision

The Book of Commandments, the earliest published compilation of Joseph Smith's revelations, contains nothing on such important events as Joseph's first vision, how the Book of Mormon came forth, the restoration of priesthood, or accounts by the witnesses to the Book of Mormon.[1] As with the priesthood restoration accounts, current LDS interpretations of Joseph's first vision simplify and retrofit later accounts to provide a seemingly authoritative, unambiguous recital.[2]

The earliest allusion, oral or written, to the first vision is the brief mention that was transcribed in June 1830 and originally printed in the Book of Commandments (24:6/D&C 20:5). The passage states that Joseph "had received a remission of his sins." Nothing is said

---

1. Book of Commandments (1833; hereafter BofC), in Wilford C. Wood, *Joseph Smith Begins His Work: The Book of Commandments*, 2 vols. (Salt Lake City: by the Author, 1962), vol. 2.

2. For the development of the first vision and its authoritative instructions to Joseph Smith, see James B. Allen, "The Significance of Joseph Smith's 'First Vision' in Mormon Thought," *Dialogue: A Journal of Mormon Thought* 1 (Autumn 1966): 29-45; rpt. in *The New Mormon History: Revisionist Essays on the Past*, ed. D. Michael Quinn (Salt Lake City: Signature Books, 1992), 37-52.

about a vision, but the later recital quoted below reveals that in his vision he received forgiveness of sins. The 1832 account (below) is the earliest explicit mention of a vision. The wording and themes and the experience itself are similar to other conversion epiphanies of the era. Joseph wrote in his own hand:

> At about the age of twelve years my mind become seriously imprest with regard to the all importent concerns for the wellfare of my immortal Soul which led me to searching the scriptures believeing as I was taught, that they contained the word of God[. T]hus applying myself to them[,] and my intimate acquaintance with those of different denominations[,] led me to marvel excedingly for I discovered that they [congregants] did not of[ten] adorn their profession by a holy walk and Godly conversation agreeable to what I found contained in that sacred depository[. T]his was a grief to my Soul[. T]hus from the age of twelve years to fifteen I pondered many things in my heart concerning the situation of the world of mankind[,] the contentions and divi[si]ons[,] the wicke[d]ness and abominations and the darkness which pervaded the minds of mankind[. M]y mind become excedingly distressed for I become convicted of my sins and by searching the scriptures I found that mankind did not come unto the Lord but that they had apostatised from the true and liveing faith and there was no society or denomination that built upon the gospel of Jesus Christ as recorded in the new testament and I felt to mourn for my own sins and for the sins of the world ... [T]herefore I cried unto the Lord for mercy for there was none else to whom I could go and obtain mercy[,] and the Lord heard my cry in the wilderness and while in the attitude of calling upon the Lord in the 16th year of my age a piller of light above the brightness of the sun at noon day come down from above and rested upon me and I was filled with the spirit of god and the Lord opened the heavens upon me and I saw the Lord and he spake unto me saying Joseph my son thy sins are forgiven thee. [G]o thy way[,] walk in my statutes and keep my commandments[;] behold I am the Lord of glory[,] I was crucifyed for the world that all those who believe on my name may have Eternal life[;] behold the world lieth in sin at this time and none doeth good no not one[;] they have turned aside from the gospel and keep not my com-

Fig. 52. Path leading from the Smith home to the traditional sacred grove in Manchester, New York. Photograph by George E. Anderson, 1907.

mandments[;] they draw near to me with their lips while their hearts are far from me[,] and mine anger is kindling against the inhabitants of the earth to visit them acording to th[e]ir ungodliness and to bring to pass that which hath been spoken by the mouth of the prophets and Ap[o]stles[;] behold and lo I come quickly[,] as it is written of me[,] in the cloud clothed in the glory of my Father[. A]nd my soul was filled with love and for many days I could rejoice with great Joy and the Lord was with me[,] but [I] could find none that would believe the hevnly vision[. N]evertheless I pondered these things in my heart ...[3] (figs. 52-53).

Typically, such youthful conversion visions did not result in a permanent change of behavior. In Joseph's case, he noted in his 1830 and 1832 statements that he became "entangled again in the vanities of

---

3. Dean C. Jessee, ed., *The Papers of Joseph Smith: Autobiographical and Historical Writings*, 2+ vols. (Salt Lake City: Deseret Book Co., 1989-), 1:5-7.

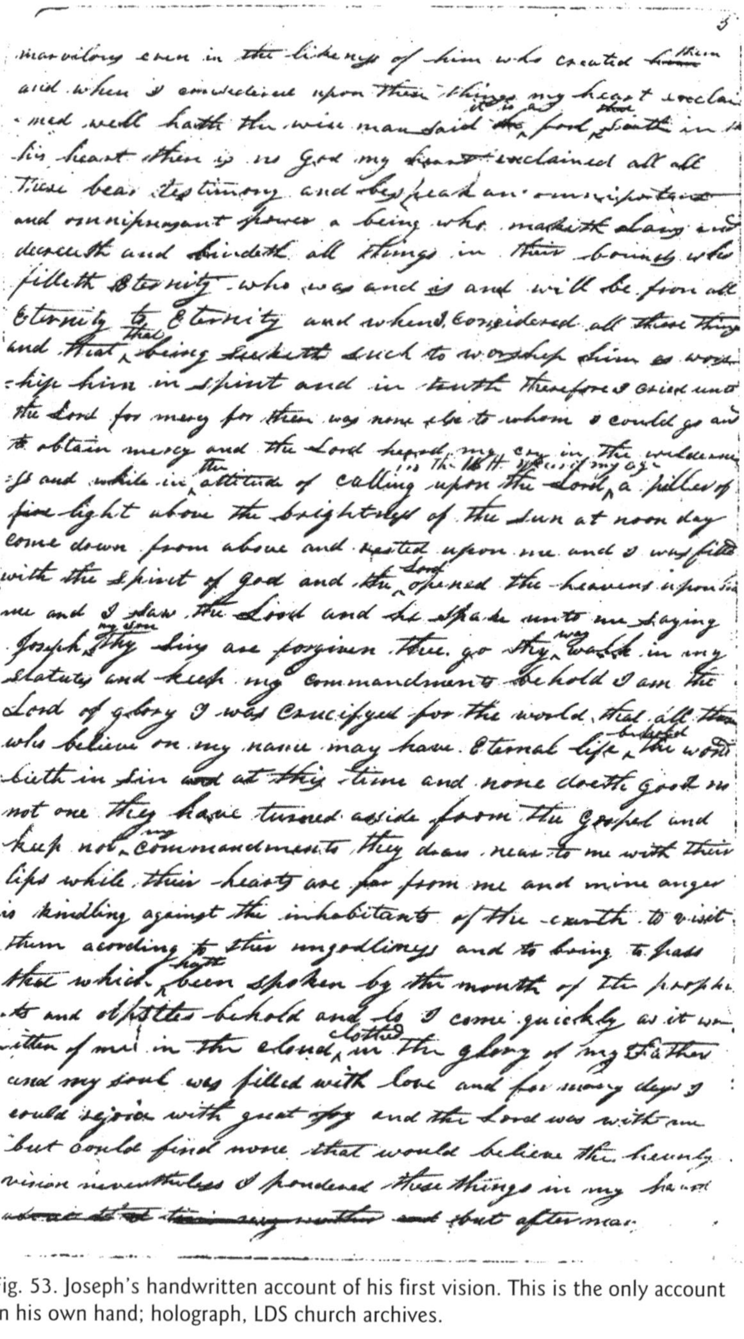

3

marvilous even in the likeness of him who created ~~him~~ them
and when I considered upon these things my heart exclai
-med well hath the wise man said ~~the~~ it is a fool that saith in his
his heart there is no God my ~~heart~~ exclaimed all all
these bear testimony and bespeak an omnipotant
and omnipreasant power a being who makith Laws and
decreeth and bindeth all things in their bounds who
filleth Eternity who was and is and will be from all
Eternity to Eternity and when I considered all these things
and that being seeketh such to worship him as wor
-ship him in spirit and in truth therefore I cried unto
the Lord for mercy for there was none else to whom I could go and
to obtain mercy and the Lord heard my cry in the wilderne
-ss and while in the attitude of calling upon the Lord in the 16th year of my age a piller of
fire light above the brightness of the sun at noon day
come down from above and rested upon me and I was filled
with the spirit of god and the Lord opened the heavens upon
me and I saw the Lord and he spake unto me saying
Joseph my son thy sins are forgiven thee. go thy way walk in my
statutes and keep my commandments behold I am the
Lord of glory I was crucifyed for the world that all those
who believe on my name may have Eternal life behold the world
lieth in sin ~~and~~ at this time and none doeth good no
not one they have turned asside from the gospel and
keep not my commandments they draw near to me with their
lips while their hearts are far from me and mine anger
is kindling against the inhabitants of the earth to visit
them acording to thir ungodliness and to bring to pass
that which hath been spoken by the mouth of the prophe
-ts and Apstles behold and lo I come quickly as it wa
-written of me in the cloud clothed in the glory of my Father
and my soul was filled with love and for many days I
could rejoice with great Joy and the Lord was with me
but could find none that would believe the hevnly
vision nevertheless I pondered these things in my heart
~~about that time my mother and~~ but after man

Fig. 53. Joseph's handwritten account of his first vision. This is the only account in his own hand; holograph, LDS church archives.

the world" and "after many days I fell into transgressions and sinned in many things which brought a wound upon my soul."[4]

The Book of Commandments emphasizes that it was the Book of Mormon—not the first vision known to the church today—that constituted Joseph's "call ... to his holy work" (24:7-11/D&C 20:6-11). Consistent with this passage are Joseph's 1832 and Oliver Cowdery's 1835 reports that cite an angel, later identified as Moroni, who called Joseph to the work, rather than Jesus in the first vision.[5] Those entering the Protestant ministry frequently mention that they experienced a vision in their youth that was God's first sign that they were called to his work.[6] It is clear from Joseph's 1830 and 1832 statements that, like his evangelical Protestant contemporaries, he too looked upon forgiveness of his sins ("receiving the testamony from on high") as the "firstly" step toward becoming a true disciple and contributing to his future ministry and "the rise of the church of Christ in the eve of time." He viewed his epiphany in evangelical Protestant fashion until he dictated his 1838 narrative.

------

4. BofC 24:6/D&C 20:5; Jessee, *Papers of Joseph Smith*, 1:7.

5. Oliver Cowdery, "Letter IV," *Latter Day Saints' Messenger and Advocate* 1 (Feb. 1835): 78-79; qtd. in *Early Mormon Documents*, ed. Dan Vogel, 3+ vols. (Salt Lake City: Signature Books, 1996-), 2:427-29.

6. Neal E. Lambert and Richard H. Cracroft, "Literary Form and Historical Understanding: Joseph Smith's First Vision," *Journal of Mormon History* 7 (1980): 33-35. I have examined the originals of the following accounts: *Memoirs of the Life and Travels of B. Hibbard* (New York: J. C. Totten, 1825), 21-26; Abel Thornton, *The Life of Elder Abel Thornton* (Providence, RI: J. B. Yerrington, 1828), 14-23; Minton Thrift, *Memoir of the Rev. Jesse Lee* (New York: Myers & Smith, 1823), 6-7, 15-17; Lorenzo Dow, *The Dealings of God, Man, and the Devil: As Exemplified in the Life, Experience, and Travels of Lorenzo Dow* (Norwich, CT: Wm. Faulkner, 1833), 9-17; H. Harvey, *A Discourse on the Life and Character of Rev. Alfred Bennett* (Homer, NY: Rufus A. Reed, 1851), 3-16; Ray Potter, *Memoirs of the Life and Religious Experience of Ray Potter* (Providence: H. H. Brown, 1829), 112-24; Eleazer Sherman, *The Narrative of Eleazer Sherman* (Providence: H. H. Brown, 1830), 1:1-21; Benjamin Putnam, *Sketch of the Life of Elder Benj. Putnam* (Woodstock, VT: David Watson, 1821), 14-21; and Eleazer Sherman, *A Discourse, Addressed to Christians of All Denominations* (Providence: H. H. Brown, 1829), 3-13.

We might expect that after the church's organization in early 1830, Joseph would cite the first vision as the source of his call since it came directly from Jesus Christ. He does not. Even in his 1832 and 1835 narratives, he does not yet mention the appearance of God the Father, his divine commission to open the last dispensation, or his appointment as the prophet of the Restoration.[7] These omissions are peculiar. In 1832 Joseph is privately chronicling his experiences in his own journal. After twelve years of reflection, to then omit the role his 1820 vision played in the Restoration—to see it as a personal conversion rather than as the beginning of a new dispensation—suggests that when he rewrote his history in 1838, he reinterpreted his experience to satisfy institutional needs.

The 1838 version adds an impressive setting and context by combining his 1820 epiphany with a major religious revival. These extended revivals caused "unusual excitement," and he "often" attended them and almost joined the Methodists, he wrote. "Great multitudes," including his mother and others in his family, joined various churches (JS—History 1:5-9). These facts best fit the 1824-25 local history rather than an 1820 setting.[8] Lucy mentioned that her participation in the revival came after Alvin's death in November 1823. She joined the Presbyterians, hoping for solace.[9] Her reason is plausible.

---

7. During 1820-34 when Joseph Smith still saw the godhead as one, only one God appears in his first vision (1832 account). From 1835 on, when he came to see two separate personages in the godhead, two personages appear (1835 and 1838 accounts). For Joseph's changing view of deity, see Boyd Kirkland, "The Development of the Mormon Doctrine of God," in *Line upon Line: Essays on Mormon Doctrine,* ed. Gary James Bergera (Salt Lake City: Signature Books, 1989), 35-52; and Dan Vogel, "The Earliest Mormon Concept of God," *Line upon Line,* 17-33; Melodie Moench Charles, "Book of Mormon Christology," in *New Approaches to the Book of Mormon: Explorations in Critical Methodology,* ed. Brent Lee Metcalfe (Salt Lake City: Signature Books, 1993), 81-114.

8. Marvin S. Hill, "The First Vision Controversy: A Critique and Reconciliation," *Dialogue* 15 (Summer 1982): 37-39; Wesley P. Walters, "New Light on Mormon Origins from the Palmyra [NY] Revival," *Dialogue* 4 (Spring 1969): 60-67.

9. Hill, "First Vision Controversy," 39. For Hyrum joining the Presby-

William Smith noted that his mother and family "belong[ed] to the Presbyterian Church, of whome the Rev. Mr Stoc[k]ton was the Presiding Pastor or Shepard."[10] Presbyterian records confirm that Benjamin B. Stockton was the pastor of the Palmyra Presbyterian Church from mid-February 1824 to September 1827 and that he participated in the very successful revivals of 1824-25.[11] The records report that 103 persons joined the Palmyra church in 1824-25, while only fourteen converted in 1820-21.[12]

Palmyra Baptist Church records for 1818-25 reveal that the only conference year to show significant growth was September 1824 to September 1825, during which membership increased from 132 to 219. No other conference year between 1818-25 had an increase of more than a dozen convert baptisms.[13]

William Smith said in 1841 that "about the year 1823, there was a revival of religion in that region, and Joseph was one of several

---

terian church in 1824-25, see E. D. Howe, *Mormonism Unvailed* (Painesville OH: by the Author, 1834), 241; qtd. in Vogel, *Early Mormon Documents*, 2:66.

10. Hill, "First Vision Controversy," 45n48; see also William Smith, "Notes Written on 'Chamber's Life of Joseph Smith' by William Smith," typescript, 18, archives, Historical Department, Church of Jesus Christ of Latter-day Saints, Salt Lake City, Utah (hereafter LDS archives); qtd. in Vogel, *Early Mormon Documents*, 1:487.

11. For Rev. Stockton's installation, see the *Wayne Sentinel* (Palmyra, NY), 18, 25 Feb. 1824; for his release, see Geneva Presbytery, "Records," 18 Sept. 1827 (C:252-54; D:83-5), Presbyterian Historical Society, Philadelphia; for "a large number" of conversions during his tenure, see James H. Hotchkin, *A History of the Purchase and Settlement of Western New York, and the Rise, Progress, and Present State of the Presbyterian Church in That Section* (New York: M. W. Dodd, 1848), 378.

12. "Presbyterial Reports to the Synod of Geneva, 1812-1828," 89 (22 March 1821), 116 (23 Sept. 1825), Presbyterian Historical Society, Philadelphia.

13. For Palmyra Baptist records, see "The First Baptized [sic] Church in Palmyra," 1818-25; and membership figures, *Minutes of the Ontario Baptist Association* (Rochester, NY: Everard Peck, 1825), 5 (28 Sept. 1825), both at the American Baptist Historical Society, Rochester, New York.

hopeful converts."[14] Oliver Cowdery said the revival that impacted Joseph and his family came in about "the year 1823." He explained: "Mr. Lane, a presiding Elder of the Methodist church, visited Palmyra and vicinity ... Large additions were made to the Methodist, Presbyterian, and Baptist churches ... [F]rom his discourses on the scriptures, and in common with others, our brother's [Joseph's] mind became awakened."[15]

Methodist church records confirm that the Reverend George Lane (fig. 22) presided over the New York, Ontario, district from July 1824 to January 1825.[16] Shortly after Lane's release, he composed a letter, published in the April 1825 issue of the *Methodist Magazine*, reporting his observations for the Ontario district for 1824-25. He wrote:

> In Palmyra ... the work commenced in the spring, and progressed moderately until the time of the quarterly meeting, which was held on the 25th and 26th of September. About this time it appeared to break out afresh ... [on] December 11th and 12th ... I found that the work, which had for some time been going on in Palmyra, had broken out from the village like a mighty flame, and was spreading in every direction. When I left the place, December 22nd, there had, in

---

14. William Smith, interview by James Murdock (Murdock read back his notes to William for correction), 18 April 1841, *The Congregational Observer* (Hartford and New Haven, CT), 3 July 1841, 1; original publication at the Connecticut State Historical Society, Hartford; rpt. in the *Peoria Register and North-Western Gazetteer*, 3 Sept. 1841; qtd. in Vogel, *Early Mormon Documents*, 1:478; William Smith, *William Smith on Mormonism* (Lamoni, IA: Herald Steam Book and Job Office, 1883), 6; *Saints' Herald*, 16 June 1883, 338; qtd. in Vogel, *Early Mormon Documents*, 1:494.

15. Oliver Cowdery, "Letter III," *Messenger and Advocate* 1 (Dec. 1834): 42; Oliver Cowdery, "Letter IV," 1 (Feb. 1835): 78; qtd. in Vogel, *Early Mormon Documents*, 2:424, 427.

16. He was installed in July 1824 and released in January 1825, *Minutes of the Annual Conferences of the Methodist Episcopal Church 1773-1828*, (1840), 1:337, 352, 373, 392, 418, 446, 470.

the village and its vicinity, upward of one hundred and fifty joined the society, besides a number [who] had joined other churches ...[17]

According to Methodist records, 208 persons joined in the Ontario district, including Palmyra, in 1824-25, while there was a loss of membership in 1820-21 totaling 81 members.[18] Notice the similarity of Reverend Lane's and Joseph Smith's descriptions of this 1824-25 revival that commenced "in the spring" (cf. JS—History 1:14) with the Methodists in the Palmyra area, then spread throughout the region, converting "great multitudes." Joseph said of the extended revival in his 1838 description:

> Some time in the second year after our removal to Manchester, [they moved from Palmyra township in 1822][19] there was in the place where we lived an unusual excitement on the subject of religion. It commenced with the Methodists, but soon became general among all the sects [Baptists and Presbyterians] in that region of country ... and great multitudes united themselves to the different religious parties (JS—History 1:5).

Oliver Cowdery's 1835 account mentions that the extended revival began "in Palmyra and vicinity."[20] Lucy elaborated: "About this time [1824] their was a great revival in religion and the whole neighborhood was very much aroused to the subject and we among the rest flocked to the meeting house."[21] Palmyra's newspaper, the *Wayne*

---

17. George Lane, "Letter from Rev. George Lane," 25 Jan. 1825, *Methodist Magazine* 8 (Apr. 1825): 159-61.

18. *Minutes of the Annual Conferences,* 1824 report: 466; 1825 report: 471; 1819 report: 330; 1820 report: 345; 1821 report: 366. The records of the Palmyra Methodist Church were destroyed in a fire at Rochester, New York, in 1933.

19. H. Michael Marquardt and Wesley P. Walters, *Inventing Mormonism: Tradition and the Historical Record* (San Francisco: Smith Research Associates, 1994), 1-8.

20. Oliver Cowdery, "Letter IV," *Messenger and Advocate* 1 (Feb. 1835): 78; qtd. in Vogel, *Early Mormon Documents,* 2:427.

21. Lucy Mack Smith, Preliminary Manuscript, 1844-45, qtd. in Vogel, *Early Mormon Documents,* 1:306. This sentence was later lined out.

Sentinel, reported the religious fervor in 1824-25.[22] It was also commonplace for religious periodicals to report on revivals. Accordingly, fifteen accounts of this 1824-25 revival have been found. There is not a single reference to a Palmyra revival between 1818 and 1821 in any of the major religious periodicals.[23]

Furthermore, it is unlikely that Lucy would have joined the Presbyterians in 1820 and then again in 1824-25. Nor is it likely that the Reverends Stockton and Lane would have worked together in the same area twice or that the Methodists, Presbyterians, and Baptists would have twice sponsored a joint revival that began in harmony and ended in turmoil and bitter sectarian strife. All of these factors indicate that Joseph's 1832 narrative is more accurate than the 1838 version in not identifying a revival preceding his forgiveness epiphany. His experience may have occurred in 1820, but the revival that the Smiths participated in occurred in 1824–25. Joseph appears to have combined these two incidents into his 1838 version. Brigham Young University professor Marvin S. Hill concurs that the revival occurred in 1824 rather than 1820.[24]

Two important questions arise from Joseph's 1838 and 1842 descriptions of his first vision that go beyond forgiveness of sins: First, was Joseph Smith "called of God" in the 1820 vision by Jesus Christ himself to restore "the fullness of the gospel"?[25] Second, what was his purpose in praying, to which the answer in 1838 was that the churches "were all wrong"? (JS—History 1:18-19, 26, 28). I will try to determine the most reasonable answers to these two important questions.

In 1838 Joseph's memory was that he was the recipient of "se-

---

22. "Communication," *Wayne Sentinel,* 15 Sept. 1824, 3; "Religious," 2 Mar. 1825, 3-4.

23. See Marquardt and Walters, *Inventing Mormonism,* 19, 36nn12, 13.

24. Hill, "First Vision Controversy," 40. Wesley P. Walters was the first to publicly question the 1820 revival date. See Walters, "New Light on Mormon Origins from Palmyra (N.Y.) Revival," *Bulletin of the Evangelical Theological Society* 10 (Fall 1967): 227-44.

25. JS—History 1:28; Jessee, *Papers of Joseph Smith,* 1:430.

vere" persecution for having talked about his 1820 vision. This is in-accurate, according to the historical record. The persecution came from talking about treasure digging and later, in 1827, about the golden plates. There is no evidence of prejudice resulting from his first vision. If his report that "all the sects ... united to persecute me" were accurate, one would expect to find some hint of this in the local newspapers, narratives by ardent critics, and in the affidavits D. P. Hurlbut gathered in 1833. The record is nevertheless silent on this is-sue. No one, friend or foe, in New York or Pennsylvania remembers either that there was "great persecution" or even that Joseph claimed to have had a vision. Not even his family remembers it.[26] It is likely that the vision was unremarkably similar to many other epiphanies of that era and no one took notice of it.

Neither Joseph nor anyone else prior to 1838 referred to the vi-sion as the source of his authority to act as God's agent of the Resto-ration. Ironically, it is during a later time of persecution in 1838, when some church leaders begin doubting his mission as a prophet, that it became important to connect his prophetic call to this vision.[27] He appears to have shifted his call from 1823 to 1820 because of the prominent apostasies over the Book of Mormon at the time.

A leadership crisis began in Kirtland on 7 November 1837. Fred-erick G. Williams, a counselor in the First Presidency, left the church.[28]

---

26. James B. Allen, "Emergence of a Fundamental: The Expanding Role of Joseph Smith's First Vision in Mormon Thought," *Journal of Mormon History* 7 (1980): 43-45; Hill, "First Vision Controversy," 31-32; JS—His-tory 1:22.

27. William I. Appleby, Biography and Journal, 30-31, LDS archives; qtd. in Vogel, *Early Mormon Documents*, 1:145-47. Although Joseph's April 1838 account was not published until 1842, it was being preached prior to publication. Appleby and a "large congregation" heard Orson Pratt relate the 1838 first vision story in September 1838 at a New Jersey school where Appleby taught. David J. Whittaker, "East of Nauvoo: Benjamin Winchester and the Early Mormon Church," *Journal of Mormon History* 21 (Fall 1995): 36n17.

28. Joseph Fielding Smith, *Essentials in Church History* (Salt Lake City: Deseret Book Co., 1966), 204, 689.

During the last week of December 1837, Martin Harris, one of the three witnesses, was excommunicated.[29] On 10 March 1838, John Whitmer, one of the eight witnesses to the Book of Mormon, was excommunicated.[30] On 25 March, Martin Harris told a public meeting that none of the witnesses had physically seen or handled the plates, that they had not seen the plates with their "natural eyes."[31] His testimony triggered a discussion led by Warren Parrish. As a result, Apostles John F. Boynton, Luke Johnson, and other church members "renounced the Book of Mormon."[32] George A. Smith attended this last meeting and wrote on 30 March: "Last Sabbath a division arose among the Parrish party about the Book of Mormon. John Boyington, W. Parrish, Luke Johnson and others, said it was nonsense."[33] Smith further recalled that about "thirty ... prominent Elders" belonging to the Parrish group, including Apostles Lyman Johnson, William Mc-Lellin, and others "renounce[d] the Book of Mormon and Joseph Smith."[34] The president of the Quorum of Twelve, Thomas B. Marsh, wrote of this meeting: "We have of late learned, that Parrish, and most of this combination have openly renounced the Book of Mormon, and become deists."[35] Abigail Holmes added that Apostle Boyington, who had "testified in my house before many witnesses that Jo-

---

29. Richard L. Anderson, *Investigating the Book of Mormon Witnesses* (Salt Lake City: Deseret Book Co., 1981), 110.

30. Ibid., 127.

31. Stephen Burnett to Lyman E. Johnson, 15 April 1838, Joseph Smith Letterbook, 2:64-66, LDS archives, qtd. in Vogel, *Early Mormon Documents*, 2:291. See also Warren Parrish to E. Holmes, 11 Aug. 1838, in *The Evangelist* (Carthage, OH), 1 Oct. 1838, 226.

32. Burnett to Johnson, 15 April 1838.

33. George A. Smith to Josiah Flemming, 30 March 1838, Kirtland Ohio, Journal History of the Church, LDS archives. George A. Smith became an apostle in April 1839. Burnett's letter to Johnson, 15 April 1838, confirms that Apostles Luke Johnson and John Boynton spoke at this meeting.

34. George A. Smith, 10 Jan. 1858, *Journal of Discourses,* 26 vols. (London and Liverpool: LDS Booksellers Depot, 1854-86), 7:115.

35. Thomas B. Marsh to Wilford Woodruff, *Elders Journal* (Far West, MO), 3 May 1838, 37.

seph Smith was a prophet of the most High God[,] had said within a few weeks in my neighbourhood that Mormonism is all a humbug from first to last."[36]

By 7 April when a church conference was held at Far West, Missouri, under Joseph's direction, five apostles were said to be out of harmony with the church. The conference minutes read:

> Pursuant to adjournment the conference convened, and opened by prayer by [Apostle] D. W. Patten who also made a few remarks respecting the twelve apostles. He spake of T. B. Marsh, Brigham Young, Orson Hyde, H. C. Kimball, P. P. Pratt, and O. Pratt, as being men of God, whom he could recommend with cheerful confidence. He spake somewhat doubtful of William Smith from something which he had heard respecting his faith in the work. He also spake of William E. McLellin, Luke Johnson, Lyman Johnson, and John F. Boynton as being men whom he could not recommend to the conference.[37]

On 13 April, Apostles Luke S. Johnson, Lyman E. Johnson, and John F. Boynton were excommunicated or left the church.[38] McLellin followed shortly thereafter.[39] They were the first four apostles to leave, and three of them—John Boynton and the Johnson brothers—

---

36. Abigail D. Holmes to James J. Strang, 6 Oct. 1850, James Jesse Strang Collection, MS 447/2:f 42, General Correspondence #390, Beinecke Library, Yale University, New Haven, Connecticut.

37. Joseph Smith Jr., Conference Minutes, *Elders Journal* 1 (July 1838), 47; also Donald Q. Cannon and Lyndon W. Cook, eds., *Far West Record: Minutes of The Church of Jesus Christ of Latter-day Saints, 1830-1844* (Salt Lake City: Deseret Book Co., 1983), 160, 161n3.

38. Smith, *Essentials in Church History*, 694-95, has John F. Boynton excommunicated on 1 January 1838 at Kirtland. Perhaps he was excommunicated twice. Luke Johnson rejoined the church in 1846. Patten would have known of Boynton's excommunication through Joseph Smith, who arrived in Far West on 12 January. Moreover, Joseph presided at the Far West conferences. On 7 April Boynton is still a member of the Twelve but out of favor. See Joseph Smith Jr., Conference Minutes, *Elders Journal* 1 (July 1838), 47, for Joseph's presence at these meetings.

39. Jessee, *The Papers of Joseph Smith*, 2:240-41.

no longer believed in the divinity of the Book of Mormon. Oliver Cowdery and David Whitmer were also excommunicated on 12-13 April, and Hiram Page and Jacob Whitmer left the church as well.[40] By the fall of 1838, Apostles Thomas B. Marsh and Orson Hyde had defected.[41] According to Dean C. Jessee, "During this time of apostasy, approximately three hundred left the Church, representing about 15 percent of the Kirtland membership."[42] Economic disillusionment over the failure of the Kirtland Anti-Safety Society may have fueled the dissent, but doctrinal disillusionment stemming from Harris's statements and the subsequent debate over the Book of Mormon continued to smolder long afterwards.

Within a month of Harris's comments, three of the apostles no longer believed in the Book of Mormon and two more were out of favor with the church (fig. 54). All three witnesses to the Book of Mormon and three of the eight had defected. The entire Whitmer clan had left the church.[43] All this must have caused considerable anxiety and cognitive dissonance within the community.

Fearing the possible unraveling of the church, Joseph Smith took to reestablishing his authority. During this week of 7-13 April, he contemplated rewriting his history.[44] On April 26 he renamed the church. The next day he started dictating a new first vision narrative.[45] He began by attacking those who were circulating unsavory "reports" regarding "the rise and progress of the Church" (see figs. 55-56), then told a revised and more impressive version of his epiphany

---

40. Anderson, *Investigating*, 39, 69, 127. Whitmer and Page left the church shortly after the April 1838 church trials.

41. Lyndon W. Cook, *The Revelations of the Prophet Joseph Smith* (Salt Lake City: Deseret Book Co,, 1985), 43 (Thomas B. Marsh), 110 (Orson Hyde).

42. Jessee, *Papers of Joseph Smith*, 2:217n2.

43. Anderson, *Investigating*, 127. Christian and Peter Whitmer Jr. died in 1835 and 1836, respectively; the three members of the Smith family remained loyal.

44. Jessee, *Papers of Joseph Smith*, 2:226-27.

45. D&C 115:3-4; ibid., 232-33.

Brigham Young   Heber C. Kimball   Orson Hyde

William E. McLellin   Parley P. Pratt   Luke S. Johnson

William Smith   Orson Pratt   John F. Boynton

Fig. 54. The original twelve apostles of the LDS church were ordained in February 1835. Photographs unavailable for Lyman E. Johnson, Thomas B. Marsh, and David W. Patten.

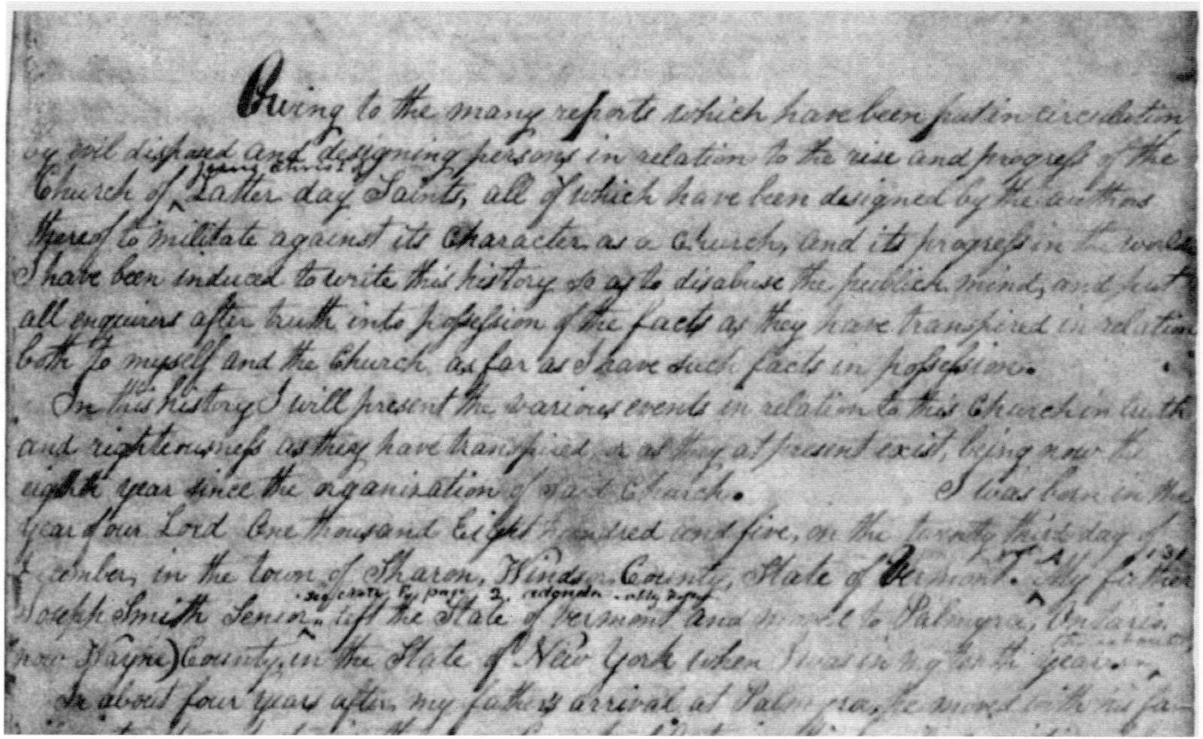

Fig. 55. Joseph Smith's history, A-1, p. 1, in the handwriting of James Mullholland; holograph, LDS church archives.

Fig. 56. Joseph Smith Jr.,
artist and date unknown;
original in Community of Christ
(RLDS) Library-Archives.

(JS—History 1:1). He announced that his initial calling had not come from an angel in 1823, as he had said for over a decade, but from God the Father and Jesus Christ in 1820 (JS—History 1:19, 28). This earlier date established his mission independent of the troubling questions and former witnesses associated with the Book of Mormon. Like the 1834-35 priesthood restoration recitals, the first vision version of April 1838 added significant material that bolstered his authority during a time of crisis.

The second question centers on Joseph's purpose in seeking the Lord in 1820. His motive for prayer differs between 1832 and 1838. What is the historical evidence regarding these differences?

Like his parents, Joseph concluded prior to 1820 that none of the churches was right.[46] He wrote in his 1832 account: "[B]y searching the scriptures I found that mankind ... had apostatized from the true

---

46. Lucy Mack Smith, *History of Joseph Smith by His Mother, Lucy Mack Smith* (Salt Lake City: Bookcraft, 1958), 36, 46-48; see also Vogel, *Early Mormon Documents*, 1:242, 255-56.

and living faith and there was no society or denomination that built upon the gospel of Jesus Christ as recorded in the new testament and I felt to mourn for my own sins and for the sins of the world."[47] In 1832 he was clearly motivated by sorrow for wrongdoing and for the fallen state of humankind. "[T]herefore I cried unto the Lord for mercy," he wrote. In this version, he knows that the pure gospel is not on the earth and therefore does not ask which church is right; rather, his concern is for the world's corruption and for his own sins. When Jesus speaks, it is to this very concern: "Thy sins are forgiven thee," is the message. He does not mention concern for doctrinal corruption. As a result, there is no injunction against joining a church.

During the leadership crisis of April 1838, Joseph remembered a different purpose in going to pray. There is nothing about forgiveness of sins. His prayer occurs within the context of a major revival. Motivated by this setting, he now says, "My object in going to enquire of the Lord was to know which of all the sects was right." While it was unnecessary to even ask this question in his 1832 report, in 1838 the matter of importance was apostasy from the only true church. In this later version, the Lord instructs him to "join none of them, for they were all wrong ... [A]ll their Creeds were an abomination in his sight." He repeats, "I was expressly commanded to 'go not after them.'"[48]

The Smiths' religiosity after 1820 is consistent with the 1832 version. First, Joseph was involved with a Methodist class in Palmyra as an exhorter.[49] Second, he reported that he "often" participated in the

---

47. Jessee, *Papers of Joseph Smith*, 1:5-6. However, by 1838 Joseph Smith would say that before his 1820 prayer, "it had never entered into my heart that all were wrong" (JS—History 1:18).

48. JS—History 1:18-20, 28; Jessee, *Papers of Joseph Smith*, 1:272-73, 430.

49. For Joseph Smith's early Methodist religious activity, see O[rsamus]. Turner, *History of the Pioneer Settlement of Phelps and Gorham's Purchase* (Rochester, NY: William Alling, 1851), 214; and Pomeroy Tucker, *The Origin, Rise, and Progress of Mormonism* (New York: D. Appleton & Co., 1867), 18; both qtd. in Vogel, *Early Mormon Documents*, 3:49-50, 94.

extended revival near his home in 1824-25. He said, "I attended their several meetings as often as occasion would permit, ... [becoming] partial to the Methodist sect, and I felt some desire to be united with them" (JS—History 1:8). During this revival Lucy, Hyrum, and other family members joined the Presbyterian church where they remained active until September 1828.[50] That same year, Joseph sought membership with the Methodists in Harmony, Pennsylvania.[51] He and his parents, while believing prior to 1820 that none of the churches was true, did not consider any unworthy to join. Had Lucy heard her son say that Jesus Christ personally instructed him "to go not after them" and to not "join any" church because "all" of the ministers, creeds, and churches "were an abomination in his sight," she and her several children certainly would not have joined the Presbyterians and worshiped with them from 1825 until 1828. Nor is it probable that Joseph would have participated with the Methodists between 1820-28.

The 1832 account describes Joseph's experience most accurately. His family's religious behavior supports the 1832 version, not the 1838 narrative. Joseph's 1832 description does not forbid him from joining a church, nor does it mention a revival or persecution. Instead, he became convicted of his sins from reading the scriptures and received forgiveness from the Savior in a personal epiphany. He stated that his call to God's work came in 1823 from an angel, later identified as Moroni. When a crisis developed around the Book of

---

50. Hill, "First Vision Controversy," 37-39, 45n48. For the family's withdrawal from the Presbyterian church in September 1828, see Milton V. Backman Jr., *Joseph Smith's First Vision: The First Vision in Its Historical Context* (Salt Lake City: Bookcraft, 1971), 182-83.

51. Joseph and Hiel Lewis, "Mormon History, A New Chapter about to be Published," *Amboy* [IL] *Journal*, 30 Apr. 1879, 1; "Review of Mormonism—Rejoinder to Elder Cadwell," *Amboy Journal*, 11 June 1879, 1; "A Word from Utah," *Amboy Journal*, 2 July 1879, 1. In these articles, Joseph Lewis, a cousin of Emma Hale Smith, reported that he and Joshua McKune, a local preacher, were present when Joseph joined the Methodist Episcopal class in Harmony, Pennsylvania, in the summer of 1828, and that it was Michael B. Morse, who married Emma's sister Trial, who accepted his request to join.

Mormon in early 1838, he conflated several events into one. Now he was called by God the Father and Jesus Christ in 1820 during an extended revival, was forbidden to join any existing church, and was greatly persecuted by institutions and individuals for sharing his vision of God. This version is not supported by the historical evidence.

It seems clear that the first vision narratives between 1832 and 1838 were expanded and became more miraculous, thus following the pattern discussed in the previous chapter with regard to priesthood restoration. Over time, spiritual events were retold in a way that was more literal, more physical, as if they occurred in the material rather than in a metaphysical realm. This may have been a function of selective memory on the one hand and, more particularly in Joseph Smith's case, a life lived as much in the invisible as in the temporal world. Like the priesthood restoration, Joseph's 1838 first vision account served an immediate, institutional purpose in consolidating his authority and quashing dissent. It happened during another time of crisis in the church. A controversy sometimes arises among church historians about whether an early or later account is the most reliable and valuable. Is it conceivably most accurate and perceptive if told immediately after an event or after a participant has had time to process what he or she experienced? In this case, where there are three evolving versions of the first vision, the earliest is the most accurate whether or not it is the most valuable.[52]

---

52. BYU professor William G. Hartley writes: "My experience with diaries and diarists convinces me that the later, reflective recollections sometimes are more important than comments recorded at the time of an event. It takes time to understand some things that are ongoing." This view is contrary to the traditional canons of historiography. Regarding Joseph Smith's narratives in particular, Hartley writes: "Joseph Smith's later perspectives on early events deserve as much trust as do his early statements. Only after years of experience and implementation was Joseph Smith able to say how priesthood offices and operations worked together or should work together realistically and functionally in a maturing church structure." William G. Hartley, review of *Power from on High: The Development of Mormon Priesthood* by Gregory A. Prince, in *BYU Studies* 37:1 (1997-98): 225-30.

Appendix

The Expanding Role of God and Christ in
Joseph Smith's Call to the Ministry

Joseph Smith wrote three accounts of the first vision in the 1830s—specifically in 1832, 1835, and 1838. In 1842 Joseph gave a fourth and final description of his vision in a letter to John Wentworth, editor of the *Chicago Democrat*. Joseph may have first alluded to this vision in the 1830 Articles and Covenants of the Church of Christ, published in the 1833 Book of Commandments. It is excerpted below. Under the second heading below are three examples from the Smith family of what their understanding was of the source of Joseph's calling. These examples are representative of what the general church membership knew, or did not know, about Joseph's vision. Next are portions of the 1832 and 1835 accounts under one heading, followed by samplings from the 1838 and 1842 accounts under another heading. These should give an idea of the evolution of the narratives.

"[H]e ... received [from Jesus] a remission of his sins ...
And [from an angel a] call ... to his holy work"
Fayette, New York, 1830

For, after that it truly was manifested unto this first elder, that he had received a remission of his sins, he was entangled again in the vanities of the world; But after truly repenting, God ministered unto him by an holy angel, whose countenance was as lightning, and whose garments were pure and white above all whiteness, and gave unto him commandments which inspired him from on high, and gave unto him power, by the means which were before prepared, that he should translate a book ... and [gave unto him a] call ... to his holy work.[53]

---

53. BofC 24:6-7, 10; cf. D&C 20:5-8, 11.

"[An] angel ... told him that he was chosen ...
to make known true religion"
Waterloo, New York; Nauvoo, Illinois, 1831, 1841, 1845

[Lucy Smith quotes from the above-cited section of the Book of Commandments in a letter to her brother, Solomon Mack, in 1831:] Joseph after repenting of his sins and humbling himself before God was visited by an holy Angel whose countenance was as lightning and whose garments were white above all whiteness and gave unto him commandments which inspired him from on high, and gave unto him by the means of which was before prepared that he should translate this book ...[54]

[In 1845 Lucy reveals more details:] After we ceased conversation he [Joseph] went to bed and was pondering in his mind which of the churches were the true one but he had not laid there long till he saw a bright light enter the room where he lay[. H]e looked up and saw an angel of the Lord standing by him[.] The angel spoke[:] I perceive that you are enquiring in your mind which is the true church[. T]here is not a true church on earth[,] no not one ... [T]here is a record for you ... but you cannot get it until you learn to keep the commandment of God[.][55]

[William Smith said in 1841:] About the year 1823, there was a revival of religion in that region and Joseph was one of several hopeful converts ... While his mind was perplexed with this subject, he prayed for divine direction; and afterwards was awaked one night by an extraordinary vision. The glory of the Lord filled the chamber with a dazzling light, and a glorious angel appeared to him, conversed with him, and told him that he was a chosen vessel unto the lord to make known true religion.[56]

---

54. Lucy Smith to Solomon Mack, 6 Jan. 1831, LDS church archives; qtd. in Vogel, *Early Mormon Documents,* 1:216.

55. Lucy Mack Smith, Preliminary Manuscript, 1844-45; qtd. in Vogel, *Early Mormon Documents,* 1:289-90.

56. William Smith, *The Congregational Observer,* 3 July 1841, 1; qtd. in Vogel, *Early Mormon Documents,* 1:478.

"[T]hy sins are forgiven thee, go thy way";
and again, "[T]hy sins are forgiven thee"
Kirtland, Ohio, 1832, 1835

[In 1832 Joseph wrote:] [T]he Lord opened the heavens upon me and I saw the Lord and he spake unto me saying Joseph my son thy sins are forgiven thee, go thy way walk in my statutes and keep my commandments[. B]ehold I am the Lord of glory[. I] was cruci-fyed for the world that all those who believe on my name may have Eternal life. ... [Three years later in a vision] an angel of the Lord came and stood before me and it was by night and he called me by name and he said the Lord had forgiven me my sins and he revealed unto me that in the Town of Manchester Ontario County N.Y. there was plates of gold ... and that I should go and get them ...[57] [Joseph said in 1835:] A personage appear[e]d in the midst of this pillar of flame ... Another personage soon appeared like unto the first, he said unto me thy sins are forgiven thee, he testified unto me that Jesus Christ is the son of God; I saw many angel[s] in this vision ... [Three years later] an angel appeared before me ... he told me of a sacred re-cord which was written on plates of gold ... and that God would give me powre [power] to translate it, with the assistance of this instru-ment [urim and thummim] [H]e then gradually vanished out of my sight, or the vision closed[.][58]

"[Jesus said I] was called of God" and
"promise[d] ... the fullness of the gospel"
Far West, Missouri; Nauvoo, Illinois, 1838, 1842

When the light rested upon me I saw two personages (whose brightness and glory defy all description) standing in the air. One of them spake unto me calling me by name and said (pointing to the other) "This is my beloved Son, Hear him." My object in going to enquire of the Lord was to know which of all the sects was right ... I

---

57. Jessee, *Papers of Joseph Smith*, 1:6-8.
58. Joseph Smith Journal, 9 Nov. 1835, 22-23, LDS church archives; qtd. in Jessee, *Papers of Joseph Smith*, 2:69-70.

was answered that I must join none of them, for they were all wrong. ... [Joseph says later in this account that his behavior] was not consistent with that character which ought to be maintained by one who was called of God as I had been.[59]

I was enwrapped in a heavenly vision and saw two glorious personages who exactly resembled each other in features, and likeness, surrounded with a brilliant light which eclipsed the sun at noon-day. They told me ... that none of them [churches] was acknowledged of God as his church and kingdom. And I was expressly commanded to "go not after them," at the same time receiving a promise that the fulness of the gospel, should at some future time be made known unto me.[60]

59. Ibid., 1:272-73, 276; cf. JS—History 1:17-19, 28d.

60. Joseph Smith, "Church History," *Times and Seasons*, 1 Mar. 1842, 706-10; qtd. in Jessee, *Papers of Joseph Smith*, 1:430.

Conclusion

That Joseph Smith literally translated ancient documents is problematic. He mistranslated portions of the Bible, as well as the Book of Joseph, the Book of Abraham, the Kinderhook plates, and a Greek psalter. There is no evidence that he ever translated a document as we would understand that phrase.

Furthermore, there are three obstacles to accepting the golden plates as the source of the Book of Mormon. First, although these records were said to have been preserved for generations by Nephite prophets, Joseph Smith never used them in dictating the Book of Mormon. If we accept the idea that he dug up a real, physical record, then we must account for the fact that he never used it in the translation process.

Second, much of the Book of Mormon reflects the intellectual and cultural environment of Joseph's own time and place. We find strands of American antiquities and folklore, the King James Bible, and evangelical Protestantism woven into the fabric of the doctrines and setting. A few people want to maintain that something like the Protestant Reformation occurred 2,500 years ago in America. It is more reasonable to accept that the evolving doctrines and practices of Protestantism down to Joseph Smith's time influenced the Book of Mormon. There is also an interesting syncretism in the Book of Mormon that shows the work of Joseph's creative mind. He draws from these major sources and fashions a message that was especially relevant to nineteenth-century America.

Third, the only other conceivable reason for preserving the gold plates would have been to show the witnesses a tangible artifact that would verify the antiquity of the translation. Yet, the eleven witnesses gazed on and handled the golden plates the same way they saw spectral treasure guardians and handled their elusive treasures, in the spirit, not in the flesh.

The remaining foundational experiences are the first vision, the angel Moroni, and priesthood restoration. These appear to have developed from relatively simple experiences into more impressive spiritual manifestations, from metaphysical to physical events. Joseph added new elements to his later narratives that are not hinted at in his earlier ones. His first vision evolved from a forgiveness epiphany to a call from God the Father and Jesus Christ to restore the true order of things. His original golden plates story was largely borrowed from his environment and then altered, becoming more religious and Christianized. His form-changing archivist became a resurrected angel named Moroni who dispensed heavenly wisdom and quoted liberally from the Bible. Likewise, Joseph's accounts of priesthood restoration developed from spiritual promptings into multiple, physical ordinations by resurrected angels. The witnesses to the Book of Mormon reportedly saw both secular and spiritual treasure guardians by "second sight" or through "the eyes of our understanding." Their testimony of the Book of Mormon was not of a secular event. Their emphasis was on seeing an angel and handling plates of gold, which was impressive for its metaphysical aspects. Today we see the witnesses as empirical, rational, twenty-first-century men instead of the nineteenth-century men they were. We have ignored the peculiarities of their world view, and by so doing, we misunderstand their experiences. Over time, we have reinterpreted their testimony so that, like with the other foundation stones, it appears to be a rational, impressive, and unique story in the history of religion.

The foundation events were rewritten by Joseph and Oliver and other early church officials so the church could survive and grow. This reworking made the stories more useful for missionary work and for fellowshipping purposes. But is this acceptable? Should we continue to tell these historically inaccurate versions today? It seems that, among the many implications that could be considered, we should ask ourselves what results have accrued from teaching an unequivocal, materialistic, and idealized narrative of our church's founding. The first question would be whether it has brought us closer to Christ. Has it made us more humble and teachable or more secure in our exclusivity and condescending toward others? Has it made us reliant on the expectation of infallible guidance and therefore, to a degree, gullible? It is appropriate to tell simplified, faith-inspiring stories to children, but is it right to tell religious allegories to adults as if they were literal history?

I cherish Joseph Smith's teachings on many topics, such as the plan of salvation and his view that the marriage covenant extends beyond death. Many others could be enumerated. But when it comes to the founding events, I wonder if they are trustworthy as history. The issue of his credibility in differentiating between history and allegory initially filled me with a sense of loss. But I realize that the focus of my worship, as a Mormon, is Jesus Christ. As I learn more about our history, I arrive at a greater commitment to Christ's teachings. As Joseph Smith himself explained in 1838: "The fundamental principles of our religion is the testimony of the apostles and prophets concerning Jesus Christ, 'that he died, was buried, and rose again the third day, and ascended up into heaven'; and all other things are only appendages to these, which pertain to our religion."[1] I have followed this encapsulation and pursued what might be considered to be a more practical approach to our religion—an emphasis on the character of Jesus Christ and his promises.[2] I like the fact that Jesus emphasized an empirical

---

1. Joseph Smith Jr., "Answers to Questions," *Elders Journal* (Far West, MO) 1 (July 1838): 42.

2. For an extended discussion of this topic, see my forthcoming book, "The Incomparable Jesus."

test of his teachings to "know" him (John 7:16-17; 2 Pet. 1:4-10) rather than a metaphysical approach to truth (Moro. 10:4-5).

To each new generation, the answer is given to an ancient query, "What shall I do to inherit eternal life? ... [C]ome follow me" (Luke 18:18, 22). In the Sermon on the Mount, Jesus explains what it means to follow him. He affirms that when we do his work and become "poor in spirit" and "mourn," we are renewed and "comforted" and receive the assurance of entering "the kingdom of heaven" (see Rev. 21-22). After each day's work at the Salt Lake County jail—teaching, counseling, giving blessings, and hearing the most serious sins in the city—I have felt "poor in spirit." But repeatedly the loving spirit of Christ has sustained and renewed me for the next day's tasks.

In the beatitudes Jesus summarizes what is expected of true disciples. Principally, a Christian (1) is meek, humble, gentle, long suffering, not easily offended, self-controlled; (2) hungers and thirsts after righteousness; (3) is more forgiving than justice requires; (4) is pure in heart and honest; (5) is a peacemaker; and (6) returns good for evil when reviled or persecuted. Jesus said that by embracing these ideals, we become "the salt of the earth" and "the light of the world" (Matt. 5:1-16). He invites the simple and the wise to his banquet; to those who respond, they find his spiritual fellowship in their toils, conflicts, and sufferings.

Jesus also asks that we become a Christian by covenant. In the LDS sacrament prayers, we ask ourselves each week if we are willing to take on us his name and remember him so that we will always have his Spirit with us (D&C 20:77-78, paraphrased). By following this ritual, we prepare ourselves for the challenges of each week. Such a commitment brings unity with Christ and the abundant life he promises which, in addition to receiving his spirit, includes peace, subtle reminders to our minds of his teachings, and that he will "manifest" or reveal himself in our life (John 10:10; see also Matt. 28:20, John 14:21, 23, 26, 27, and Rev. 21-22).

As a fourth-generation Latter-day Saint, with children and grandchildren in the fifth and sixth generations, I am proud of my heritage and have a mixture of confidence in, and anxiety for, the future. Recently the church has reemphasized the importance of centering our worship in Christ. This is apparent at the upper levels of the church, but little has yet changed at the local level. In many sacrament meetings, the tendency remains to simply mention Jesus' name and then talk about other matters rather than to discuss him and his ministry. In our Sunday classes, the Gospels are taught for several months once every four years; the lives and teachings of modern prophets are studied each year. As the apostle Paul, who was capable of speaking on a variety of religious subjects, said of the early church: "I determined not to know any thing among you, save Jesus Christ, and him crucified" (1 Cor. 2:2). I would hope for a greater focus on Jesus Christ in our Sunday meetings.

There are many people, both in our church and in other traditions, who write and comment about religion in ways that differ from the official canon. These people can and do persuade belief. In the early 1980s, Seventh-day Adventist scholars discovered that over 80 percent of church founder Ellen G. White's revelations in her "key-stone" book, *The Great Controversy,* came directly from existing nineteenth-century sources. Other revelatory writings and teachings, including some of her visions, also show unacknowledged literary borrowings.[3] The Adventist leadership has responded by making the church more Christ-centered. More recently, the Community of Christ (RLDS) went through a similar process. Today, anyone willing to covenant with Christ is invited to join either church and partake of the sacrament with them, regardless of their belief in the claims of their founding prophet.

As Latter-day Saints, our religious faith should be based and evaluated by how our spiritual and moral lives are centered in Jesus Christ, rather than in Joseph Smith's largely rewritten, materialistic, idealized, and controversial accounts of the church's founding. I hope that this study contributes in some way toward that end.

---

3. Douglas Hackleman, "Ellen White's Habit," *Free Inquiry,* Fall 1984, 16-22; Walter Rea, "Who Profits from the Prophet?" ibid., 23-29, esp. 29.

Selected Bibliography

Allen, James B. "The Significance of Joseph Smith's 'First Vision' in Mormon Thought," *Dialogue: A Journal of Mormon Thought* 1 (Autumn 1966): 22-45. Reprinted in D. Michael Quinn, ed., *The New Mormon History: Revisionist Essays on the Past.* Salt Lake City: Signature Books, 1992, pp. 37-52.

———. "Emergence of a Fundamental: The Expanding Role of Joseph Smith's First Vision in Mormon Religious Thought," *Journal of Mormon History* 7 (1980): 43-61.

Anderson, Richard L. *Investigating the Book of Mormon Witnesses.* Salt Lake City: Deseret Book Co., 1981.

Anderson, Rodger I. *Joseph Smith's New York Reputation Reexamined.* Salt Lake City: Signature Books, 1990.

Ashment, Edward H. "The Facsimiles of the Book of Abraham," *Sunstone* 4 (Dec. 1979): 33-51.

Backman, Milton V., Jr. *American Religions and the Rise of Mormonism.* Salt Lake City: Deseret Book Co., 1970.

———. *Joseph Smith's First Vision: The First Vision in Its Historical Context.* Salt Lake City: Bookcraft, 1971.

Baer, Klaus. "The Breathing Permit of Hor: A Translation of the Apparent Source of the Book of Abraham," *Dialogue: A Journal of Mormon Thought* 3 (Autumn 1968): 109-34.

Bergera, Gary James, ed. *Line upon Line: Essays on Mormon Doctrine.* Salt Lake City: Signature Books, 1989.

Bleiler, E. F., ed. *The Best Tales of Hoffmann: By E. T. A. Hoffmann.* New York: Dover Publications, Inc., 1967.

Bushman, Richard L. *Joseph Smith and the Beginnings of Mormonism.* Urbana: University of Illinois Press, 1984.

Cannon, Donald Q., and Lyndon W. Cook, eds. *Far West Record: Minutes of The Church of Jesus Christ of Latter-day Saints, 1830-1844.* Salt Lake City: Deseret Book Co., 1983.

Carlyle, Thomas. *German Romance: Specimens of Its Chief Authors.* 4 vols. Edinburgh: William Tait; and London: Charles Tait, 1827.

Hansen, Klaus J. *Mormonism and the American Experience.* Chicago: University of Chicago Press, 1981.

Hill, Donna. *Joseph Smith: The First Mormon.* Garden City, NY: Doubleday, 1977.

Hill, Marvin S. *Quest for Refuge: The Mormon Flight from American Pluralism.* Salt Lake City: Signature Books, 1989.

———. "The First Vision Controversy: A Critique and Reconciliation," *Dialogue: A Journal of Mormon Thought* 15 (Summer 1982): 31-46.

———. "Secular or Sectarian History? A Critique of 'No Man Knows My History,'" *Church History* 43 (Mar. 1974): 79-96.

Howard, Richard P. *Restoration Scriptures: A Study of Their Textual Development.* Independence, MO: Herald Publishing House, 2nd ed., 1995.

James, William. *The Varieties of Religious Experience.* New York: New American Library, 1958.

Jessee, Dean C., comp. and ed. *The Papers of Joseph Smith: Autobiographical and Historical Writings.* 2 vols. Salt Lake City: Deseret Book Co., 1989-1992.

———. *The Personal Writings of Joseph Smith.* Salt Lake City: Deseret Book Co., 1984.

Journal of Discourses of the Church of Jesus Christ of Latter-day Saints. 26 vols. London and Liverpool: LDS Booksellers Depot, 1854-86.

Lambert, Neal E., and Richard H. Cracroft, "Literary Form and Historical Understanding: Joseph Smith's First Vision," *Journal of Mormon History* 7 (1980): 31-42.

Larson, Charles M. *By His Own Hand upon Papyrus: A New Look at the Joseph Smith Papyri.* Grand Rapids, MI: Institute for Religious Research, 1992.

Larson, Stan. *Quest for the Gold Plates: Thomas Stuart Ferguson's Archaeological Search for The Book of Mormon.* Salt Lake City: Freethinker Press in association with Smith Research Associates, 1996.

Marquardt, H. Michael, and Wesley P. Walters, *Inventing Mormonism: Tradition and the Historical Record.* San Francisco: Smith Research Associates, 1994.

Metcalfe, Brent Lee, ed. *New Approaches to the Book of Mormon: Explorations in Critical Methodology.* Salt Lake City: Signature Books, 1993.

————. Unpublished response to Blake T. Ostler's "The Book of Mormon as a Modern Expansion of an Ancient Source," 1987 (copy in my possession).

Nibley, Preston. *The Witnesses of the Book of Mormon.* Salt Lake City: Deseret Book Co., 1968.

Ostler, Blake T. "The Book of Mormon as a Modern Expansion of an Ancient Source," *Dialogue: A Journal of Mormon Thought* 20 (Spring 1987): 66-123.

Prince, Gregory A. *Power from on High: The Development of Mormon Priesthood.* Salt Lake City: Signature Books, 1995.

Quinn, D. Michael. *Early Mormonism and the Magic World View.* Salt Lake City: Signature Books, 2nd ed., 1998.

Ritner, Robert K. "The 'Breathing Permit of Hor' Thirty-four Years Later," *Dialogue: A Journal of Mormon Thought* 33 (Winter 2000): 97-119.

Roberts, B. H. *Studies of the Book of Mormon.* Brigham D. Madsen, ed. Urbana: University of Illinois Press, 1985.

Smith, Lucy Mack. *History of Joseph Smith by His Mother, Lucy Mack Smith.* Salt Lake City: Bookcraft, 1958.

Stendahl, Krister. "The Sermon on the Mount and Third Nephi," in *Reflec-*

tions on Mormonism, Judaeo-Christian Parallels. Truman G. Madsen, ed. Provo, UT: Religious Studies Center, 1978.

Taylor, Alan. "The Early Republic's Supernatural Economy: Treasure Seeking in the American Northeast, 1780-1830," *American Quarterly* 38 (Spring 1986): 6-34.

Thomas, Mark D. "Revival Language in the Book of Mormon," *Sunstone* 8 (May-June 1983): 19-25.

Thompson, Stephen E. "Egyptology and the Book of Abraham," *Dialogue: A Journal of Mormon Thought* 28 (Spring 1995): 143-60.

Van Wagoner, Richard S., and Steven C. Walker. "Joseph Smith: 'The Gift of Seeing,'" *Dialogue: A Journal of Mormon Thought* 15 (Summer 1982): 48-68.

Vogel, Dan, ed. *Early Mormon Documents.* 5 vols. Salt Lake City: Signature Books, 1996-.

———. *Indian Origins and the Book of Mormon: Religious Solutions from Columbus to Joseph Smith.* Salt Lake City: Signature Books, 1986.

———, ed. *The Word of God: Essays on Mormon Scriptures.* Salt Lake City: Signature Books, 1990.

Walker, Ronald W. "Martin Harris: Mormonism's Early Convert," *Dialogue: A Journal of Mormon Thought* 19 (Winter 1986): 29-43.

———. "The Persisting Idea of American Treasure Hunting," *BYU Studies* 24 (Fall 1984): 429-59.

Whitman, Jason. "The Book of Mormon," *The Unitarian* (Boston), 1 Jan. 1834.

Wilson, John A., and Richard A. Parker, et al. "The Joseph Smith Egyptian Papyri: Translations and Interpretations," *Dialogue: A Journal of Mormon Thought* 3 (Summer 1968): 67-105.

Wood, Wilford C. *Joseph Smith Begins His Work.* 2 vols. Salt Lake City: by the Author, 1958-1962.

Index

A

Aaron's breastplate, 159, 160, 192

Address to All Believers in Christ, 198

Anderick, S. F., 42n12

Anselm of Canterbury, 129

Anselmus, 136; parallels to Joseph Smith, 147-70, 151-52n28

Anthon, Charles, 5, 168

anti-Mormons, viii

Antiquities of the Jews, 16

Apocrypha, possible influence of on Book of Mormon, 55; Nephi's name in, 70, 70n2

Appleby, William I., 245n27

Arabic, 167, 168

Arminianism, 123

Articles of Faith, 39

Athay, R. Grant, 21-22

Atlantis, 138, 147, 148, 151n27, 153, 154

Augustine, 132

Austin, Addison, 8

B

Bainbridge (NY). *See* South Bainbridge (NY)

baptism, infant, 46; authority needed to perform, 46

Baptist(s), 176, 241, 242, 244

Barrows, Ethan, 201

Beman, Alva, 184

Bennett, Alfred, 111, 113

Benton, A. W., 8

Bible, vii, x, xiii, 9, 40, 46, 47, 57, 58, 64, 66, 109, 110, 126, 130, 135, 159, 260; Smith's revision of, 1, 11-12, 259; use of during Book of Mormon translation, 10, 48, 69-93, 259; Smith's revisions in, not supported in ancient texts, 11; Smith's revisions in, conflict with current LDS teachings on godhead, 11-12; study of by Smith family, 43; Smith believed corrupt, 82, 122; concept of authority in, 220, 221, 223. *See also* Book of Mormon, *influence of Bible (apocrypha) on*

Blood, William, 159, 161

Howe, E. D., 44, 228, 231

Hurlbut, D. P., 227, 228, 245

Huss, 132

Hyde, Orson, 47, 247, 248

hypnotism. *See* Mesmerism

I

Improvement Era, 16

Indian Origins and the Book of Mormon, 56

Indians. *See* Native Americans

Ingersoll, Peter, reported Smith confessed inability to see through stone, 8, 9; reported on Smith treasure seeing, 188

Institute of Early American History and Culture, 194

intellects (souls), 22n50

intelligences (souls), 24

interpreters, 2, 4, 5; described as spectacle-like, 2, 4, 5; seen in vision of three witnesses, 197. *See also* seer stone; spectacles (magic); urim and thummim

J

James, William, 132

Jaredites, 31, 41

Jefferson, Thomas, xi, 125

Jessee, Dean C., 248

John (ancient apostle); record of, 1, 4

John the Baptist, 217, 223, 224, 224n17, 225, 228, 229, 230

Johnson, D. Lynn, 34

Johnson, Luke S., 200, 204, 246, 246n33, 247

Johnson, Lyman E., 200, 201, 204, 246, 247

Joseph Fielding Smith Institute for Church History, viii

Josephus, Flavius, 16-19, 29

K

Kane, Elizabeth, 140, 200

Kelley, Edmund L., 142

Kidd, Captain, 188

Kimball, Heber C., 158, 161, 191, 247

Kinderhook (IL), 30

Kinderhook plates, 1, 30-34; Smith translated, 30-31, 42, 259; Smith published facsimile of, 32-33; hoax exposed, 33-34. *See also* plates (gold)

Kirkland, Boyd, 122

Kirtland (OH), 19, 26, 140, 146, 183, 212, 227, 231, 247n38, 248, 256

Kirtland Anti-Safety Society, 248

Knight, Joseph, Jr., 145n21

Knight, Joseph, Sr., 2, 144, 145, 157, 160; described Smith's method of translation, 5, 7; attempted to sell Book of Mormon's copyright in Canada, 65-66; dug for treasure with Smith, 188

Knight, Newel, 188

Knight, Sally, 188

Kolob, 24

L

Lamanites, 41, 42, 62

Landers, John, 200

Lane, George, 44, 100, 101, 106, 109, 117, 242

Lapham, Fayette, 145

Lawrence, Samuel, 184

Lazarus, 48

Lee, John D., 201

Lewis, Joseph, 253n51

liahona, 75, 77

Liliputian race, 183

Lindhorst, Archivarius, 138; parallels

reproduce stolen 116 pages, 7; translated from behind curtain, 10, 82-83; of Bible, 11-12, 259; believed Bible corrupt, 82; of Egyptian papyri, 12-30, 259; studied Hebrew, 19; owned Thomas Dick's *Philosophy of a Future State*, 22, 23; had Egyptian papyri cut into smaller pieces, 29; of Kinderhook plates, 30-34, 42, 259; published facsimile of Kinderhook plates, 31-32; of Greek psalter, 34-36, 259

—*as author of Book of Mormon*, 39-67; ignorance of, overstated by apologists, 40; creative enough to have written Book of Mormon, 40-42; named skeleton Zelph, 41-42; education of, 42-43, 43n16; intelligent but unschooled, 43-44; knowledgeable about the Bible, theology, and American antiquities, 44-67, 84; received revelation to sell Book of Mormon's copyright in Canada, 65-66; ability to speak Bible language, 46-47; dictation of Book of Mormon became progressively easier, 66; autobiographical material of included in Book of Mormon, 70; synthesized material from environment, 135; parallels to E. T. A. Hoffmann, 136, 144, 146, 147-74

—*visions and revelations of*, first vision of, xiii, 21, 235-58, 260; claims of regarding priesthood restoration, xiii, 215-34, 260; revelations of, 6; returned plates to angel, 193; altered revelations to include reference to angelic ordinations, 228, 229-30, 230n39; vision of "angels," 148-49; encountered evil force while trying

to get plates, 150-52; angel appeared under apple tree, 154-55; appearances of Moroni to, 149, 153, 156, 161, 166, 172

Smith, Joseph, Sr., 145, 154, 160, 164, 167, 171n59, 173, 193, 233; reported plates kept in mountain during translation, 4; taught school, 43; refused to attend church meetings, 65; dream of reflected in Book of Mormon, 70-71; related story of Joseph's finding plates, 151; mentioned cave in Hill Cumorah, 159, 191; witness to gold plates, 175; member of money-digging company, 184, 194; searched for treasure on Hill Cumorah, 185, 185n26; statements about locations of treasures, 187-88

Smith, Lucy, 42, 65, 66, 144, 144-45n21, 162, 193, 198, 256; related husband's early dreams, 70-73; related story of Joseph Jr. getting plates, 150, 152, 172, 190; owner of corner from stone treasure box, 178; follower of James J. Strang, 211; described manner in which Smith received authority to baptize, 215-16, 218n3; joined Presbyterian church, 240, 244, 253; described Palmyra revival, 243; withdrew from Presbyterian church 1828, 253n50

Smith, Samuel, 191-92, 233; witness to gold plates, 175, 205; baptism of, 216

Smith, Simon, 199

Smith, Wallace B., xi

Smith, William, 65, 241, 247, 256; reported father taught school, 43; follower of James J. Strang, 211; blessing of by Joseph Smith, 233, 234

Sodus, Wayne County (NY), 139

South Bainbridge (NY), 8, 176, 187

Southerton, Simon, 56-57n36

Southport Telegraph, 209

spectacles (magic), 160

Stafford, John, 43

Stafford, Joshua, 187, 187n28

Stafford, William, 186, 187n28

Stendahl, Krister, 69, 74, 81, 91, 93

Stevenson, Edward, 5, 199

Stockton, Benjamin, 241, 244

Stoddard, Lucy, 100-101

Stowell, Josiah, attempts to sell Book of Mormon's copyright in Canada, 65-66; hired Smith, 176; money digger, 184

Strang, James J., 207-13, 231-32n40

Stringfellow, Douglas R., 131-32

Susquehanna River, 188

T

Talmage, James E., 39

Taylor, Alan, 194

Taylor, Thomas, 21

temple, Egyptian, 16; LDS, 21, 124

Thomas, Mark D., 119, 123

Thompson, Jonathan, 187, 187n30

Thornton, Abel, 106-107, 111, 113

Times and Seasons, 31

Towner, Joseph, 110

Townsend, Jesse, 177, 198

translation, of Book of Mormon, 1, 162, 174, 217; of Bible, 1, 11-12, 144-45n21; of Egyptian papyri, 1, 12-25; not supported by Egyptologists, 12-16, 19, 20; of Kinderhook plates, 1, 30-34; of Greek psalter, 1, 34-36; of record of John, 1; Book of Mormon, literal, 1n1; done without plates, 2-4; Smith's method not scholarly, 5, 7; "by gift and power of God," 7, 11,

49; theory of conceptual method, 10; in story of "The Golden Pot," 138, 153

Traughber, John L., 181

Tucker, Pomeroy, 47, 177, 185n26

Turley, Theodore, 205

Turner, Orsamus, 184

Tyler, Daniel, 205

U

Underwood, Grant, 128

Unitarian, 95, 125

Unitarian(s), 96, 123

Universalist(s), 96, 125, 126-29, 129n63, 176

urim and thummim, 5, 9, 62, 160, 161, 166, 170, 190, 207, 215-16, 257. *See also* interpreters; seer stone; spectacles (magic)

V

Varieties of Religious Experience, 132

Veronica, 156-57, 164, 165, 166

View of the Hebrews, 58-64

Vogel, Dan, 56, 207

Voree Herald, 211, 212

W

Walker, Lucy, 30

Walker, Ronald W., 176, 177

Walker, Sylvia, 187

Walters, Luman, 139, 140, 140n10, 141, 142, 142n17, 144, 174

Walters, Wesley P., 37n77

Waterloo (NY), 256

Wayne Sentinel, 243-44

Welch, John W., 83

Wentworth, John, 146, 255

Wesley, John, 109, 132